Nevertheless

Nevertheless

Machiavelli, Pascal

Carlo Ginzburg

Translation editor Gregory Elliott

VERSO
London • New York

First published in English by Verso 2022
Originally published in Italian as *Nondimanco:
Machiavelli, Pascal*, Adelphi Edizioni 2018
© Carlo Ginzburg 2018, 2022
Translation © Chapter 7: Francis Mulhern 2022
Preface, Chapter 7 postscript, Chapter
10 and Appendix: Gregory Elliott 2022

The translation of this work has been funded by SEPS –
Segretariato Europeo per le Pubblicazioni Scientifiche

Via Val d'Aposa 7 – 40123 Bologna – Italy
seps@seps.it – seps.it

1 3 5 7 9 10 8 6 4 2

Verso
UK: 6 Meard Street, London W1F 0EG
US: 20 Jay Street, Suite 1010, Brooklyn, NY 11201
versobooks.com

Verso is the imprint of New Left Books

ISBN-13: 978-1-83976-014-3
ISBN-13: 978-1-83976-015-0 (UK EBK)
ISBN-13: 978-1-83976-016-7 (US EBK)

British Library Cataloguing in Publication Data
A catalogue record for this book is available from the British Library

Library of Congress Control Number: 2021947716

Typeset in Sabon LT by Hewer Text UK Ltd, Edinburgh
Printed and bound by CPI Group (UK) Ltd, Croydon CR0 4YY

Contents

Preface

1. First things first – the subtitle: *Machiavelli, Pascal.*[1] Why the comma?

The comma is an ambiguous punctuation mark, indicating either a conjunction or a disjunction. In this instance, both. *Nevertheless* begins by arguing that Machiavelli learned from medieval casuistry how to reflect on rules and exceptions and ends by analysing Pascal's savage polemic against casuistry. What makes it possible to ponder Machiavelli and Pascal conjointly?

The answer is: political theology – a notion the contemporary reader immediately associates with Carl Schmitt. Here is the celebrated opening of chapter 1 of his book *Political Theology* (1922; 2nd edition, 1934), followed by the no less famous start of chapter 3:

> Sovereign is he who decides on the exception . . .
>
> All significant concepts of the modern theory of the state are secularized theological concepts not only because of their historical development – in which they were transferred from theology to the theory of the state, whereby, for example, the omnipotent God became the omnipotent lawgiver – but also because of their systematic structure, the recognition of which is necessary for a sociological consideration of these concepts. The exception in jurisprudence is analogous to the miracle in theology.[2]

---

1 In this preface I draw on some passages from my preface to *A Historical Approach to Casuistry: Norms and Exceptions in Comparative Perspective* (Bloomsbury, 2018), a collection of essays edited by Lucio Biasiori and myself.

2 Carl Schmitt, *Political Theology: Four Chapters on the Concept*

And now Pascal (*Pensées*, fragment 280):

States would perish if their laws were not often stretched to meet necessity, but religion has never tolerated or practised such a thing. So either compromises [*accommodements*] or miracles are needed.[3]

As is well known, Schmitt often refrained from citing his sources, even when he read them polemically. As far as I know, neither Schmitt nor his countless followers, commentators and critics have ever mentioned this *pensée* of Pascal.[4] But in this instance to speak of sources would be at once too little and too much. Too little, because Pascal's comparison between political exceptions and miracles anticipates, in a few dense lines, the theme of political theology formulated by

---

of Sovereignty, tr. George Schwab (Chicago: University of Chicago Press, 2005), pp. 5, 36. (*Politische Theologie. Vier Kapitel zur Lehre von der Souveränität*, Munich: Duncker & Humblot, 2nd edn, 1934, p. 11: 'Souverän ist, wer über den Ausnahmezustand entscheidet'; p. 49: 'Alle prägnanten Begriffe der modernen Staatslehre sind säkularisierte theologische Begriffe. Nicht nur ihrer historischen Entwicklung nach, weil sie aus der Theologie auf die Staatslehre übertragen wurden, indem zum Beispiel der allmächtige Gott zum omnipotenten Gesetzgeber wurde, sondern auch in ihrer systematischen Struktur, deren Erkenntnis notwendig ist für eine soziologische Betrachtung dieser Begriffe. Der Ausnahmezustand hat für die Jurisprudenz eine analoge Bedeutung wie das Wunder für die Theologie.')

3 Blaise Pascal, *Pensées*, tr. A. J. Krailsheimer (Harmondsworth: Penguin, 1983), fr. 280, p. 118. (*Pensées*, ed. M. Le Guern [Paris: Gallimard, 1977], fr. 263 [Brunschvicg fr. 614], p. 196: 'Les États périraient si on ne faisait ployer souvent les lois à la nécessité, mais jamais la Religion n'a souffert cela et n'en a usé. Aussi il faut ces accommodements ou des miracles.')

4 Two particularly significant examples: Jan Assmann, *Herrschaft und Heil: Politische Theologie in Altägypten, Israel und Europa* (Munich: Hanser, 2000), who cites the opening of chapter 3 of Schmitt's *Political Theology* (see above), and Giorgio Agamben, *State of Exception*, tr. Kevin Attell (Chicago: University of Chicago Press, 2005), who refers to the miracle as 'the paradigm of the state of exception' (p. 56). Assmann sets out from Schmitt's thesis only to invert it from a historical-religious point of view, while Agamben does so to develop it from a philosophical perspective.

Schmitt.[5] Too much, because for Schmitt political theology was a programme of action that presupposed not only revelation but revelation based on Catholic anti-Judaism (which in Schmitt's case survived the fall of the Nazi regime he actively supported).[6] The target of Schmitt's political theology was the anonymous author of the *Tractatus theologico-politicus*, or 'the Jew Spinoza', as Schmitt unfailingly characterized him. 'The most brazen insult ever done to God and man, and which justifies all the anathemas of the synagogue', wrote Schmitt in his diary (7 October 1947), 'consists in the *sive* in the formula *Deus sive Natura* [God, or Nature]'.[7] As Spinoza explains in chapter 6 of the *Tractatus*, the formula implied rejection of the very idea of miracles: 'Nature therefore always observes laws and rules which involve eternal necessity and truth – albeit not all are known to us – and therefore also a fixed and immutable order.'[8]

---

5 The studies by Heinrich Meier have been particularly useful to me: *Carl Schmitt and Leo Strauss: The Hidden Dialogue*, tr. J. Harvey Lomax (Chicago: University of Chicago Press, 1995), and *The Lesson of Carl Schmitt: Four Chapters on the Distinction between Political Theology and Political Philosophy*, tr. Marcus Brainard (Chicago: University of Chicago Press, 1998), pp. 151ff. Specifically, see Raphael Gross, *Carl Schmitt and the Jews: The 'Jewish Question', the Holocaust, and German Legal Theory*, tr. Joel Golb, foreword by Peter C. Caldwell (Madison: University of Wisconsin Press, 2007). And see also Carl Schmitt, *Glossario*, ed. Petra Dal Santo (Milan: Giuffrè, 2001), which collects Schmitt's diaries for 1947–1951, with a preface by J. H. Kaiser that justifies Schmitt's persistent anti-Semitism with anti-Semitic arguments (an eloquent example is the entry dated 19 November 1947 on p. 65).

6 Catholic anti-Judaism, ever present and never recanted, explains Schmitt's silence on the theological-religious roots of secularization, highlighted by Sigrid Weigel, *Walter Benjamin: Images, the Creaturely, and the Holy*, tr. Chadwick Truscott Smith (Stanford, CA: Stanford University Press, 2013). The intertwinement of anti-Judaism and anti-Semitism is amply documented in Gross's *Carl Schmitt and the Jews*.

7 Schmitt, *Glossario*, p. 41.

8 Benedict de Spinoza, *Theological Political Treatise*, ed. Jonathan Israel, trs. Michael Silverthorne and Jonathan Israel (Cambridge: Cambridge University Press, 2007), p. 83.

'Political theology' is not a neutral category. In this case, as always, it is necessary to analyse the research tools, bringing to light their presuppositions and implications.

2. In a famous passage (*The Prince*, chapter 6), Machiavelli pays an ambiguous tribute to Moses (and his 'great master'), comparing him with more or less mythical sovereigns of secular antiquity:

> However, to come to those who have become rulers through their own ability and not through luck or favour, I consider that the most outstanding were Moses, Cyrus, Romulus, Theseus and others of that stamp. And although one should not reason about Moses, as he was a mere executor of things that had been ordered for him by God, nonetheless he should be admired even if only for that grace which made him deserving of speaking with God. But let us consider Cyrus and others who have acquired or founded kingdoms. They will all be found remarkable, and if their actions and methods are considered, they will not appear very different from those of Moses, who had such a great master.[9]

Moses, Cyrus and Theseus return at the end of *The Prince* (chapter 26) when Machiavelli evokes the present situation of Italy, 'more enslaved than the Hebrews, more oppressed than the Persians, more scattered than the Athenians'. Machiavelli

---

9 Niccolò Machiavelli, *The Prince*, eds. Quentin Skinner and Russell Price, tr. Russell Price (Cambridge: Cambridge University Press, 2016), p. 20. ('Ma per venire a quelli che per propria virtù e non per fortuna sono diventati principi, dico che li più escellenti sono Moisè, Ciro, Romulo, Teseo e simili. E benché di Moisè non si debba ragionare sendo stato uno mero essecutore delle cose che erano ordinate da Dio, *tamen* debba essere ammirato *solum* per quella grazia che lo faceva degno di parlare con Dio. Ma consideriamo Ciro e li altri che hanno acquistato o fondati regni: li troverrete tutti mirabili, e, se si consideranno le azioni e ordini loro particulari, parranno non discrepanti da quelli di Moisè che ebbe sì gran precettore': *Il principe*, ed. Mario Martelli, Edizioni nazionale delle Opere, section 1, vol. I [Rome: Salerno Editrice, 2006], pp. 113–15.)

recalls the miraculous signs that accompanied the Exodus of the Hebrews from Egypt: 'Very unusual events, which are signs from God, have recently been observed here: the sea has opened; a cloud has shown you the way; water has flowed from the rock; manna has rained down here.'[10] The reference implicit in this coolly rhetorical outburst was the 'miraculous' election of Cardinal Giovanni de' Medici, who became Pope Leo X.

Obviously, we are far removed from Pascal. For him miracles – something God alone, the God of the Bible not of the philosophers, could perform – possessed a profound, literal, existential significance. But at the same time, as we saw in the fragment cited above, for Pascal the miracle was comparable to the exception to the political and moral rule – hence to Machiavelli's 'nevertheless'. Chapter 7 is devoted to an analysis of Pascal's reading of Machiavelli.

3. The first seminar in which I had the good fortune to participate was Arsenio Frugoni's on *Il principe* at the Scuola Normale di Pisa in 1957–1958 (I was eighteen). Almost fifty years later, in January 2002, I read *The Prince* with my students at UCLA. The choice of this subject, following the attack on the Twin Towers of 11 September 2001, seemed obvious. Secularization was an open problem, which demanded reflection. In the months preceding the seminar, I began to explore the possible link between Machiavelli and casuistry: a research scheme possibly triggered, without me having realized it, by the gesture with which Benedetto

---

10 Machiavelli, *The Prince*, pp. 88–9 ('Più stiava che li Ebrei, più serva che e' Persi, più dispersa che li Ateniesi' / 'qui si veggano estraordinarii sanza essemplo condotti da Dio: el mare s'è aperto, una nube vi ha scorto el cammino, la pietra ha versato acqua, qui è piovuto la manna': *Il principe,* pp. 312, 315). On the instrumental use of political messianism by Machiavelli (who was anything but a good Christian), important indications are supplied by Gaetano Lettieri, 'Nove tesi sull'ultimo Machiavelli', *Humanitas,* new ser., 72/5–6 (Sep.–Dec. 2017), pp. 1034–89, esp. pp. 1043–4 n. 18. And see Lettieri's 'Agostino, Aurelio', in *Enciclopedia machiavelliana,* vol. I, ed. Gennaro Sasso and Giorgio Inglese (Rome: Istituto della Enciclopedia Italiana, 2014), pp. 15–26.

Croce dismissed it, after having evoked it. The research programme outlined in chapter 1 has been pursued in the subsequent chapters from different, partial angles, but not, I hope, irrelevant ones. Also a discussion (here virtually absent) of Machiavelli and the republican tradition will, if I am not mistaken, have to settle accounts with the interpretation proposed here.

Over the years, this research trajectory has intersected on the one hand with the coordination of a project on the comparative history of casuistry, funded by the International Balzan Prize Foundation, and on the other with the invitation to deliver the Tanner Lectures at Harvard. In both instances I presented the results of my research on Pascal's *Provincial Letters* and their echoes. Machiavelli drew me towards Pascal, including the Pascal who was a reader of Machiavelli – the 'most religious' Machiavelli referred to (as we shall see in chapter 9) by a reader of the *Provincial Letters*. Pascal, Machiavelli.

I am grateful to my students at UCLA; the Università degli Studi, Siena; and the Scuola Normale Superiore, Pisa, who many years ago participated in my seminars on Machiavelli (in particular, Fabio Paglieri and my friend Carlo Pincin for their contributions to the Sienese seminar on the *Ghiribizzi*); Quentin Skinner for his extraordinary intellectual generosity; Homi K. Bhabha for having invited me to give the Tanner Lectures, reworked here in chapters 7–9; Robert A. Maryks for having agreed to comment on them at Harvard; Ann Blair and Robert Darnton for their warm hospitality; Marcelo Barbuto for the bibliographical supplementation of chapters 1 and 7; Suzanne Werder (Balzan Foundation) for having made the project on the comparative history of casuistry possible; Laura Tita Farinella (Biblioteca dell'Archiginnasio, Bologna) for having guided my research on the reception of Pascal; Monsignor Alejandro Cifres (Archive of the Congregation for the Doctrine of the Faith) and Marco Grillo (Vatican Secret Archive) for having allowed me to consult the documents from the trial of Galileo Galilei; the Vatican Apostolic Library in Vatican City and the Royal Library of Turin, which permitted me to reproduce pages of manuscripts in their possession; Stefano Zamponi for having replied, with the competence peculiar to him, to my questions on the documents of the Galileo trial; Perry Anderson, Franco Bacchelli, Lucio Biasiori, Maria Luisa Catoni, Gaetano Lettieri, Martin Rueff and Sanjay Subrahmanyam for their valuable criticisms. I recall with regret Francesco Orlando, who many years ago nudged me towards Pascal.

In preparing this text for the press, I have received irreplaceable help from Francesca Savastano: once again, I am profoundly grateful to her.

I dedicate this book to my brother Andrea, who was not able to see it completed.

The essays collected below have been partially rewritten (especially the seventh). Original publication details are as follows (three of the essays have not previously been published):

1. 'Machiavelli, l'eccezione e la regola. Linee di una ricerca in corso' (Machiavelli, the exception and the rule), *Quaderni storici* 38/112 (April 2003), pp. 195–213.

2. 'Diventare Machiavelli. Per una nuova lettura dei *Ghiribizzi al Soderini*' (Becoming Machiavelli: A new reading of the *Ghiribizzi al Soderini*), *Quaderni storici* 41/121 (April 2006), pp. 151–64.

3. 'Pontano, Machiavelli and Prudence', in *From Florence to the Mediterranean and Beyond: Essays in Honour of Anthony Molho*, ed. Diogo Ramada Curto et al. (Florence: Leo S. Olschki, 2009), pp. 117–25.

4. 'Intricate Readings: Machiavelli, Aristotle, Thomas Aquinas', *Journal of the Warburg and Courtauld Institutes* 78 (2015), pp. 157–72.

5. 'Moulding the People: Machiavelli, Michelangelo', in *Soredemo: Makiaverri, Pasukalu*, tr. Tadao Uemura (Tokyo: Misuzu Shobo, 2020), pp. 88–118.

6. 'Machiavelli e gli antiquari' (Machiavelli and the antiquarians), in *L'Europa divisa e i nuovi mondi. Per Adriano Prosperi*, vol. II, ed. Massimo Donattini, Giuseppe Marcocci and Stefania Pastore (Pisa: Edizioni della Normale, 2011), pp. 3–8.

7. 'Machiavelli, Galileo and the Censors' (not including the

postscript added in this book), *New Left Review* 2/123 (May/June 2020), pp. 91–109.

8. '*Virtù*, Justice, Force: On Machiavelli and Some of His Readers', unpublished.

9. 'Oblique Words: In the Workshop of the *Provincial Letters*', unpublished.

10. 'Ironic and Ambiguous Euclid: Two Notes in Connection with Bayle', unpublished.

Appendix: 'Noterella su *Il Gattopardo*. Leggere tra le righe' (Reading between the lines – a short note on *The Leopard*), *L'Indice dei libri del mese* 32/5 (May 2015), p. 8.

Machiavelli, the Exception and the Rule

1.[1] 'Machiavellian' or, as we read in one of the most widely disseminated Italian dictionaries, 'cunning and unscrupulous ... astute, devious'.[2] Scrutiny of the dictionaries of many other languages would, of course, yield similar results: the tangible sign of a polemic that has gone on for centuries. Certainly, the scholarly discussion of Machiavelli's writings and activity has moved on to a different level. In recent decades, the stereotypical negative image of Machiavelli has started to turn into its opposite, especially in the anglophone world. Machiavelli has become the model of the virtuous citizen, who teaches the importance of republican values – liberty and the ability to sacrifice oneself for the common good – to present-day democracies.[3]

---

1   I have presented different versions of these pages in the Department of History, UCLA, in June 2002; at the Center for Humanities, Princeton, in October 2002; and at a conference in memory of Giovanni Aquilecchia held in London at the Warburg Institute in November 2002. The bibliographical references have been reduced to a minimum. I am grateful to Franco Bacchelli for his observations.

2   *Il nuovo Zingarelli*, entry on 'Machiavellico' (N. Zingarelli, *Vocabolario della lingua italiana* [Bologna: Zanichelli, 2001], p. 1030).

3   See, for example, Quentin Skinner, 'Machiavelli's *Discorsi* and the Pre-Humanist Origins of Republican Ideas', in *Machiavelli and Republicanism*, ed. Gisela Bock, Quentin Skinner and Maurizio Viroli (Cambridge: Cambridge University Press, 1990), pp. 121–41; J. G. A. Pocock, *The Machiavellian Moment* (Princeton, NJ: Princeton University Press, 1975); Maurizio Viroli, 'Machiavelli and the Republican Idea of Politics', in *Machiavelli and Republicanism*, pp.

This striking transformation of Machiavelli's image is the result of a series of analytical studies by scholars from England, the United States and New Zealand. These studies share some methodological assumptions, to which I shall return shortly, and by the fact that they focus mainly on Machiavelli's *Discourses on Livy* rather than on *The Prince*. One has the impression that for many recent scholars Machiavelli's most famous work has become an unacknowledged source of intellectual, as well as moral and political, embarrassment.

The need to reconcile the contradictions, genuine or presumed, between *The Prince* and the *Discourses* has been stated countless times. The road I shall follow is, if I am not mistaken, in many respects new. The tools I shall use are context and language – Skinner's and Pocock's methodological watchwords, but employed differently.

2. We know very little about Machiavelli's youth. Carlo Dionisotti spoke once of 'that initial tangle, mysterious for us, comprising reflections, rejections and choices, from which Machiavelli's vocation as a writer, and more specifically as a poet, originated'.[4] The emergence of Machiavelli's vocation as a thinker (not easily distinguishable from the poet and the writer) is equally obscure. But there is a document, often inadequately used by scholars, that sheds some invaluable light on Machiavelli's intellectual formation – namely, the *Libro di ricordi*, covering the years 1475–1487, kept by his father, Bernardo.[5] Bernardo Machiavelli had a degree

---

144–71. Among the dissenting voices, see Leo Strauss, *Thoughts on Machiavelli* (Glencoe, IL: Free Press, 1958); Harvey C. Mansfield, 'Bruni and Machiavelli on Civic Humanism', in *Renaissance Civic Humanism*, ed. James Hankins (Cambridge: Cambridge University Press, 2000), pp. 223–46; and Paul A. Rahe, 'Situating Machiavelli', in *Renaissance Civic Humanism*, pp. 270–308, esp. p. 306.

4 Carlo Dionisotti, *Machiavellerie* (Turin: Einaudi, 1980), p. 230.

5 Bernardo Machiavelli, *Libro di ricordi*, ed. Cesare Olschki (Florence: Le Monnier, 1954), and see the facsimile reprint, with a postface by Leandro Perini (Rome: Edizioni di Storia e Letteratura, 2007). The comments of Sebastian de Grazia, *Machiavelli in Hell* (Princeton, NJ: Princeton University Press, 1989), pp. 5–6, are

in law and, like many other Florentines of similar social standing, recorded a series of ordinary events of various kinds in his logbook: purchasing a cow and some books, lending a small sum of money, the beginning of the educational career of his son Niccolò (born in 1469) and so on.

As is obvious, the books listed in the *Libro di ricordi*, carefully identified by the editor, do not amount to an exhaustive description of Bernardo's library.[6] But they give us an idea of the books available to his son as he grew up. Some were to have a lasting impact on him.

3. I shall start with Machiavelli's best-known play, *Mandragola* (The Mandrake), probably begun around 1514 and staged for the first time in Rome in 1520.[7] Its plot is well known. Nicia, an elderly lawyer, desperately hopes that Lucrezia, his young wife, will bear him a child. Callimaco, a young man in love with Lucrezia, instructed by the parasite Ligurio, disguises himself as a doctor and tells Nicia that his wife will become pregnant if she drinks a potion made from a miraculous plant, the mandrake. But there is a problem. The first person to have sex with a woman after she has imbibed a mandrake potion will die. Hence, the sham doctor concludes, Lucrezia, to spare Nicia's life, must sleep with a stranger (Callimaco himself, in another disguise). Nicia is

---

superficial. On Bernardo, see Felix Gilbert, *Machiavelli and Guicciardini: Politics and History in Sixteenth-Century Florence* (Princeton, NJ: Princeton University Press, 1965), pp. 318–22 (which mentions the *Dialogus* by Bartolomeo Scala cited above, but without examining it), and the extremely useful postface by Perini. And see the entry 'Machiavelli, Bernardo' by A. Guidi, in *Enciclopedia machiavelliana*, vol. II, ed. Gennaro Sasso and Giorgio Inglese (Rome: Istituto della'Enciclopedia Italiana, 2014), pp. 109–12.

6 Roberto Ridolfi's exclamation ('What the heck? Among so many books, was there no Bible in the Machiavelli home?': *Vita di Machiavelli*, 5th rev. edn, vol. II [Florence: Sansoni, 1972], p. 424 n. 7) is senseless. (I refer to the exclamation, not to the lack of a Bible: see instead Perini in his postface to the *Libro di ricordi*, p. 268 n. 16.)

7 For this date, see Pasquale Stoppelli, *La 'Mandragola': storia e filologia. Con l'edizione critica del testo secondo il Laurenziano Redi 129* (Rome: Bulzoni, 2005).

immediately convinced and asks Timoteo, a friar from a nearby convent, to persuade Lucrezia to commit adultery.

Mandragola is a black comedy, and the friar is the blackest character of all – a sordid blend of hypocrisy and cynicism. The scene in which he pursues the virtuous wife to overcome her scruples is rightly famous. Let me quote from the first part of the dialogue between the friar and Lucrezia (act 3, scene 11):

Fra Timoteo: To tell you the truth I have been poring over my books for hours, studying the case, and after careful research I find that there are numerous considerations on our side, both general and particular . . .

There are many things which, far off, seem strange, terrifying, and intolerable, but when you come close appear natural, bearable, and homely; because of this one says that fear of the evil is greater than the evil itself. And this is such a matter . . .

I want to go back to what I first said to you. As far as conscience is concerned, you have to accept this common rule: that where there is a certain good and an uncertain evil, the good must never be sacrificed for fear of the evil. Here we have a certain good – that you will conceive a child, gaining a soul for our Almighty Saviour: the uncertain evil is that the man who shares your bed after you have taken the potion might die; but it may well turn out that he does not die. Nevertheless, as there is some doubt, it is better for Messer Nicia not to run any risk. As for the act itself, it is foolish to call that a sin, for it is the will that commits a sin, not the body; the real sin is to displease your husband, and you will be pleasing him; or to take pleasure in the act, and you are displeased about it. Besides this, it is the outcome of any action that we have to bear in mind: the outcome of yours will be to content your husband and fill a place in Paradise. The Bible says that Lot's daughters, believing themselves left alone in the world, lay with their father; and, because their intention was good they did not sin.

Lucrezia: What are you persuading me to do?[8]

---

8 *The Mandragola*, act 3, scene 11, in *The Literary Works of Machiavelli*, ed. and tr. J. R. Hale (Oxford: Oxford University Press,

The friar's crafty, enticing speech, which prompts Lucrezia's indignant response, suggested the term 'casuistry' to Luigi Russo, in a book that more than half a century ago left its mark on Italian studies of Machiavelli.[9] Benedetto Croce had already applied this term to Fra Timoteo.[10] Russo forced Croce's hint,

---

1961), pp. 37–8. (I have made a few modifications.) For the original text, see Niccolò Machiavelli, *La mandragola*, in *Teatro*, ed. Pasquale Stoppelli, Edizione nazionale delle Opere, section 3, vol. I (Rome: Salerno Editrice, 2017), pp. 191–4:

Fra Timoteo: Veramente io sono stato in su' libri più di dua ore a studiare questo caso, e, dopo molta esamina io truovo dimolte cose che in particulare e in generale fanno per noi. . . .

E' sono molte cose che discosto paiano terribili, insopportabili, strane, che quando tu ti appressi loro le riescono umane, sopportabili, domestiche; e però si dice che sono maggiori li spaventi che e mali: e questa è una di quelle . . .

Io voglio tornare a quello ch'io dicevo prima. Voi avete, quanto alla consciènza, a pigliare questa generalità: che dove è un bene certo e un male incerto, non si debba mai lasciare quel bene per paura di quel male. Qui è un bene certo: che voi ingraviderete, acquisterete una anima a messer Domenedio. El male incerto è che colui che iacerà con voi dopo la pozione si muoia. E' si truova anche di quelli che non muoiano, ma perché la cosa è dubbia, però è bene che messer Nicia non corra quel pericolo. Quanto allo atto che sia peccato, questo è una favola, perché la volontà è quella che pecca non el corpo; e la cagion del peccato è dispiacere al marito, e voi li compiacete; pigliare piacere, e voi ne avete dispiacere. Oltr'a di questo, el fine si ha a riguardare in tutte le cose; el fine vostro è riémpiere una sedia in paradiso e contentare el marito vostro. Dice la Bibbia che le figliuole di Lotto, credendosi essere rimase sole nel mondo, usorono con el padre; e perché la loro intenzione fu buona, non peccorono.'

Lucrezia: Che cosa mi persuadete voi?

---

9 Luigi Russo, *Machiavelli* (Rome: Tumminelli, 1945), pp. 136–7: 'Subtle casuistry . . . This page anticipates the casuistry that was to assume an official character in the seventeenth and eighteenth centuries. Machiavelli writes its first tract in this speech by his friar.' Russo's book contained a twofold dedication, to the memory of Nello Rosselli and Leone Ginzburg.

10 Cf. Benedetto Croce, 'La "commedia" del Rinascimento', in *Poesia popolare e poesia d'arte*, 2nd rev. edn (Bari: Laterza, 1946), pp. 244–5.

identifying Fra Timoteo as a 'precursor' of casuistry, indeed as the author of its 'first treatise': the tradition of moral theology ferociously satirized by Pascal in the mid-seventeenth century in the *Provincial Letters*. But what does 'precursor' signify? Here, as ever, 'precursion' – a typical idealistic category – rather than untying an interpretative knot, points to its existence.[11] Where, we must ask, do Fra Timoteo's arguments come from?

The answer is easier for us today than it was half a century ago. Casuistry, liquidated by Pascal, has long since been redis-covered as a topic for research and theoretical reflection. It might even be said that it has become fashionable.[12] Reading a recent essay on the roots of casuistry, I chanced upon a passage from a prayer by St Bernardino of Siena which, translated, runs as follows:

> Evil can be permitted for two reasons: first, for the good that arises thereby; second, for the greater evil that thereby is avoided. In order to avoid a greater evil, evil is permitted in three ways: first, in order to avoid a spiritual evil in the soul, which is the greater evil, by permitting a bodily evil in the body, which is the lesser evil; second, in order to avoid a greater spiritual evil by permitting a lesser spiritual evil, just as a lesser sin is often permitted in order to avoid a greater one; third, in order to avoid a greater bodily evil by permitting another bodily evil that is lesser.[13]

---

11 On precursors, see Eugenio Garin, *La filosofia come sapere storico* (Bari: Laterza, 1959).

12 The revival of interest began with Albert R. Jonsen and Stephen Toulmin, *The Abuse of Casuistry* (Berkeley: University of California Press, 1988) and Edmund Leites, ed., *Conscience and Casuistry in Early Modern Europe* (Cambridge: Cambridge University Press, 1988).

13 Franco Mormando, S. J., '"To Persuade Is a Victory": Rhetoric and Moral Reasoning in the Sermons of Bernardino of Siena', in *The Context of Casuistry*, ed. James F. Keenan, S. J., and Thomas A. Shannon (Washington, DC: Georgetown University Press, 1995), pp. 55–84, esp. p. 80. See also Bernardino of Siena, *Opera omnia*, vol. IV (Florence: Collegii S. Bonaventurae, Ad Claras Aquas, 1956), pp. 258–9 (*De prohibitione usurae*, sermon XXXVIII).

In his prayer, Bernardino of Siena spoke of usury, not carnal relations, but his arguments bear a surprising resemblance to Fra Timoteo's. Why? The explanation is simple. Bernardino cited in support of his claims Gerard of Siena, who in turn referred to the text of another famous canonist, the *Quaestiones mercuriales super regulis juris* by Giovanni d'Andrea.[14] This book is also mentioned by Bernardo Machiavelli in his *Libro di ricordi*, along with two other legal works he bought on 3 January 1476: the *Novella super sexto Decretalium*, also by d'Andrea, and *Lectura super quinque libros Decretalium* by Niccolò de' Tudeschi (also known as Panormitanus).[15]

Giovanni d'Andrea, a renowned professor of canon law, taught at the universities of Padua and Bologna. He died in Bologna in 1348, probably from the plague. In the section on usury in his *Quaestiones mercuriales* (Rome, 1472), we find, besides the passage on corporal evil as a lesser evil quoted by Bernardino of Siena in his sermon, a remark on the reasons for choosing the lesser evil. In support of this thesis, Giovanni d'Andrea wrote, could be cited arguments drawn from 'divine and civil law as well. As regards the former, in Genesis 18 [in fact, 19] we read that Lot forced his daughters into prostitution so that a greater evil, namely sodomy, might be averted.'[16] It will

---

14 See Lawrin Armstrong, *The Idea of a Moral Economy: Gerard of Siena on Usury, Restitution, and Prescription* (Toronto: University of Toronto Press, 2016) – on Giovanni d'Andrea, cf. pp. 5, 25.

15 Bernardo Machiavelli, *Libro di ricordi*, pp. 39, 240–1. On Giovanni d'Andrea, 'fons et tuba juris', see J. T. Noonan Jr, *The Scholastic Analysis of Usury* (Cambridge, MA: Harvard University Press, 1957), pp. 65–7 and passim, citing J. F. von Schulte, *Die Geschichte der Quellen und Literatur des canonischen Rechts*, vol. II (Stuttgart: Enke, 1887) pp. 205–15.

16 Giovanni d'Andrea (Joannes Andreae), *Quaestiones mercuriales super regulis juris* (Rome, 1472), Gesamtkat. d. Wiegendr. 1734: 'Ulterius ad maiorem evidentiam istius articuli est sciendum quod sicut tactum fuit superius circa principium quaestionis malum potest permitti duabus de causis, sive vel propter bonum quod inde oritur vel propter malum quod inde vitatur. Maius autem malum vitatur et permittitur tribus modis. Primo quando vitatur malum spirituale in anima, quod est maius, propter malum corporale in corpore, quod est

be recalled that Fra Timoteo relied on the same chapter of Genesis to convince Lucrezia, though he chose a different episode, the one dealing with Lot's intercourse with his two daughters (Gen. 19:31–36).

On 1 July 1486 Bernardo Machiavelli noted that Niccolò, then seventeen years old, gave 'a barrel of red wine' to a bookseller called Francesco d'Andrea di Bartolomeo as payment for the binding of two works by Giovanni d'Andrea: the *Novella* and his *Quaestiones mercuriales*. A month earlier, the same bookseller had received a payment from Bernardo for binding another book: Livy's history of Rome.[17] Long before he drew his merciless portrait of the lawyer Nicia, Niccolò had started to make good use of his father's library.

4. 'To tell the truth,' Fra Timoteo told Lucrezia, 'I have been poring over my books for hours, studying the case, and after careful research I find that there are numerous considerations on our side, both general and particular.' Fra Timoteo was telling the truth.[18] Certainly, the relationship between his arguments

---

minus. Secundo, quando vitatur unum malum spirituale quod est maius propter minus malum spirituale, sicut sepe permittitur minus peccatum ut vitetur maius. Tercio, quando vitatur unum malum corporale maius propter aliud corporale quod est minus . . . Ad IX quando arguebatur quod duobus malis concurrentibus semper minus est eligendum, quod probatur per ius divinum et civile. Per ius divinum primo quia invenimus in lege mosaica scilicet Gen. xviii, quod Loth tradidit filias suas fornicationi ut vitaretur maius malum, scilicet sodomiticum.' (I have consulted a microfilm of the copy Ross. 2152 in the Vatican Apostolic Library, Vatican City, deposited in the Charles E. Young Research Library, UCLA.) Bernardo Machiavelli may have bought a copy of a different edition, published in Rome by Georg Lauer in 1476 (Gesamtkat. d. Wiegendr. 1736). For other editions of the *Quaestiones mercuriales*, cf. Gesamtkat. d. Wiegendr. 1734–41. Olschki suggests that Bernardo may have owned a copy of the Pavia edition of 1483 (*Libro di ricordi*, pp. 260–1). But this is impossible since he bought the book in 1477.

17 Bernardo Machiavelli, *Libro di ricordi*, pp. 222–3.

18 Machiavelli, *La mandragola*, p. 37. In a response to a series of questions Guicciardini asked him about *La mandragola*, Machiavelli wrote, 'And honestly, like Fra Timoteo, I've leafed through many books

and the scholastic tradition has been highlighted many times. But even the essay dedicated to this topic, around half a century ago, by the Finnish scholar Lauri Huovinen remained conjectural, attributing to Machiavelli an indirect knowledge of the arguments put forward by St Bonaventure and Aquinas, mediated by Savonarola's sermons.[19] The comparison with Giovanni d'Andrea's *Quaestiones mercuriales* confronts us with a certain fact that casts an unexpected light on Machiavelli's way of working. This is not some mere scholarly curiosity. As Francesco De Sanctis wrote, faced with Fra Timoteo even Machiavelli 'loses his good humour and grace, and resembles instead an anatomist who strips the flesh and exposes the nerves and tendons. In his imagination there is not laughter and there is not indignation in the presence of Timoteo, but the fearful detachment with which he depicts the prince, or adventurers or the nobleman'.[20] Let us now try to examine the frequently signalled proximity between *The Prince* and *Mandragola*, starting from the distinction made by Giovanni d'Andrea between general principles (such as the condemnation of usury) and derogation from principles dictated by circumstances (and hence the admissibility of usury).[21] This way of reasoning, typical of the casuistic tradition of scholastic provenance, takes us straight to the heart of *The Prince*.

---

to find the basis for this harrow' (*Opere*, ed. Corrado Vivanti, vol. II [Turin: Einaudi, 1999], p. 407 [16–20 October 1525]). I am grateful to Adrián López Denis for having brought this reference to my attention. Isaiah Berlin maintains that Fra Timoteo, like all the characters in *La mandragola*, violate their professed principles: '[He] never attempted to practice the maxims of the Fathers and the Schoolmen with which he liberally seasons his speeches' ('The Originality of Machiavelli' [1972], in *Against the Current* [Princeton, NJ: Princeton University Press, 2001], pp. 25–79, esp. p. 72 n. 1). In fact, Fra Timoteo precisely lives in accordance with his maxims.

19   Lauri Huovinen, 'Der Einfluss des theologischen Denkens des Renaissancezeit auf Machiavelli. "Mandragola", die Scholastiker und Savonarola', *Neuphilologische Mitteilungen* 57/1 (1956), pp. 1–13.

20   Francesco De Sanctis, *Storia della letteratura italiana*, ed. N. Gallo, vol. II (Turin: Einaudi, 1958), p. 603.

21   Noonan, *Scholastic Analysis of Usury*, pp. 65–7.

As is well known, there is a turning point in *The Prince*, emphatically signalled by Machiavelli himself. It is the celebrated opening of chapter 15:

It remains now to consider in what ways a ruler should act with regard to his subjects and allies. And since I am well aware that many people have written about this subject I fear that I may be thought presumptuous, for what I have to say differs from the precepts offered by others, especially on this matter. But because I want to write what will be useful to anyone who understands, it seems to me better to concentrate on what really happens rather than on theories or speculations. For many have imagined republics and principalities that have never been seen or known to exist. However, how men live is so different from how they should live that a ruler who does not do what is generally done, but persists in doing what ought to be done, will undermine his power rather than maintain it. If a ruler who wants always to act honourably is surrounded by many unscrupulous men his downfall is inevitable. Therefore, a ruler who wishes to maintain his power must be prepared to act immorally when this becomes necessary.[22]

---

22 Niccolò Machiavelli, *The Prince*, ed. Quentin Skinner and Russell Price, tr. Russell Price (Cambridge: Cambridge University Press, 2016), pp. 54–5. (*Il principe*, pp. 215–16: 'Resta ora a vedere quali debbano essere e' modi e governi di uno principe co' sudditi o con li amici. E perché io so che molti di questo hanno scritto, dubito, scrivendone ancora io, non essere tenuto prosuntuoso, partendomi massime nel disputare questa materia dalli ordini delli altri; ma, sendo l'intento mio, scrivere cosa utile a chi la intende, mi è parso più conveniente andare drieto alla verità effettuale della cosa che alla immaginazione di essa. E molti si sono immaginati republiche e principati, che non si sono mai visti né conosciuti essere in vero, perché elli è tanto discosto da come si vive a come si doverrebbe vivere, che colui che lascia quello che si fa per quello che si doverrebbe fare, impara più presto la ruina che la perservazione sua, perché uno omo che voglia fare in tutte le parte professione di buono conviene che ruini fra tanti che non sono buoni. Onde è necessario a uno principe, volendosi mantenere, imparare a potere essere non buono e usarlo e non usarlo secondo la necessità.') On this passage as a turning point in *The Prince*, see Federico Chabod, 'Machiavelli's Method and Style', in

As and when necessary, or as circumstances dictate. The next three chapters of *The Prince* duly retrace an identical trajectory of the general principle towards derogation.

Chapter 16: 'To begin, then, with the first of the above-mentioned qualities, I maintain that it would be desirable to be considered generous; *nevertheless [nondimanco]* if generosity is practiced in such a way that you will be considered generous, it will harm you.'[23]

Chapter 17: 'Turning to the other previously mentioned qualities, I maintain that every ruler should want to be thought merciful, not cruel; *nevertheless [nondimanco]*, one should take care not to be merciful in an inappropriate way. Cesare Borgia was considered cruel, yet his harsh measures restored order to the Romagna, unifying it and rendering it peaceful and loyal.'[24]

Chapter 18: 'Everyone knows how praiseworthy it is for a ruler to keep his promises, and live uprightly and not by trickery. *Nevertheless [nondimanco]*, experience shows that in our times the rulers who have done great things are those who have set little store by keeping their word, being skillful rather in cunningly deceiving men; they have got the better of those who have relied on being trustworthy.'[25]

Machiavelli and the Renaissance, tr. David Moore (Cambridge, MA: Harvard University Press, 1960), pp. 126–48, esp. pp. 143–4.

23 Ibid., pp. 55–6. (*Il principe*, p. 219: 'Cominciandomi adunque alle prime soprascritte qualità, dico come sarebbe bene essere tenuto liberale; *nondimanco* la liberalità, usata in modo che tu sia tenuto, ti offende.')

24 Ibid., p. 58. (*Il principe*, p. 226: 'Scendendo appresso alle altre parte e qualità preallegate da me, dico che ciascuno principe debbe desiderare di essere tenuto piatoso e non crudele: *nondimanco* debbe avvertire di non usare male questa pietà. Era tenuto Cesare Borgia crudele, nondimanco quella sua crudeltà aveva racconcia la Romagna, unitola, ridottola in pace e in fede.')

25 Ibid., p. 61. (*Il principe*, pp. 234–5: 'Quanto sia laudabile in uno principe mantenere la fede e vivere con integrità e non con astuzia, ciascuno lo intende; *nondimanco* si vede per esperienza ne' nostri tempi quelli principi avere fatto grandi cose, che della fede hanno tenuto poco conto e che hanno saputo con la astuzia aggirare e' cervelli delli òmini, e alla fine hanno superato quelli che si sono fondati in sulla lealtà.')

5. Reading Machiavelli in unmediated fashion, ignoring the endless debates occasioned by his writings, is obviously impossible. In this instance, the normal relationship between history and historiography assumes especially intricate forms. We need to know whether (and, if so, how) our reading may have been influenced, directly or indirectly, by previous research, perhaps forgotten or even unbeknown to us. A brief historiographical digression is therefore unavoidable.

The passages quoted above, drawn from a much vaster sequence, indicate Machiavelli's fondness for the adverb *nondimanco* ('nevertheless'): a factor ignored by those scholars who limit their analysis of Machiavelli's language to the words *virtù* and *fortuna*.[26] Fredi Chiappelli is, of course, a different case. In his *Nuovi studi sul linguaggio di Machiavelli*, he noted the frequency of *nondimeno* and *nondimanco* in Machiavelli's diplomatic writings (*Legazioni e commissarie*), of which he was in the process of preparing an edition (subsequently interrupted); and he linked these words to a marked propensity for concessive and counter-concessive sentences.[27] In this context Chiappelli did not repeat a previous reference to the broader implications of *nondimeno* and *nondimanco*. In *Studi sul linguaggio del Machiavelli*, he had already interpreted an instance of *nondimanco* in *The Prince* (chapter 11) as evidence of an alleged tension in Machiavelli's work between two contradictory approaches, the first objective and scientific, the second emotional and artistic.[28]

This interpretation is unconvincing. In general, as has been noted countless times, in Machiavelli's texts it is difficult to distinguish between artistic component and scientific component. More specifically, in the passage from *The Prince* analysed by Chiappelli

26 See Pocock, *Machiavellian Moment*, pp. 156–82.

27 Fredi Chiappelli, *Nuovi studi sul linguaggio di Machiavelli* (Florence: Le Monnier, 1969), pp. 115–25.

28 Fredi Chiappelli, *Studi sul linguaggio di Machiavelli* (Florence: Le Monnier, 1952), p. 107ff. In his *Nuovi studi*, p. vii, Chiappelli stresses 'the homogeneity of the Machiavellian language of *negotia* with the brilliant language of *otia*' – a remark that might have been the starting point for a fuller analysis.

we recognize the linguistic and conceptual dynamic described above, although here geared to the sarcasm that pervades the entire chapter entitled 'Ecclesiastical Principalities':

> However, since they are controlled by a higher power, which the human mind cannot comprehend, I shall refrain from discussing them; since they are raised up and maintained by God, only a presumptuous and rash man would examine them.
>
> *Nevertheless*, someone might ask me how it has happened that the temporal power of the Church has become so great . . .[29]

The syntactical construction is the usual one, although this time it is directed to indicating that the putative exception conforms, ironically, to the rule. The passages quoted above proceed inversely, from the rule to the exception. The significance of this argumentative strategy has been overlooked by both generalists and contextualists. By 'generalists' I mean those scholars who identify Machiavelli's modernity with the discovery of a series of universal principles about politics, rooted in his own political and intellectual experience. By 'contextualists' I mean those who stress Machiavelli's attempt to root his general principles, invariably and exclusively, in specific contexts and circumstances. In fact, Machiavelli's political reflection focuses as much on the exception as on the rule. Above all, however, it focuses on the tension between them, usually expressed by the words *nondimeno* or *nondimanco*.

In his *Studi sul linguaggio di Machiavelli*, Chiappelli ascribed to the author of *The Prince* the aim of 'producing a casuistry based on necessity'.[30] In these words we hear an echo of Croce's

---

29 Machiavelli, *The Prince*, p. 40. *Il principe*, p. 176:

'Ma sendo quelli [principati ecclesiastici] retti da cagione superiori, alle quali mente umana non aggiugne, lascerò el parlarne, perché, sendo essaltati e mantenuti da Dio, sarebbe offizio di uomo prosuntuoso e temerario discorrerne.

Nondimanco, se alcuno mi ricercassi donde viene che la Chiesa nel temporale sia venuta a tanta grandezza . . .'

30 Chiappelli, *Studi*, p. 48.

essay 'Machiavelli e Vico. La politica e l'etica'. To fully understand the content of these famous pages, it is imperative to specify the context, which is frequently ignored.[31] Prior to publication in *La Critica* (and subsequently as a chapter in his *Elementi
di politica* [1925]), the essay had appeared in *Giornale d'Italia*, 4
July 1924.[32] Croce was prompted to publish a text of this kind in
a daily paper by his polemical target, which was implicit and yet
self-evident: Mussolini's 'Prelude to Machiavelli', published in
Gerarchia in April 1924.[33] In this brief, cursory piece, based
exclusively on *The Prince*, Mussolini underscored Machiavelli's
praise of force and his contempt (which Mussolini stated he fully
shared) for human beings.[34] Croce's response came out amid the
Matteotti Crisis. The socialist deputy had disappeared on 10
June, kidnapped and murdered (it later turned out) by a Fascist
squad; his body was found near Rome on 16 August. On 26 June
Croce had unenthusiastically supported Mussolini's government
in a confidence vote.[35] A few days later, in a series of reflections
rendered tragically pertinent by political circumstances, Croce
stressed Machiavelli's stern and rueful moral consciousness, the
religious tones of his attitude towards politics, and his 'yearning'
for 'an unattainable society of good and pure men'.[36] According

31   What follows is not mentioned by Gennaro Sasso, 'Benedetto
Croce interprete di Machiavelli', in *Benedetto Croce*, ed. Francesco
Flora (Milan: Malfasi, 1953), pp. 305–22.

32   Silvano Borsari, ed., *L'opera di Benedetto Croce. Bibliografia*
(Naples: Istituto Italiano per gli Studi Storici, 1964), no. 1783.

33   Benito Mussolini, 'Preludio al Machiavelli', *Scritti e discorsi*, vol.
IV, *Il 1924* (Milan: Hoepli, 1934), pp. 105–10. The April 1924 issue of
Gerarchia appeared towards the end of the month (ibid., p. 105).

34   Mussolini, 'Preludio', p. 108 ('Machiavelli è uno spregiatore
degli uomini . . . Di tempo ne è passato, ma se mi fosse lecito giudicare
i miei simili e contemporanei, io non potrei in alcun modo attenuare il
giudizio di Machiavelli. Dovrei, forse, aggravarlo').

35   Renzo De Felice, *Mussolini il fascista* (Turin: Einaudi, 1966),
pp. 652–3, quoting a passage from the interview Croce gave to
Giornale d'Italia after the confidence vote.

36   Benedetto Croce, 'Machiavelli e Vico. La politica e l'etica', in
Elementi di politica (Bari: Laterza, 1925), pp. 59–67. The introduction
is dated July 1924; printing was completed in October 1924; the book

to Croce, the continuation of Machiavelli's thought was to be sought 'neither from those Machiavellians who embraced his casuistry and political prescriptions, and wrote on *raison d'état*, often mixing moralistic trivialities with these precepts', nor from anti-Machiavellians. The 'true and worthy' successor to Machiavelli, who 'discovered the necessity and autonomy of politics', Croce explained, was Giambattista Vico.[37] Casuistry was a peripheral element in the nucleus of Machiavelli's political thought, inspired by an austere morality. And yet, according to Croce, it unquestionably formed part of it.

After the collapse of Fascism, Croce, then in his eighties, returned to Machiavelli and the relationship between morality and politics, characterizing it as 'una questione che forse non si chiuderà mai' – a question that might never be resolved.[38] In this late essay Croce criticized a book by Goffredo Quadri, which underscored the link between Machiavelli's ideas on politics and late-medieval theological and legal casuistry.[39] Croce refuted Quadri's argument with reference to Pascal and Schleiermacher, who had demonstrated that casuistry was alien to reflection on morality.[40]

Croce had apparently forgotten that two decades earlier he himself had referred to 'casuistry' in connection with Machiavelli. His refutation of Quadri's argument relied upon an implicit, bizarre syllogism or pseudo-syllogism: Machiavelli was a profoundly moral thinker; casuistry is foreign to moral thought;

---

was distributed in 1925. As is well known, Croce's conversion to a militant opposition to Fascism was signalled by his 'La protesta contro il "Manifesto degli intellettuali fascistici"', dated 1 May 1925, *La Critica* XXIII (1925), pp. 310–12.

37 Croce, *Elementi*, p. 64. In an essay on modern studies of Machiavelli, Russo (*Machiavelli*, p. 305) rephrased Croce's comment, making not Machiavelli but his seventeenth-century readers and commentators the casuists.

38 Benedetto Croce, 'La questione del Machiavelli', in *Indagini su Hegel* (Bari: Laterza, 1952), pp. 164–76 (a text originally published in *Quaderni della critica* 5/14 [July 1949], pp. 1–9, under the title 'Una questione che forse non si chiuderà mai: La questione del Machiavelli').

39 Goffredo Quadri, *Niccolò Machiavelli e la costruzione politica della coscienza morale*, 2nd rev. edn (Florence: La Nuova Italia, 1971).

40 Croce, *Indagini*, p. 173.

therefore Machiavelli had nothing to do with casuistry. While Quadri is a sloppy, superficial scholar, he does deserve recognition for having grasped – in the revised and expanded edition of his own book, which was different from the one criticized by Croce – the significance of a book where Machiavelli's name is never mentioned: Alessandro Bonucci's *La derogabilità del diritto naturale nella Scolastica* (1906) – roughly, 'Exceptions to natural law in Scholasticism'.[41] Most of the medieval debates analysed by Bonucci revolve around passages from the Bible. Moses, for instance, is said to have allowed repudiation of a first wife and remarriage, on the basis of the principle *permisit fieri mala, ne fierent pejora* ('he permitted the bad in order to avoid something worse').[42] In his *Quaestiones mercuriales*, as Bonucci noted, Giovanni d'Andrea illustrated the same principle, recalling God's toleration of both Jewish sacrifices and usury.[43] With this we are back to *Mandragola* and Fra Timoteo's speech; we are also back to *The Prince* and *Discourses on Livy*. The following passage from the latter will demonstrate the consistency of Machiavelli's thought: 'Although employing deceit in every action is detestable', we read in the *Discourses* (book III, chapter 40), 'in waging war, it is, *nevertheless*, a laudable and glorious thing'.[44] As usual, Machiavelli starts out from the universal

---

41 Quadri (*Niccolò Machiavelli*, 1971 edn, p. 230) characterizes it as a 'magnificent book'; and see also ibid., p. 264 (as well as the entry on 'Bonucci, Alessandro' by P. Craveri and F. Parente in *Dizionario biografico degli Italiani*). Much less useful, because imprisoned in abstract, teleological categories, are the studies by Rodolfo de Mattei collected in *Dal premachiavellismo all'antimachiavellismo* (Florence: Sansoni, 1969) – see esp. the first part, 'Aspetti di premachiavellismo', pp. 3–48.

42 Alessandro Bonucci, *La derogabilità del diritto naturale nella Scolastica* (Perugia: Bartelli, 1906), p. 55.

43 Ibid., p. 276.

44 Niccolò Machiavelli, *Discourses on Livy*, tr. Julia Conaway Bondanella and Peter Bondanella (Oxford: Oxford University Press, 2008), p. 348. (Machiavelli, *Discorsi sopra la prima deca di Tito Livio*, ed. Corrado Vivanti [Turin: Einaudi, 1983], p. 503: 'Ancora che lo usare la fraude in ogni azione sia detestabile, *nondimanco* nel maneggiare la guerra è cosa laudabile e gloriosa'.) On this passage, see Strauss, *Thoughts on Machiavelli*, pp. 237–8.

moral rule and arrives at local exceptions. But in this passage the exception is not simply admissible, it is 'laudable and glorious'.

6. 'In the vast literature inspired by Machiavelli', wrote John Humphreys Whitfield, 'proof has been largely missing.'[45] To stress (as did Quadri) the pervasiveness of scholastic philosophy in Machiavelli's age does not amount to proof.[46] But proof of Machiavelli's reworking of Giovanni d'Andrea's *Quaestiones mercuriales* in the scene from *Mandragola* confronts us with something different. We can easily imagine the young Machiavelli browsing through his father's books, coming across pages that fired his intelligence and imagination. But who would have guessed that such stimulation could derive from a scholastic treatise on canon law? Which aspects of scholastic philosophy aroused Machiavelli's curiosity? And what did he make of such reading?

For a long time such questions could not have been raised, or even contemplated. In a typical passage, Luigi Russo contrasted Machiavelli's sequential reasoning, 'which will subsequently be that of Galileo and all modern scientific prose', with scholasticism's pyramidal reasoning, based on a series of concealed syllogisms descending from a single universal premise.[47] As incarnations, respectively, of the Renaissance and the Middle Ages, Machiavelli and scholasticism seemed like completely incompatible entities. Today, the picture has changed (notwithstanding the presence of variously argued theories of modernity). The research of Anneliese Maier and Paul Oskar Kristeller has shown the extent to which scholastic philosophy mattered during the so-called Renaissance.[48]

---

45 John Humphreys Whitfield, *Discourses on Machiavelli* (Cambridge: Heffer, 1958), p. 181.

46 See Quadri, *Niccolò Machiavelli*, 1971 edn, pp. 9, 11.

47 Russo, *Machiavelli*, pp. 79, 81.

48 P. O. Kristeller, *Medieval Aspects of Renaissance Learning*, ed. E. P. Mahoney (Durham, NC: Duke University Press, 1974). See esp. the second essay, 'Thomism and the Italian Thought of the Renaissance'

Nevertheless, as far as Machiavelli is concerned, there remains something to be learned in this respect.

But first we should recall something important. In 1639 Gabriel Naudé compared Thomas Aquinas's remarks on tyranny to Machiavelli's *Prince*, noting that both writers advised tyrants to assume an outwardly religious appearance. With the malice of the *libertin érudit*, Naudé commented, 'Bizarre advice, coming from a saint.'[49] Naudé merely gave an ironic twist to a serious comparison that had been made some years earlier by Kaspar Schoppe, in the context of an implicit defence of Machiavelli's ideas.[50] In the entry on 'Machiavel' in his *Dictionnaire*, Pierre

---

(1967), pp. 29–91. For an early version of Kristeller's interpretation, see his 'Florentine Platonism and Its Relations with Humanism and Scholasticism' (1939), in *Studies in Renaissance Thought and Letters*, vol. III (Rome: Edizioni di Storia e Letteratura, 1993), pp. 39–48. Old commonplaces are tenacious, even, exceptionally, in the pages of a scholar like Dionisotti (*Machiavellerie*, p. 2): 'A scholastic tradition: pre-humanist and now discarded in Italy, but still alive abroad' (in connection with a comparison between the writings of Pier Andrea da Verrazzano and Machiavelli's *Decennale*).

49 Gabriel Naudé, *Considérations politiques sur les coups d'état* (Hildesheim-Zurich-New York: Georg Olms, 1993) (a facsimile of the 1st edn, Rome, 1639), pp. 12–14. See, e.g., 'Et les mesme Aristote [...] lorsqu'il a traitté de la Politique et des gouvernemens opposez à la Monarchie, Aristocratie et Democratie, qui sont la tyrannie, l'olygarchie et l'ochlocratie, il donne aussi bien les preceptes de ces trois vicieux que des legitimes. Enquoy il a esté suivy par sainct Thomas en ses Commentaires, où après avoir blasmé et dissuadé par toutes raisons possibles la domination tyrannique, il donne neantmoins les advis et les regles communes pour l'établir, au cas que quelqu'un soit si méchant que de le vouloir faire. Et qu'ainsi ne soit, voilà ses propres mots tirez du Commentaire sur le cinquième des Politiques texte XI: *Ad salvationem tyrannidis*. [...] Voilà certes des preceptes bien estranges en la bouche d'un Sainct, et qui ne different en rien de ceux de Machiavel et de Cardan.'

50 Cf. Kaspar Schoppe, *Paedia politices* (Rome: Ex typographia Andreae Phaei, 1623) (which does not mention Machiavelli), based on his unpublished treatise *Machiavellica*. See Mario D'Addio, *Il pensiero politico di Gaspare Scioppio e il machiavellismo del Seicento* (Milan: Giuffrè, 1962), p. 416ff; Giuliano Procacci, *Studi sulla fortuna del Machiavelli* (Rome: Istituto Storico Italiano per l'Età Moderna et Contemporanea, 1965), pp. 679, 328 (and see below chapters 4 and 7).

Bayle quoted Naudé's comments extensively, with obvious relish.[51] Schoppe, Naudé and Bayle were all unaware that the pages on tyranny ascribed to Aquinas were in fact by one of his continuators, Peter of Auvergne.[52] But the convergences between *The Prince* and the pseudo-Aquinas pointed out by Naudé have been there for scholars to see for almost four centuries, without having the slightest influence on the interpretation of Machiavelli. As to the history of Machiavelli's reception, naturally, Naudé is conspicuously present.[53]

All this shows that *Rezeptionsgeschichte* cannot be regarded as a domain independent of actual historical analysis.[54] In his commentary on *The Prince* (published in 1891 and in many respects still unsurpassed), Lawrence Burd remarked in a note to chapter 18 that there was nothing 'unnatural' in the resemblance pointed out by Naudé, since both Aquinas and Machiavelli depended on Aristotle.[55] Burd's remark, which echoed Bayle's, failed to elicit any scholarly interest. The possibility of a relationship between Machiavelli, Aristotle and Aquinas never came to be regarded as an admissible research topic. Yet the question has continued to arise from time to time, a broken line that never turned into an arrow (but see chapter 4 below).

In 1942 Jacques Maritain, an exile from Nazi-occupied France, published an essay entitled 'The End of Machiavellianism': an appeal to democratic states, starting

---

51 Pierre Bayle, *Dictionnaire historique et critique*, 5th rev. edn, corrected and expanded, vol. III (Amsterdam-Leyden-The Hague-Utrecht: Pierre Brunel, 1740), p. 246.

52 See Lidia Lanza, 'Aspetti della ricezione della *Politica* aristotelica nel XIII secolo: Pietro d'Alvernia', *Studi medievali*, 3rd ser., 35/2 (1994), pp. 643–94.

53 Procacci, *Studi sulla fortuna del Machiavelli*. The whole of chapter 3 ('Machiavelli aristotelico') is important. Only in exceptional cases (p. 285) does Procacci attach exegetical value to the reception reconstructed by him.

54 On this point, see below, chapter 4, pp. 63–7.

55 Niccolò Machiavelli, *Il principe*, ed. L. A. Burd and introd. Lord Acton (Oxford: Clarendon, 1891), p. 304.

with the United States, to fight totalitarian regimes, the embodiment of modern Machiavellianism. In the section dealing directly with Machiavelli, which is comparatively short, Maritain wrote, 'What makes the study of Machiavelli extremely instructive for a philosopher is the fact that nowhere is it possible to find a more purely artistic conception of politics. And here is his chief philosophical fault, if it is true that politics belongs to the field of the "praktikon" (to do), not of the "poietikon" (to make), and is by essence a branch – the principal branch, according to Aristotle – of ethics.'[56]

Maritain, a neo-Thomist philosopher and an authority on Aquinas, only referred explicitly to Aristotle. Leo Strauss, who echoed – without acknowledgement – a passage from Maritain's essay, dropped the allusion to Aquinas.[57] The implications of Maritain's piece were developed – also without explicit acknowledgement – by Charles Singleton, the leading Dante scholar and translator of his day, in an essay entitled 'The Perspective of Art' (1953). This conversational, unassuming piece, without footnotes and scholarly references, includes a fictional dialogue between Machiavelli and two characters from Plato's *Republic*. In my view, Singleton's pages are among the most profound on Machiavelli's thought ever written.[58] If I am not mistaken, they went unnoticed by Machiavelli scholars, with the exception of Isaiah Berlin, who

---

56 Jacques Maritain, 'The End of Machiavellianism', *Review of Politics* 4/1 (1942), pp. 1–33, esp. p. 7.

57 Ibid., p. 20: 'Among modern states, there is one state to whose political instinct and understanding Machiavellianism is basically repugnant, this one is the United States'; Strauss, *Thoughts on Machiavelli*, p. 13: 'The United States of America may be said to be the only country in the world which was founded in explicit opposition to Machiavellian principles.' Maritain's words are preceded by the remark that only Christian politics could confront Machiavellianism in all its forms – a passage which Strauss understandably ignored.

58 C. S. Singleton, 'The Perspective of Art', *Kenyon Review* 15/2 (1953), pp. 169–89. At p. 170 Singleton refers to 'certain neo-Thomists'. Singleton relied heavily on Maritain's *Art et scholastique* (1927) in his *An Essay on the* Vita Nuova (Cambridge, MA: Harvard University Press, 1949), pp. 116, 165.

briefly summarized their content.[59] Singleton's argument, in a nutshell, is that Machiavelli detached himself from the Aristotelian-Thomistic tradition because he shifted politics from the sphere of *doing* to the sphere of *making*, from *agere* to *facere*.[60] His enduring originality consisted in conceiving of politics as an 'art' in the Aristotelian-Thomistic sense: an activity devoid of moral connotations and oriented to the production of objects.

All this may seem somewhat removed from serious historico-philological research on Machiavelli's work. It should be noted that Singleton himself concluded his conversation in a deliberately minor key:

> The considerable time which was taken in my beginning to find and distinguish the perspective of art in the thought of Thomas Aquinas must have left you wondering what I intended to make of the fact that we *then* find that frame of thought in Machiavelli. Am I suggesting that Machiavelli was a student of the *Summa*? And that he took the conception from there, gleefully saying, 'Ah, here's something I can use!' But I know that you don't think I mean this. What then is the connection or interest?

According to Singleton, the answer was 'a pattern of thought.'[61] But perhaps we can come up with a more precise answer.

7. We seem to be confronted with two different questions: the relationships between Machiavelli and Aquinas on the one hand and between Machiavelli and Aristotle on the other. But we are dealing (see below, chapters 2 and 4) with related questions. Machiavelli also (not exclusively, but also) read Aristotle through the filter of Aquinas. A filter used critically: a warning to be borne in mind amid attempts to transform Machiavelli into a good Christian.[62] One distinguished scholar has been heard to wonder

---

59   Berlin, 'The Originality of Machiavelli', p. 35.
60   This objection had already been formulated by Schoppe, *Paedia politices*, p. 17ff (and see chapter 4 below).
61   Singleton, 'The Perspective of Art', p. 188.
62   Cf. the essays on Machiavelli and religion published in *Journal*

whether the famous passage in chapter 6 of *The Prince* on Cyrus, Romulus, Theseus and Moses, 'who had such a great master', really implied 'impious thoughts', since its language seemed 'irritatingly orthodox'.[63] Irony is an implicit rhetorical figure: not everyone gets it. It is worth recalling that Agostino Nifo, the Aristotelian philosopher who plagiarized *The Prince* when it was still circulating in manuscript, suppressed the name of Moses in that passage to avoid scandalizing his readers.[64]

But the inclusion of Moses in this company was not Machiavelli's invention. Discovery of its source throws some interesting light on how Machiavelli worked. He drew his inspiration from Valerius Maximus, specifically from section I, 2 of *Facta et dicta memorabilia* (Memorable doings and sayings), entitled 'On feigned religion' (*De simulata religione*). Once again we are approaching a topic apparently untouched by Machiavelli scholars.[65] True, Walker mentioned Valerius Maximus among Machiavelli's possible sources, listing the earliest editions of his work (Johann Mentelin, Strasbourg 1470; Vindelinus de Spira, Venice 1471; in aedib. Aldi Romani, Venice 1502).[66] But those editions do not include the section 'On Feigned Religion', revealed as a genuine text of Valerius Maximus's by the German humanist Johannes Cuspinianus. Shortly afterwards, Aldo Manuzio inserted it into a 1501 printing, together with a grateful letter

of the History of Ideas 60/4 (1999); Maurizio Viroli, *Il Dio di Machiavelli e il problema morale dell'Italia* (Bari: Laterza, 2005).

63 Pocock, *Machiavellian Moment*, p. 170.

64 Procacci, *Studi*, p. 12.

65 Valerius Maximus goes unmentioned in the first three volumes of Gennaro Sasso, *Machiavelli e gli antichi* (Milan: Ricciardi, 1987–1988). Volume IV (1997) contains two references to him. As regards the second of them, it is noted that we are dealing with 'obvious ideas, which cannot have been foreign to Machiavelli' (p. 301). Even Bayle's mention of Christoph Adam Rupert, *Dissertationes mixtæ ad Valerii Maximi exemplorum memorabilium libros IX* (Nuremberg: Johann Tauber, 1663), as a source of Alberico Gentili's judgement on Machiavelli, did not inspire research on what Machiavelli might have found of interest in Valerius Maximus.

66 Niccolò Machiavelli, *The Discourses*, vol. II, ed. L. J. Walker (New Haven, CT: Yale University Press, 1950), p. 292.

22

addressed to Cuspinianus.[67] Naturally, Moses did not figure in the section *De simulata religione,* or in other passages of Valerius Maximus. He appeared in the commentary on Valerius Maximus that Badius Ascensius, the Parisian printer and humanist, added as a supplement to the fifteenth-century commentary by Oliverius Arzignanensis.

Here is the passage from Valerius Maximus: 'Numa Pompilius, wishing to bind the Roman people with rituals, tried to make it appear that he had meetings by night with the goddess Aegeria and that at her prompting he instituted rituals that would be acceptable to the immortal gods.'[68]

In his commentary, Badius quoted Livy's well-known passage on Numa (*Ab urbe condita,* I, 19) and concluded, 'Just as, therefore, Moses truthfully (*vere*) declared to have received from God a law and that law had been written by God's own hand, so too (*ita*) pagan founders of laws added the authority of some divinity, knowing that it is difficult for men to obey other men.'[69]

---

67 Cf. H. G. Fletcher III, *New Aldine Studies* (San Francisco: Rosenthal, 1988), pp. 109–11. The part that has recently come to light was first published in Leipzig in 1501 by Martin of Würzburg.

68 Valerius Maximus, *Facta et dicta memorabilia,* I.2.1, ed. J. Briscoe, p. 26, quoting from Julius Paris's epitome: 'Numa Pompilius, ut populum Romanum sacris obligaret, volebat videri sibi cum dea Aegeria congressus esse nocturnos, eiusque monitu quae se accepta diis immortalibus sacra forent instituere.' The translation in the text above is that of D. R. Shackleton Bailey (Loeb Classical Library, 2000).

69 *Valerius Maximus cum commentario historico videlicet ac litterato Oliverii Arzignanensis et familiari admodum ac succincto Jodoci Badii Ascensi, qui quattuor et viginti exempla Aldino auspicio nuper inventa simili commentatione declaravit, et totum opus gemina tabella altera titulorum, altera litterarum illustravit. Additis Theophili lucubrationibus nec non pene vivis imaginibus, que priscorum gesta referre videntur,* D. Lu. Ant. de Giunta (Venetiis: 1513), c. xiiir: 'Sicut ergo Moses vere asseruit se legem a deo deique digitis scriptam accepisse, ita ethnici quoque legum latores numinis alicuius interposuerunt authoritatem, scientes difficile esse hominem homini parere.' According to Paolo Camerini, *Annali dei Giunti,* vol. I, *Venezia* (Florence: Sansoni, 1962), pt. 1, p. 154, para. 159, this edition is a reprint of the one published by Bartolomeo Zanni in 1508 – an incorrect statement, I presume, since the latter did not include Badius's commentary, first published in Paris in 1510.

Well-wrought sentences that Machiavelli must have read and reread with relish. In them he will have found a familiar argument. In a dialogue entitled *De legibus et iudiciis*, written circa 1483 but not published, by the Florentine chancellor Bartolomeo Scala, the divine origins of law were exemplified by comparing Moses, 'whom, as they say, spoke with God' (*qui cum deo fertur locutus*), to Minos: two names followed shortly by those of Zoroaster, Charondas, Hermes Trismegistus, Lycurgus, Draco, Solon, Numa, Zalmoxis and Mohammed.[70] The legislators appealed to nature, which assumes different names in different religions (hence including the 'evil sect' of Mohammed); what decrees the laws is well-ordered reason, 'the likeness of divinity'. This argument was put forward by the other participant in the dialogue: Bernardo Machiavelli. It is impossible to decide to what extent Bartolomeo Scala attributed his own ideas to Bernardo. But it is notable that in these

---

70 Lamberto Borghi, ed., 'Bartholomeus Scala de legibus et iudiciis dialogus', *La Bibliofilía* 42/8–10 (Aug.–Oct. 1940), pp. 256–82, esp. p. 273: 'Nos Moysem, qui cum deo fertur locutus, ut amicus ad amicum solet, tabulas dictante domino quas scripsisset postquam cum eo quadraginta dies totidemque fuisset noctes, quibus quidem nec panem gustavisset aut aquam, tradidisse hominibus primum leges pie credimus; etsi Minoem alii, nonnulli Rhadamantum primos in Creta posuisse leges tradunt.' The new edition of the *Dialogus*, edited by Alison Brown (by whom see also *Bartolomeo Scala, 1430–1497, Chancellor of Florence: The Humanist as Bureaucrat* [Princeton, NJ: Princeton University Press, 1979], esp. pp. 288–96), for no reason corrects '*qui*' into '*quem*', contrary to the only manuscript: 'Nos Moysem quem, cum Deo fertur locutus [...] tradidisse hominibus primum leges pie credimus.' See Bartolomeo Scala, *Humanistic and Political Writings*, ed. Alison Brown (Tempe, AZ: Medieval and Renaissance Texts and Studies, 1997), pp. 338–64 (esp. pp. 355, 549 n. 93, correctly n. 94). A recent English translation skips the word '*fertur*', thereby changing the meaning of the entire passage: 'As people of faith, we devoutly believe that Moses spoke directly with God.' See Bartolomeo Scala, *Dialogue on Laws and Legal Judgements*, tr. David Marsh, in *Cambridge Translations of Renaissance Philosophical Texts*, vol. II, ed. Jill Kraye (Cambridge: Cambridge University Press, 1997), pp. 173–99, esp. p. 187. See now the entry 'Scala, Bartolomeo' by L. Boschetto in *Enciclopedia machiavelliana*, vol. II, pp. 492–5.

pages Bernardo, after having repeatedly referred to Plato and
his followers, 'who wish to be called Platonists', stressed the
etymology of the word *religio*, invoking alongside the familiar
names of Cicero and Lactantius that of Lucretius. The cohesive
function of religion (from *re-ligare*) was illustrated with words
from the poem that Bernardo's son transcribed in its entirety
some years later. The line forcefully stated the author's aim to
untie human minds from religion's knots: *et artis religionum
animos nodis ex(s)olvere pergo* (*De rerum natura*, I, 931–2 ;
repeated at IV, 6–7).[71]

Badius's commentary on Valerius Maximus was published in
Paris in 1510 and 1513, and twice in Milan in 1513.[72] But
Machiavelli probably consulted a different edition, published in
Venice by Lucantonio Giunta (a branch of the same family of
publishers operating in Florence). The colophon of this printing is
dated 24 August 1513. A few months later, on 10 December,
Machiavelli wrote the famous letter to Francesco Vettori in which
he informed him that he had 'composed a little book *On*

---

71   On Machiavelli's transcription of *De rerum natura*, see the entry
'Lucrezio Caro, Tito' by Alison Brown and Gennaro Sasso in *Enciclopedia
machiavelliana*, vol. II, pp. 97–9, 99–101. See also P. A. Rahe, 'In the
Shadow of Lucretius: The Epicurean Foundations of Machiavelli's
Political Thought', *History of Political Thought* 28/1 (2007), pp. 30–55,
and Alison Brown, 'Machiavelli and the Influence of Lucretius', in *The
Return of Lucretius to Renaissance Florence* (Cambridge, MA: Harvard
University Press, 2010), p. 68ff. For a close rereading of the rediscovery of
Lucretius outside the banal filter of 'modernity', cf. Pierre Vesperini,
Lucrèce. Archéologie d'un classique européen (Paris: Fayard, 2017), p.
213ff (there is no discussion of Machiavelli, briefly mentioned at p. 243).

72   Philippe Renouard, *Bibliographie des impressions et des
oeuvres de Josse Badius Ascensius, imprimeur et humaniste, 1462–
1535*, vol. III (Paris: Paul et fils et Guillemin, 1908), pp. 316–19, lists
the following Paris or Milan editions: J. Badius (Paris, 1510); G. A.
Scinzenzeler for J. J. de Legnano and brothers (Milan, 1513); L. Vegius
(Milan, 1513); and J. Badius and J. Petit (Paris, 1513). According to
Ennio Sandal, *Editori e tipografi a Milano nel Cinquecento*, vol. II
(Baden-Baden: Koerner, 1978), p. 270, the edition published by Vegio
is a reprint of the one published by Minuziano in 1508 – an incorrect
statement, for the reasons given above (see n. 68).

Principalities ... even though I am still revising and adding to it'.[73]
8. Machiavelli knew (in Badius's words) 'how difficult it is for men to obey other men'. For this reason he was convinced that no power could be maintained without religion: a bond based on appearances. 'For the common people are impressed by appearances and outcomes and everywhere the common people are the vast majority' (*The Prince*, chapter 18).[74] Such is the rule; knowledge of the 'actual reality' is an exception – the property of a few.

---

73 Machiavelli, *The Prince*, appendix A, pp. 93–4 (*Opere*, vol. II, p. 296: 'Uno opusculo *De principatibus* ... che tuttavolta io lo ingrasso e ripulisco').

74 Ibid., p. 63; tr. modified (*Il principe*, p. 119: 'El vulgo ne va preso con quello che pare e con lo evento della cosa, e nel mondo non è se non vulgo'). And see the entry 'Religione' by E. Cutinelli-Rendina in *Enciclopedia machiavelliana*, vol. II, pp. 392–400.

2

Becoming Machiavelli: A New Reading of the Ghiribizzi al Soderini

1. The so-called *Ghiribizzi al Soderini* is the draft of a letter that Machiavelli possibly didn't send.[1] A single copy of the draft exists, made in the late sixteenth century by Giuliano de' Ricci, one of Machiavelli's nephews. The discovery of the original, found by Jean-Jacques Marchand among the Carte Capponi in the Vatican Library, prompted renewed debate over the dating of the draft, the circumstances of its composition, and the identity of the addressee.[2] After an intense discussion, virtually

---

[1] The following text is a revised version of the one presented at the conference on Machiavelli held at Columbia University on 24 October 2003.

[2] Roberto Ridolfi and Paolo Ghiglieri, 'I *Ghiribizzi* al Soderini', *La Bibliofilía* 72/1 (1970), pp. 53–74; Mario Martelli, 'I "Ghiribizzi" a Giovan Battista Soderino', *Rinascimento*, 2nd ser., 9 (1969) (but 1972), pp. 147–80; Roberto Ridolfi, 'Ancora sui *Ghiribizzi* al Soderini', *La Bibliofilía* 74/1 (1972), pp. 1–7; Mario Martelli, 'Ancora sui "Ghiribizzi" a Giovan Battista Soderini', *Rinascimento*, 2nd ser., 10 (1970) (but 1973), pp. 3–27; Gennaro Sasso, 'Qualche osservazione sui *Ghiribizzi al Soderino*', in *Machiavelli e gli antichi*, vol. II (Milan: Ricciardi, 1988), pp. 3–56; R. Ridolfi, 'Ultime postille machiavelliane', *La Bibliofilía* 77 (1975), pp. 65–9; Carlo Pincin, 'Osservazioni sul modo di procedere di Machiavegli nel *De principatibus*, XV–XXV', in *Essays Presented to Myron P. Gilmore*, vol. I, *History*, ed. Sergio Bertelli and Gloria Ramakus (Florence: La Nuova Italia, 1978), pp. 209–30; Paolo Ghiglieri, 'Noterella all'edizione dei *Ghiribizzi*', *La Bibliofilía* 82/1 (1980), pp. 81–2; and Mario Martelli, 'I dettagli della

unanimous agreement was reached on the following points: the draft was not written in 1512, as previously thought, but 1506; the addressee, traditionally identified as Pier Soderini, the *gonfaloniere* of Florence, was in fact the latter's nephew, Giovan Battista Soderini; the draft was not written in Florence after the return of the Medici, but in all likelihood in Perugia, immediately after Pope Julius II's entry into the city.

As Ridolfi immediately remarked, the correction of the date of the draft had important implications, since various passages of the *Ghiribizzi* anticipate, sometimes almost to the letter, fragments of *The Prince* and the *Discourses*.[3] Mario Martelli, one of the scholars who had contributed to establish the document's context, declared himself to be of a different opinion. At the time of Machiavelli's first appearance on the public stage in 1498, he was already the possessor of a 'doctrine', but more than that, a doctrine which had already assumed a fixed, timeless form. This, Martelli concluded, 'rendered hopeless any attempt to "historicize"' Machiavelli's political thought, 'which (leaving to one side its scientific value) is shaped like the immobile water of a ruby which, on contact with reality, is dramatically filled with images'.[4]

These words elicited a sarcastic comment from Carlo Dionisotti.[5] I do not share all Dionisotti's views on the *Ghiribizzi*, but their starting point is undeniable: the importance, here as ever, of dating. Elsewhere I have sought to reconstruct elements of the initial, highly obscure phase of Machiavelli's intellectual development.[6] Here I shall take a further step in the same direction.[7]

---

filologia' (2001), in *Tra filologia e storia. Otto studi machiavelliani*, ed. Francesco Bausi (Rome: Salerno Editrice, 2009), pp. 278–335, esp. pp. 281–303. See, in addition, the entry 'Ghiribizzi al Soderino' by Rinaldo Rinaldi in *Enciclopedia machiavelliana*, vol. I, pp. 617–20.

3 Ridolfi, 'I *Ghiribizzi* al Soderini', pp. 65–6.
4 Martelli, 'I "Ghiribizzi" a Giovan Battista Soderini', p. 179 n. 1.
5 Carlo Dionisotti, *Machiavellerie* (Turin: Einaudi, 1980), p. 83.
6 See chapter 1 above.
7 The following paragraph is based on a seminar held in 2003 by the present writer at the Università degli Studi in Siena. I am grateful

2. Machiavelli begins the draft of his letter by commenting on some points in a short message from Giovan Battista Soderini, dated 12 September 1506.[8] Then something else happens almost immediately. We get the impression that an unexpected thought crossed Machiavelli's mind, a silent event which the rapid handwriting records with stenographic precision. Machiavelli leaves aside the private (and, to us, largely obscure) issues he had started to comment upon, and embarks on a series of more general considerations: a dense, urgent reflection on *fortuna* and its impact on human actions. Probably, as has been suggested, this unexpected development led Machiavelli not to send his letter, but to convert the draft into the tercets of the chapter 'Di Fortuna', precisely dedicated to Giovan Battista Soderini.[9]

Can we locate the turning point in Machiavelli's draft, or the moment when a private letter changed into an intense, general meditation? To answer this question, we must examine the draft's physical appearance more closely.

The *Ghiribizzi* occupies three full folio pages written recto and verso, plus five lines of a fourth (fols 219r–221r), of the Vatican Codice Capponi 107 (vol. II). In writing his draft Machiavelli added some short notes in the margins; in all likelihood, notes he intended to develop in the final version of the letter. The precise point where these addenda were to be inserted

to Carlo Pincin for his expert, generous help, and to all the members of the seminar, especially Fabio Paglieri, who made a decisive contribution to the development of the hypothesis presented here.

8 Niccolò Machiavelli, *Opere*, vol. II, ed. Corrado Vivanti (Turin: Einaudi, 1999), pp. 135–8, esp. p. 135. Corrado Vivanti follows the critical edition by Roberto Ridolfi and Paolo Ghiglieri. Both the letter from Giovan Battista Soderini, and the beginning of the *Ghiribizzi*, have been interpreted as a series of coded allusions of a sexual nature: cf. Paul Larivaille, '"*Delenda est civitas Pisarum*"? *Ghiribizzi* intorno a un enigma machiavelliano', *Interpres* 31 (2012/2013), pp. 182–249, esp. pp. 182–9.

9 Martelli, 'I "Ghiribizzi" a Giovan Battista Soderini', p. 155ff. See Niccolò Machiavelli, *Capitoli*, ed. Giorgio Inglese (Rome: Bulzoni, 1981), pp. 113–23.

is only indicated in two cases. I shall examine one of them, quoting from Ridolfi and Ghiglieri's critical edition:

[fol 221r] Conoscho voi et la bussola della navigatione vostra; et quando potessi essere dannata, che non può, io non la dannerei, veggiendo ad che porti vi habbi guidato et di che speranza vi possa nutrire. [marginal addition] Donde io credo, non con lo spechio vostro, dove non si vede se non prudentia, ma <per> quello de' più, che si habbi nelle cose ad vedere el fine et non el mezo, et vedendosi con varij governi conseguire una medesima cosa et diversamente <oper>ando have[re] uno medesimo fine; et quello che manchava ad questa opinione, le actioni di questo pontefice et li effecti loro vi hanno adgiunto. Hannibale et Sci<pione> // [fol 221v] oltre alla disciplina militare, che nell'uno et nell'altro excelleva etc.[10]

My translation:

I know you and the compass of your navigation; even if it could be blamed, which it cannot be, I should not, since I see what ports it has guided you to and what hopes it may foster in you. [*marginal addition*] Hence I think not according to your perspective, wherein nothing but prudence is visible, but to the perspective of the many, which must see the ends, not the means, of things. And I see that steering along a variety of routes can bring about the same thing and that acting in different ways can bring about the same end – whatever this conviction may have lacked has been filled in by this pope's actions and their outcomes. Take Hannibal and Scipio: in addition to their military training, in which they were equally preeminent etc.[11]

One has the impression that something is amiss in this

---

10 Ridolfi and Ghiglieri, 'I *Ghiribizzi* al Soderini', pp. 71–2.
11 *Machiavelli and His Friends: Their Personal Correspondence*, tr. and ed. James B. Atkinson and David Sices (DeKalb: Northern Illinois University Press, 1996), p. 134; tr. slightly modified.

passage. The transition from 'uno medesimo fine' ('et vedendosi con varij governi conseguire una medesima cosa et diversamente, <oper>ando have[re] uno medesimo fine'), to the
next sentence ('et quello che mancava ad questa opinione, le
actioni di questo pontefice et li effecti loro vi hanno adgiunto')
has something awkward about it, syntactically and logically.
What is initially presented as a fact – 'et vedendosi con varij
governi . . .' – is subsequently characterized as *'questa opinione'*. This minor inconsistency points to a much more serious
textual problem. As has been said, the passage just cited
includes a marginal addition, clearly marked in the manuscript
by two inverted hooks, which begins with the words 'Donde io
credo, non con lo spechio vostro' (Hence I think not according
to your perspective). But if the start of the addendum is clear,
the end isn't. There are good reasons to believe that the addendum was much longer than was thought by its original editors,
Ridolfi and Ghiglieri, followed by subsequent scholars. An
examination of the manuscript indicates that, after having
filled the left margin of folio 221r, Machiavelli continued writing two lines at the bottom of the same page, which fill all the
space between the left margin and the right margin (figure 1,
overleaf).

Hence when Machiavelli wrote these two lines, the bottom of
folio 221r was still empty. The editors of the *Ghiribizzi* did not
realize that the addendum, following the words *'Hannibale et
Sci<pione>'*, continues on the next page covering folio 221v in
its entirety (figure 2).

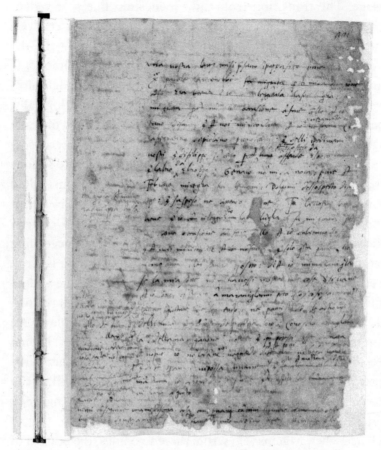

Fig. 1 N. Machiavelli, *Ghiribizzi* (codex *Capponi*, 107, vol. II, c. 221r, Biblioteca Apostolica Vaticana, Città del Vaticano).

Once the long addition is properly reinserted, the junction between its conclusion and the main text reads as follows:

Ma donde nascha che le diverse operationi qualche volta equalmente giovino o equalmente nuochino, io non lo so, ma desiderrei bene saperlo; pure, per intendere l'opinione vostra, io userò presuntione ad dirvi la mia. [*end of the marginal addition*] Et quello che manchava ad questa opinione, le actioni di questo pontefice et li effecti loro vi hanno adgiunto.

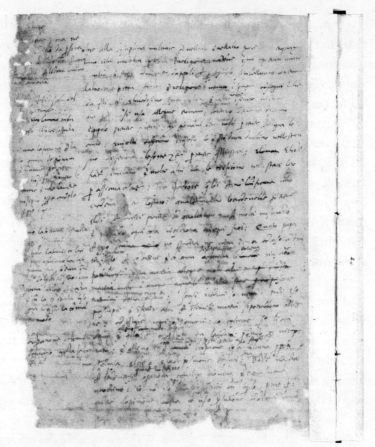

Fig. 2 N. Machiavelli, *Ghiribizzi* (codice *Capponi*, 107, vol. II, c. 221v, Biblioteca Apostolica Vaticana, Città del Vaticano).

My translation:

But the reason why different actions are sometimes equally useful and sometimes equally detrimental I do not know – yet I should very much like to; so, in order to learn your view, I shall be presumptuous enough to give you mine. [*end of the marginal addition*] And whatever this view may have lacked, has been filled in by this pope's actions and their outcomes.[12]

---

12   *Machiavelli and His Friends*, pp. 134–5; tr. slightly modified.

By inserting the reference to the pope's actions after the long marginal addition, the awkwardness mentioned previously disappears. We are faced, above all, with an admission of ignorance: 'Ma *donde nascha* che le diverse operationi qualche volta equalmente giovino o equalmente nuochino, io non lo so' (my emphasis). (But *the reason why* different actions are sometimes equally useful and sometimes equally detrimental I do not know.) There follow, in rapid succession, '*l'opinione vostra*', '*la mia [opinione]*', 'questa *opinione*' (your view, mine, *this* view). '*This* view' is then presented in the last part of the draft (fol 222r–v), which begins '*Io credo*' (I believe). This sequence seems to me much more consistent with Machiavelli's style and logic.

3. Here I shall point out some implications of the reading proposed. If the sentence 'et quello che manchava ad questa opinione, le actioni di questo pontefice et li effecti loro vi hanno adgiunto' (and whatever this view may have lacked has been filled in by this pope's actions and their outcomes) is the resumption of the long marginal addition, its opening will read as follows:

[fol 221r] Donde io credo, non con lo spechio vostro, dove non si vede se non prudentia, ma <per> quello de' più, che si habbi nelle cose ad vedere el fine et non el mezo, et vedendosi con varij governi conseguire una medesima cosa et diversamente <oper>ando have[re] uno medesimo fine. Hannibale et Sci<pione> // [*fol 221v*] oltre alla disciplina militare, che nell'uno et nell'altro excelleva etc.[13]

Here is the translation:

Hence I think not according to your perspective, wherein nothing but prudence is visible, but to the perspective of the many, which must see the ends, not the means, of things. And I see that steering along a variety of routes can bring about the same thing and that acting in different ways can bring about the same end.

---

13 Ridolfi and Ghiglieri, 'I *Ghiribizzi* al Soderini', pp. 71–2 (rev.).

Take Hannibal and Scipio: in addition to their military training, in which they were equally preeminent etc.

The beginning of the long marginal addition thus signals the transition from the passage of the response to Giovan Battista Soderini to what is, above all, a self-reflection. The sentence 'vedendosi con varij governi conseguire una medesima cosa et diversamente <oper>ando have[re] uno medesimo fine' (steering along a variety of routes can bring about the same thing and that acting in different ways can bring about the same end) prompted the reference to Hannibal and Scipio: a theme which will surface again at the end of the draft. How can we explain this sudden transition?

My answer will be inevitably long and tortuous. I will begin by translating Machiavelli's sentence into French: 'Par divers moyens on arrive à pareille fin' (by different means we arrive at the same end): the title of the first of Montaigne's essays. Montaigne, who could not have known the *Ghiribizzi al Soderini*, which remained unpublished until 1786, had read *The Prince* and the *Discourses*, which echoed ideas and words from the *Ghiribizzi*. But much more importantly in this context is a work read by Machiavelli and Montaigne: Plutarch's *Lives* (echoed countless times in the *Essays*, starting with the one that opens the volume). But which Plutarch?

4. On 21 October 1502, Biagio Buonaccorsi wrote a letter to his friend and colleague Niccolò Machiavelli. At the time, Machiavelli was at Imola, performing his duties as an ambassador at the court of Cesare Borgia. Answering a letter by Machiavelli that has been lost, inter alia, Buonaccorsi wrote, 'We have tried to locate some *Lives* of Plutarch, and there are none for sale in Florence. Be patient, because we have to write to Venice; to tell you the truth, you can go to the devil for asking so many things.'[14]

---

14 *Machiavelli and His Friends*, p. 55. (Machiavelli, *Opere*, vol. II, p. 53: 'Abbiamo fatto cercare delle *Vite* di Plutarco, et non se ne truova in Firenze da vendere. Abbiate pazienzia, che bisogna scrivere a Venezia; a dirvi il vero, voi siate lo'nfracida a chiedere tante cose'.)

What impelled Machiavelli to try to get hold of Plutarch's *Lives* so urgently was (as Gennaro Sasso has observed) his first encounter with Cesare Borgia.[15] This is one of many examples of Machiavelli's inclination to connect 'l'esperienza delle cose moderne' and 'la lezione delle antiche'. However, no one has inquired as to the physiognomy of the Plutarch read by Machiavelli – in Latin, of course, since he was unable to read Greek.[16]

Latin editions of Plutarch's *Lives* available in early sixteenth-century Italy were expensive folio volumes. In all likelihood, in 1502 Machiavelli did not own a copy of *Lives*: otherwise he would not have asked Buonaccorsi to procure one. The edition Machiavelli received was probably the one published by Donnino Pinzi in Venice in the same year, 1502.[17] The book opens with a dedicatory letter by the editor, Gerolamo Squarciafico from Alessandria, addressed to Giovan Francesco Bragadin, a Venetian jurist. Having emphasized the efforts he had made to furnish an accurate text of Plutarch, Squarciafico bitterly lamented the current state of publishing: the correction of texts was entrusted indifferently to the educated and the ignorant; the printing press had fallen into the hands of people who did not know Latin. 'Nearly all books', Squarciafico concluded, 'are soiled and corrupted, so that the authors, if they came to life again, would not recognize those books as their own.'[18] When read today, this

---

15   Gennaro Sasso, *Machiavelli e gli antichi*, vol. III (Milan and Naples: Ricciardi, 1988), p. 194.

16   Sasso, in his essay on 'Machiavelli e i detrattori, antichi e nuovi, di Roma' (*Machiavelli e gli antichi*, vol. I [Milan and Naples: Ricciardi, 1987], pp. 401–536), offers a conjecture as to the Latin translation of Plutarch's *De fortuna Romanorum* that Machiavelli may have read (p. 431 n.). But the bulk of the analysis is conducted on the Greek text.

17   Plutarchus, *Vitae* (Venetiis: Doninum Pincium, 1502). I consulted the copy in the UCLA library (Young Research Library, Special Collections: SCB 140942* AMEIP). This edition is mentioned, along with others, in Machiavelli, *Opere*, vol. II, p. 1477.

18   Plutarchus, *Vitae* (Venetiis: Donnino Pinzi, 1502), ante-frontispiece: 'Sed nunc pariter docti et indocti emendandi provinciam sibi assumunt. Praeterea, haec impressoria ars in manus quorundam illiteratorum incidit, a quibus libri fere omnes coinquinantur et corrumpuntur, ut si auctores reviviscerent suos protinus esse negarent.'

last remark is unintentionally comic: among the significant new additions to his list, Squarciafico mentioned some lives – of Socrates, Epaminondas and Attila (!) – which were not by Plutarch. But the 1502 edition included other, equally spurious lives, which warrant a longer comment. This touches on facts which, though well known to historians of both the classical tradition and Italian humanism, seem not to have attracted the attention of Machiavelli scholars.

The history of the first Latin translation of Plutarch's *Lives*, published in Rome in 1470, has been reconstructed by Vito Giustiniani in minute detail.[19] The editor, Giovanni Antonio Campano, assembled a number of translations, prepared by various Italian humanists over several decades, in two sumptuous folio volumes, which he dedicated to Cardinal Francesco Piccolomini. The dedication copy of this rare work, decorated with beautiful illuminated initials, is owned by the Biblioteca Comunale degli Intronati in Siena.[20] Each life is preceded by the translator's dedicatory letter. As Giustiniani noticed, this first Latin edition also included texts that were not by Plutarch: among them, Donato Acciaiuoli's lives of Hannibal and Scipio and comparison between them.[21] They were composed, as Acciaiuoli explained in his dedicatory letter to Piero de' Medici, utilizing a series of passages by Greek and Roman historians.[22]

---

19 Vito R. Giustiniani, 'Sulle traduzioni latine delle "Vite" di Plutarco nel Quattrocento', *Rinascimento*, 2nd ser., 1 (1961), pp. 3–62. See also Marianne Pade, 'A Checklist of the Manuscripts of the Fifteenth-Century Latin Translations of Plutarch's *Lives*', in Italo Gallo, ed., *L'eredità culturale di Plutarco dall'antichità al Rinascimento, Atti del VII convegno plutarcheo* (Naples: D'Auria, 1998), pp. 251–87.

20 Giustiniani mentions three other copies, held by the British Library, France's Bibliothèque Nationale and the Biblioteca Nazionale Centrale in Florence. The Newberry Library, Chicago, owns another copy.

21 Giustiniani, 'Sulle traduzioni latine', p. 25 and passim.

22 Plutarch, *Vitae* (Rome: Ulrich Han, 1470), vol. I, c. 139r: 'Itaque constitui animo duorum praestantissimorum docum Annibalis et Scipionis gesta, quae ex variis auctoribus tum Graecis tum Latinis collegeram, praesenti volumine complecti, idque sicut alias lucubrationes meas nomini tuo [Piero de' Medici] dicare.' (The passage is quoted by B. Scardigli, 'C'è qualcosa di plutarcheo nella vita di Scipione dell'Acciaiuoli?', in *L'eredità*

In Plutarch's project, based on a comparison between illustrious Greeks and Romans, there was no room for the Carthaginian Hannibal. Donato Acciaiuoli filled the gap, transforming the comparison suggested by Livy (book XXX, 30–31) into a Plutarchian pastiche.[23]

A pastiche, not a forgery. But in the table of contents of Campano's edition, Acciaiuoli as an author of lives *à la manière de Plutarque* was equated with Acciaiuoli the translator of Plutarch's *Lives*.[24] In the reprint of Campano's edition, published in Strasbourg a few years later, the life of Scipio was presented as written by Plutarch and translated by Donato Acciaiuoli.[25] Another reprint, published in Venice in 1478 by Nicolas Jenson, removed all dedicatory letters: Acciaiuoli appeared as author of both lives, Hannibal's and Scipio's.[26] These two continued to be reprinted as writings by Plutarch until 1561, the year in which a Heidelberg professor, Wilhelm Holtzmann, better known under the humanistic name Xylander, published a new Latin translation of Plutarch's work.[27] The editions of Plutarch's *Lives* in Greek, and the translations, like Amyot's, based on the Greek original, ignored Acciaiuoli's pastiches. But some editions of Amyot's translation included, in a separate appendix, Scipio's

---

culturale di Plutarco, p. 289 n.) See Monica Affortunati and Barbara Scardigli, 'La vita "plutarchea" di Annibale. Un'imitazione di Donato Acciaiuoli', *Atene e Roma* 37/2–3 (1992), pp. 88–105. Machiavelli's comparison between Hannibal and Scipio is mentioned on p. 92, without linking it to the texts compiled by Donato Acciaiuoli.

23 Andreola Rossi, 'Parallel Lives: Hannibal and Scipio in Livy's Third Decade', *Transactions of the American Philological Association* 134/2 (2004), pp. 359–81.

24 Giustiniani, 'Sulle traduzioni latine', p. 11.

25 Here is the title: 'Plutarci Historiographi Greci de vita atque gestis Scipionis Africani traducti in Latinum linguagium per Donatum Acciaiolum': see Plutarch, 2 vols, *Vitae*, (Strasbourg: Adolf Rusch, [no date, but after 1470–1471]). I consulted the copy in the Newberry Library, Chicago.

26 See Plutarch, *Vitae* (Venice: Nicolaus Jenson, 1478).

27 Giustiniani, 'Sulle traduzioni latine', pp. 6–7, 25. See *Plutarchi Opus, quod Parallela et Vitas appellant*, tr. Guilielmo Xylandro Augustano (Heidelberg: Ludovicus Lusius, 1561).

and Hannibal's lives as works by Plutarch, without mentioning Acciaiuoli's name.[28]

Not everyone was taken in. In his life of Scipio, Acciaiuoli had referred to Cornelia, the mother of Tiberius and Caius Gracchus, observing that ancient authors provided conflicting information about her: 'Polybius, Plutarch and other eloquent authors say ...' '*Plut[archus]*. *Videtur hec vita non esse composita da Plut[archo]*' (Plutarch: it seems that this life was not written by Plutarch), dryly noted an anonymous sixteenth-century reader (possibly a Venetian antiquarian), in the margin of a copy, now owned by the Regenstein Library in Chicago, of the Latin translation of the *Lives* published in Venice by Giovanni Ragazzo in 1491.[29]

Did Machiavelli doubt the authenticity of Hannibal's and Scipio's lives? Or did he read them as the work of Plutarch, '*gravissimo scrittore*' (a most authoritative writer) (*Discourses*, II, 1)?[30] Even if the first hypothesis is considered more plausible, it must be admitted that the Plutarchian model which inspired Donato Acciaiuoli shaped Machiavelli's reflections on Scipio and Hannibal, the mild general and the ferocious one: a parallel which, having made its appearance in the *Ghiribizzi*, reappeared in *The Prince* (chapter 18) and the *Discourses* (III, 21).

---

28 See Plutarque, *Les Vies d'Hannibal et de Scipio l'African*, tr. Charles de l'Ecluse, in *Les vies des hommes illustres*, vol. VI, tr. Jacques Amyot (Paris: Vascosan imprimeur du Roy, 1567), with separate pagination; *Les Vies des hommes illustres*, vol. II, tr. Jacques Amyot (Paris: Olivier de Harsy, 1578), p. 973ff. Contrary to Scardigli ('C'è qualcosa di plutarcheo'), Amyot did not think that the two lives were by Plutarch. Montaigne read Plutarch in Amyot's translation or in the 1565 edition (which did not contain the two spurious lives), or in 'one of the subsequent editions', writes Pierre Villey, without dwelling on the differences between these editions (*Les sources des Essais* [Bordeaux: F. Pech, 1920], vol. IV of Montaigne, *Essais*, ed. Fortunat Strowski, 5 vols [Bordeaux: F. Pech, 1906–1933]).

29 Plutarch, *Vitae* (Venice: Ioannem Rigatium de Monteferrato, 1491), pt. 1, c. 178 (Joseph Regenstein Library, Chicago: alc Incun. 1491.P7).

30 Machiavelli, *Discorsi*, ed. Corrado Vivanti (Turin: Einaudi, 1983), p. 215.

This recurrent theme has been variously interpreted by Machiavelli scholars. According to Martelli, Machiavelli started out from the references to Hannibal and Scipio scattered in the texts of minor fifteenth-century writers like Antonio Bonciani, Antonio di Meglio and Francesco Accolti.[31] Dionisotti reacted impatiently to this suggestion, recalling Machiavelli's famous letter to Francesco Vettori.[32] But Machiavelli's splendid words on the 'antique corti degli antiqui uomini' (the venerable courts of the ancients) cannot be taken on trust. His image of Greek and Roman antiquity was, inevitably, different from ours.

5. The *Ghiribizzi al Soderini* was written immediately after Pope Julius II entered Perugia, on 13 September 1506. He entered unarmed (a circumstance that Machiavelli possibly exaggerated). Years later (*Discourses*, I, 27), Machiavelli criticized the cowardice (*viltà*) of Giampaolo Baglioni, the tyrant of the city, who did not dare to kill the pope: a gesture that would have made him glorious. In the *Ghiribizzi* Machiavelli had made a different point: 'This pope, who has no scales or measuring stick in his house, obtains through chance – and disarmed – what ought to be difficult to attain even with organization and with weapons.'[33] Julius's gesture showed that sometimes impetuous decisions, made without reflection, could be crowned with success. Machiavelli continued by comparing Scipio and Hannibal and their respective attitudes, which were so different. Men, he observed, should learn to adapt to a constantly changing world. But since they are unable to change their own character, they are headed for defeat.

Machiavelli developed these reflections in *The Prince*, chapter 25, devoted to Fortuna and her role in human affairs. Once again he referred to Pope Julius II, who 'always acted impetuously, and found the times and circumstances so suited to his

---

31   Martelli, 'I "Ghiribizzi" a Giovan Battista Soderini', p. 164ff, esp. p. 172.
32   Dionisotti, *Machiavellerie*, p. 84.
33   *Machiavelli and His Friends*, p. 135.

way that he was always successful ... With [his] swift initiative, then, Julius achieved what no other pope, acting with consummate prudence, could have attained'.[34] Some years earlier, confronted with Julius's unexpected success in boldly entering Perugia, Machiavelli had begun to reflect on the limits of 'human prudence'. In this reflection he was helped, once again, by Donato Acciaiuoli – this time undisguised.

6. In his *Libro di ricordi* Bernardo Machiavelli, Niccolò's father, recorded the acquisition of Donato Acciaiuoli's commentary on Aristotle's *Nicomachean Ethics* (1478).[35] Elsewhere I have shown that in a scene from *La mandragola* Machiavelli drew inspiration from a page in another book in his father's library – a treatise by the medieval jurist Giovanni d'Andrea.[36] Given this precedent, the possibility that Machiavelli had read Acciaiuoli's commentary on the *Nicomachean Ethics* cannot be discounted.[37]

A book that might have introduced Machiavelli to the thought of Aristotle deserves close attention. Here I will limit myself to a

---

34 Niccolò Machiavelli, *The Prince*, ed. Quentin Skinner and Russell Price, tr. Russell Price (Cambridge: Cambridge University Press, 2016), p. 86. The passage is listed by Martelli among the texts echoing the *Ghiribizzi al Soderini* ('I "Ghiribizzi"', p. 176).

35 Cf. Bernardo Machiavelli, *Libro di ricordi*, pp. 141–2. Donato Acciaiuoli, *Expositio super libros Ethicorum Aristotelis* (Florence: Sanctum Jacobum de Ripoli, 1478). See Luca Bianchi, 'Un commento "umanistico" ad Aristotele. L'"Expositio super libros Ethicorum" di Donato Acciajuoli', *Rinascimento* 30 (1990), pp. 29–55; David A. Lines, 'Ethics as Philology: A Developing Approach to Aristotle's *Nicomachean Ethics* in Florentine Humanism', in *Renaissance Readings of the 'Corpus Aristotelicum'*, ed. Marianne Pade, Conference Proceedings, Copenhagen, 23–25 April 1998 (Copenhagen: Museum Tusculanum Press, 2001), pp. 27–42 (with other bibliographical information).

36 See chapter 1 above, pp. 4–9.

37 According to Gennaro Sasso, Acciaiuoli's comments focused on an author – Aristotle – whose work Machiavelli partially knew, although it was never fundamental for him (review of Roberto Ridolfi, *Vita di Niccolò Machiavelli* [Rome: Belardetti, 1954], *Rivista storica italiana* 66/2 [1954], p. 306).

few passages. At the beginning of the *Nicomachean Ethics* (1094a 9–15) we read,

> As there are many actions, arts, and sciences, their ends also are many; the end of the medical art is health, that of shipbuilding a vessel, that of strategy victory, that of economics wealth. But where such arts fall under a single capacity [*hupo mian tina dynamin*] – as bridle-making and the other arts concerned with the equipment of horses fall under the art of riding, and this and every military action under strategy, in the same way other arts fall under yet others – in all of these the ends of the master arts are to be preferred to all the subordinate ends; for it is for the sake of the former that the latter are pursued.[38]

Here is Acciaiuoli's comment:

> One must note that here the philosopher calls these arts 'virtues' [*virtutes*]. According to some people, the Greek text reads *dinamin*; according to others, *aretin*, that is virtue. If one reads 'virtue', this word must be taken as a reference to the force and power [*pro vi et potentia*] which is in every art, which could properly be called 'faculty', since it is indifferently and equally usable in both directions. Medicine, for instance, is called power [*potentia*], because it is the capacity [*potens*] to procure health and to destroy it.[39]

Here, as elsewhere, Acciaiuoli used Giovanni Argiropulo's lectures on Aristotle. Only a scrutiny of the Greek manuscripts

---

38 Aristotle, *Ethica Nicomachea*, tr. W. D. Ross (Oxford: Oxford University Press, 1925).

39 Donato Acciaiuoli, *In expositionem*, fol viiv: 'Notandum quod philosophus appellat istas artes hic virtutes. Nonnulli habent in textu greco dinamin, nonnulli aretin i. virtutem. Quod si dicat virtutem, tunc illa accipienda est pro vi et potentia quae est in qualibet arte, quae apellari proprie facultas potest, cum sit ad utramque partem indifferenter et aeque disposita. Veluti medicina dicitur potentia: quia potens est ad faciendum et corrumpendum sanitatem.'

of the *Nicomachean Ethics* held in Florentine libraries would reveal whether any of them contain, in the passage cited above (1094a 10), the reading ἀρετήν in place of that accepted by modern editors: δύναμιν. But no reader of Machiavelli will prove indifferent as to the interpretation of the word *virtus* in terms of *vis* and *potentia* proposed by Acciaiuoli. We shall have to return to this point. Here it will suffice to highlight Acciaiuoli's emphasis on the neutrality of medicine and the other arts (a few lines later, he refers to rhetoric).⁴⁰ Obviously, Acciaiuoli is expounding Aristotle's ideas. The Latin word *ars* is a translation of the Greek word τέχνη. Equally Aristotelian is the distinction between the two principles dealing with contingent things: prudence (*prudentia*) and art (*ars*). 'The principle of action (*principium agendi*) that is prudence, is different from the principle of making (*principium faciendi*) that is art', wrote Acciaiuoli. '*Aliud est actio, aliud est effectio*': acting and making are different things.⁴¹ Virtue (*virtus*, as previously defined) pertains to art, not prudence.⁴²

The possibility that the young Machiavelli had read Acciaiuoli's commentary in the paternal library is very attractive. Occasional references to philosophical concepts like 'form' and 'matter', cited in chapter 6 of *The Prince*, might have implied a deeper familiarity, direct or mediated, with Aristotle's writings, which would throw a different light on the *Ghiribizzi*. In these reflections scribbled in haste, Machiavelli sought to make sense of the unpredictability of human actions (like the pope's) whose conformity with the times (*riscontro*) could be the result

---

40   Ibid., fol a viiv: 'Ars disserendi et oratoria est potens ad probandum et suadendum contraria interdum de eodem: veluti quod voluptas sit bonum, et sit malum.'

41   Ibid., fol s viv: 'In prima parte ostendit duos esse habitus qui versantur circa ea que possunt aliter se habere: quorum unus est principium agendi idest prudentia, alter principium faciendi idest ars ... Aliud est actio, aliud est effectio, et aliud agere quod est prudentiae et aliud facere quod est artis.'

42   Ibid., fol s ixv: 'Artis est virtus. At prudentiae non est virtus. Ergo prudentia non est ars.'

of different trajectories.[43] To adapt to a changing world dominated by Fortune, recourse to 'art' was required.

7. The Aristotelian distinction between art and prudence, so emphatically stressed in Acciaiuoli's commentary, must be borne in mind in order to appreciate the bold novelty of Machiavelli's expression *'arte dello stato'* (only approximately translatable as 'art of the state'), used by him in rare but significant passages. Many years ago, Dolf Sternberger noted the absence in *The Prince* of terms etymologically linked to 'political' and 'politics'. Maurizio Viroli has taken up this observation, rightly noting that such an absence signals Machiavelli's deliberate detachment in *The Prince* from the classical and medieval tradition, inspired by Aristotle, founded on the πόλις and the common good.[44] But Viroli proposes to relate the expression *'arte dello stato'*, which appears in the correspondence between Machiavelli and Francesco Vettori, to this tradition. The only – late – example cited by Viroli in support of his interpretation demonstrates that it is groundless: James Harrington's definition of

---

43 In the *Ghiribizzi*, contrary to what, led astray by a Nietzschean interpretation of Machiavelli, is argued by Miguel E. Vatter (*Between Form and Event: Machiavelli's Theory of Political Freedom* (Dordrecht: Kluwer, 2000), pp. 137–65, esp. p. 144ff), the term 'riscontro' does not signify 'clash' but 'coformity'. In the language of Machiavelli and his contemporaries, the two meanings coexisted: see the entries on 'Riscontro' and 'Riscontrare' in Sergio Battaglia, *Grande dizionario della lingua italiana*. But in the *Ghiribizzi*, as in the bulk of the passages in Machiavelli listed in the entry 'Riscontro' (by Carlo Galli) in *Enciclopedia machiavelliana*, vol. II, pp. 427–33, the prevalent meaning is 'conformity'. See the fine essay by Christian Lazzeri, 'Prudence, éthique et politique de Thomas d'Aquin à Machiavel', in *De la prudence des anciens comparée à celle des modernes. Sémantique d'un concept, déplacement des problématiques*, ed. André Tosel (Paris: Les Belles Lettres, 1995), pp. 79–128 (with pertinent observations on the *Ghiribizzi*).

44 Maurizio Viroli, 'Machiavelli and the Republican Idea of Politics', in *Machiavelli and Republicanism*, ed. Gisela Bock, Quentin Skinner and Maurizio Virol (Cambridge: Cambridge University Press, 1990), pp. 144–71.

government as an art in accordance with prudence, ancient and modern alike.[45] No follower of Aristotle would have accepted a definition based on the alleged accord of concepts deemed so heterogeneous.

In fact, for Machiavelli *arte dello stato* and *politica* (or *vivere politico*, mentioned in *Discourses*, I, 25) had different if not opposite meanings. Sternberger, who rightly noted this, missed the implications of the expression *arte dello stato*, perhaps because he was diverted by the idea that Machiavelli was familiar with the late medieval Aristotelian tradition rather than the texts of Aristotle himself.[46] But Machiavelli knew both, since he had probably read Aristotle's *Politics* in an edition furnished with the commentary by Aquinas and his continuator Peter of Auvergne.[47] In his plagiarism of *The Prince*, published in 1523, the Aristotelian Agostino Nifo evoked the neutrality of medical books, which deal both with poisons as well as their antidotes. The same argument was advanced, in defensive accents, in the dedicatory letter with which the printer accompanied the edition of *The Prince*, published in Florence in 1532 after Machiavelli's death.[48] Art, as a morally neutral sphere, provided both a starting point and, at the same time, a justification for Machiavelli's new, scandalous *arte dello stato*: an expression born with *The Prince* and bound up with it.[49]

---

45 James Harrington, *The Commonwealth of Oceana, The Political Works*, ed. J. G. A. Pocock (Cambridge: Cambridge University Press, 1977), p. 161: 'Government (to define it *de jure* or accordingly to ancient prudence) is an art whereby a civil society . . .' etc.

46 Dolf Sternberger, *Machiavellis 'Principe' und der Begriff des Politischen* (Wiesbaden: Steiner, 1974), pp. 42, 67–8 n. 9.

47 On this see chapter 6 below. Some acute observations can be found in Lazzeri, 'Prudence, éthique et politique de Thomas Aquin à Machiavel'.

48 Luigi Firpo, 'Le origini dell'antimachiavellismo', in *Scritti sul pensiero politico del Rinascimento e della Controriforma* (Turin: UTET, 2005), pp. 24–56.

49 Machiavelli to Francesco Vettori, 9 April 1513; 'Pure, se io vi potessi parlare, non potre' fare che io non vi empiessi il capo di castellucci, perché la Fortuna ha fatto che, non sapendo ragionare né dell'arte della seta é dell'arte della lana, né de' guadagni né delle

8. In reflections set down in the essay 'The Perspective of Art' Charles Singleton advanced an argument close to the one I outlined here. By transferring politics from the sphere of acting (*agere*) to that of making (*facere*), from the domain of prudence to that of art, Machiavelli ended up advancing a view of politics completely different from the traditional perception of it. Singleton based his interpretation on an extremely insightful reading of *The Prince* and (to a much lesser extent) the *Discourses*. The evidence presented here strongly supports Singleton's interpretation, as well as those who had preceded him on the same road.[50]

Singleton's unconventional essay apparently escaped scholarly attention, with one (possibly unique) exception: Isaiah Berlin. In a highly critical survey of studies on Machiavelli (all deemed inadequate for one reason or another), Berlin referred briefly to Singleton's essay in a section devoted to 'aesthetic interpretations' of Machiavelli's thought.[51] But this was a curious allocation, since in Singleton's essay *arte*, like its Latin and Greek counterparts (*ars*, *techne*), refers to both arts and techniques – a modern distinction that would have seemed incomprehensible to Machiavelli.

---

perdite, e' mi conviene ragionare dello stato, e mi bisogna o botarmi di stare cheto, o ragionare di questo' (Machiavelli, *Opere*, vol. II, p. 241) ('Yet if I were able to speak with you, you couldn't keep me from filling your head with castles in Spain, because Fortune has decreed that since I cannot discuss silk-making or wool-manufacture, or profit and losses, I have to discuss matters of state. I must either make a vow of silence or talk about that subject') (tr. Allan H. Gilbert, *The Prince and Other Works*, p. 228); Machiavelli to Francesco Vettori, 10 December 1513: 'Et per questa cosa [*Il principe*], quando la fussi letta, si vedrebbe che quindici anni che io sono stato a studio all'arte dello stato, non gl'ho né dormiti né giuocati' (Machiavelli, *Opere*, vol. II, p. 297) ('This work, if they should read it, will reveal that I have not been asleep or wasted my time during the fifteen years that I have been engaged in studying statecraft') (*arte dello stato*) (tr. Russell Price, in *The Prince*, appendix A, pp. 94–5).

50 See chapters 1 and 6.

51 Isaiah Berlin, 'The Originality of Machiavelli', in *Against the Current*, ed. Henry Hardy (Princeton, NJ: Princeton University Press, 2001).

9. Neither Singleton's argument, nor that presented here, takes into account Machiavelli's republican ideas. In reality, the dramatic doubts recorded in the *Ghiribizzi* did not affect those ideals: on the contrary. In a page of the *Discourses* (III, 9), Machiavelli implicitly resumed his earlier reflections in Perugia, in order to stress the superiority of republics over principalities:

> Hence it arises that a republic has greater life and has good fortune longer than a principality, for it can accommodate itself better than one prince can to the diversity of times through the diversity of the citizens that are in it. For a man who is accustomed to proceed in one mode never changes, as was said; and it must be of necessity that when the times change not in conformity with his mode, he is ruined.[52]

A distant but crystal-clear echo, which confirms the importance of the *Ghiribizzi*: a crucial moment in the process whereby Machiavelli became himself.

Appendix
Ghiribizzi Scri<pti> <in> P[eru]gia al Soderin<o>

[fol 221r] // Una vostra lettera mi si presentò in pappafico; pure, <dopo> dieci parole la riconobbi, et veramente io credo la frequentia di Piombino per conoscervi; et delli impedimenti vostri et di Filippo son certo, perché io so che l'uno è offeso da el poco lu<me> et l'altro da el troppo. Gennaio non mi dà noia,

---

52 Niccolò Machiavelli, *Discourses on Livy*, tr. Harvey C. Mansfield and Nathan Tarcov (Chicago: University of Chicago Press, 1996), p. 240. (*Discorsi*, p. 410: 'Quinci nasce che una repubblica ha maggiore vita ed ha più lungamente buona fortuna che uno principato, perché la può meglio accomodarsi alla diversità de' temporali, per la diversità de' cittadini che sono in quella, che non può uno principe. Perché un uomo che sia consueto a procedere in uno modo, non si muta mai, come è detto; e conviene di necessità, quando e' si mutano i tempi disformi a quel suo modo che rovini.')

pure che febraio mi regha fra le mani. Dolgomi del sospecto di Filippo, et suspeso ne attendo el fine. (α) Fu la vostra lettera breve et io rileggiendo la feci lungha. Fummi grata, perché mi dette occasione ad fare quello che io dubitavo di fa<re>, et che voi mi ricordate che io non faccia; et solo questa parte ho riconosciuta in lei sanza proposito. Di che io mi maravigler<ei>, se la mia sorte non mi havessi mostre tante cose et sì varie, che io sono constrecto ad maraviglarmi poco o confessare non havere gustate né leggiendo né pratichando le actioni delli huomini et e' modi del procedere loro. Conoscho voi et la bussola della navigatione vostra; et quando potessi essere dannata, che non può, io non la dannerei, veggiendo ad che porti vi habbi guidato et di che speranza vi possa nutrire. [*marginal addition*] Donde io credo, non con lo spechio vostro, dove non si vede se non prudentia, ma <per> quello de' più, che si habbi nelle cose ad vedere el fine et non el mezo, et vedendosi con varij governi conseguire una medesima cosa et diversamente <oper>ando have[re] uno medesimo fine. Hannibale et Sc<ipione> // [fol 221v] // oltre alla disciplina militare, che nell'uno et nell'altro excelleva equalmente, (β) l'uno con la crudeltà, perfidia, inreligione mantenne e' suoi exerciti uniti in Italia, et fecesi admirare da popoli, che per seguirlo si ribellavano da e' Romani; l'altro, con la pietà, fedeltà et religione, in Spagna hebbe da quelli popoli el medesimo seguito; (γ) et l'uno et l'altro hebbe infinite victorie. Ma perché non si usa allegare e' Romani, Lorenzo de' Medici disarmò el popolo per tenere Firenze; messer Giovanni Bentivogli per tener Bologna lo armò; (δ) e' Vitelli in Castello et questo duca d'Urbino nello stato suo disfeciono le forteze per tenere quelli stati; el conte Francesco in Milano et molti altri le edificorno nelli stati loro per assicurarsene. Tito imperadore, quel dì che non beneficava uno, credeva perdere lo stato; qualchun altro, lo crederrebbe perdere el dì che facessi piacere ad qualchuno. A molti, misurando et ponderando ogni cosa, rieschono e' disegni suoi. (ε) Questo papa, che non ha né stadera né canna in casa, ad caso conseguita, et disarmato, quello che con l'ordine et con l'armi difficilmente li doveva riuscire. Sonsi veduti o veggonsi tucti e' soprascripti, et infiniti altri che in simili materia si potrebbono allegare, adquistare regni o domarli o cascarne secondo li accidenti; et alle volte quello modo del procedere che adquistando era laudato, (ζ) perdendo è vituperato et alle volte dopo una lunga prosperità, perdendo, non se ne incolpa cosa alcuna propria, ma se ne accusa el cielo et la dispositione de' fati. Ma donde nascha che le diverse operationi qualche volta equalmente giovino o equalmente nuochino, io non lo so, ma desiderrei bene saperlo; pure, per intendere l'opinione vostra, io userò presuntione ad dirvi la mia. [*end of the marginal addition*] Et quello che manchava ad questa opinione, le actioni di questo pontefice et li effecti loro vi hanno adgiunto. // [fol 222r] // Io credo che come la natura ha facto ad l'huomo diverso volto, così li habbi facto diverso ingegno et diversa fantasia. Da questo nascie che ciascuno secondo lo ingegno et fantasia sua si governa. Et perché da l'altro canto e' tempi sono varij et li ordini delle cose sono diversi, ad colui succedono *ad votum* e' suoi desiderij, et quello è felice che riscontra el modo del procedere suo con el tempo, et quello, per opposito, è infelice che si diversifica con le sua actioni da el tempo et da l'ordine delle cose. Donde può molto bene essere che dua, diversamente operando, habbino uno medesimo fine, perché ciascuno di loro può conformarsi con el riscontro suo, perché e' sono tanti ordini di cose quanti sono provincie et stati. Ma perché e' tempi et le cose universalmente et particularmente si mutano spesso, et li huomini non mutono le loro fantasie ne e' loro modi di procedere, adcade che uno ha un tempo buona fortuna et uno tempo trista. Et veramente chi fussi tanto savio, che conoscessi e' tempi et l'ordine delle cose et adcomodassisi ad quelle, harebbe sempre buona fortuna o e' si guarderebbe sempre da la trista, et verrebbe ad essere vero che 'l savio comandassi alle stelle et a' fati. Ma perché di questi savi non si truova, havendo li huomini prima la vista corta et non potendo poi comandare alla natura loro, ne segue che la fortuna varia et comanda ad li huomini, et tiegli sotto el giogo suo. Et per verificare questa opinione, voglio che mi bastino li exempli soprascripti, sopra e' quali io la ho fondata, et così desidero che l'uno sostengha l'altro. Giova ad dare reputatione ad uno dominatore nuovo la crudeltà, perfidia et inreligione in quella provincia dove la humanità, fede et religione è lungo tempo abbundata, non altrimenti che si giovi la humanità, fede et religione dove la crudeltà, perfidia et inreligione è regnata un pezo; perché, come le cose amare perturbano el gusto et le dolci lo stuchano, così li huomini infastidiscono del bene, et del male si dolgono. Queste // [fol 222v] // cagioni, infra le altre, apersono Italia ad Annibale et Spagna ad Scipione, et così ognuno riscontrò el tempo et le cose secondo l'ordine del procedere suo. Né in quel medesimo tempo harebbe facto tanto proficto in Italia uno simile ad Scipione né uno simile ad Annibale in Spagna, quanto l'uno et l'altro fece nella provincia sua.

Marginal notes:

(α) Chi non sa schermire radviluppa chi sa di scherma

(β) Infine <non> consiglar persona né piglar consiglo da persona, <excepto> un consiglar generale che ognun facci quello che li detta l'animo et con audacia

(γ) Li huomini s'infastidiscono del bene et del male si dolgo[no]; l'amaro turba el gusto, el dolce lo stucha

(δ) Tentare la fortuna che la <è> amica de' giovani, et mutare secondo e' tempi. Ma non si può havere le fortezze et non le havere; non si può essere crudele et pio, etc.

(ε) <Co>me la fortuna si stracha, così si ruina l'huomo, la famiglia, la ciptà; ogniuno ha la fortuna sua fondata in sul modo del procedere suo, et ciascuna di loro si stracha et quanto la è stracha bisogna racquistarla con un altro modo

(ζ) La comparatione del cavallo <et> del morso circha le forteze

(Original preserved in the Vatican Apostolic Library, Vatican City: Codice Capponi, 107, vol. II, fols 221r–222v (modern numbering). Reproduced above is the version edited by R. Ridolfi and P. Ghiglieri, 'I *Ghiribizzi* al Soderini', *La Bibliofilía* 72/1 (1970), pp. 53–74, with one variation justified above: the last two lines of folio 221v have been transferred to the end of the marginal addendum that begins at folio 221r.)

3

Pontano, Machiavelli and Prudence

1. Among the Florentine humanists who used to meet in the 'Orti Oricellari' in the opening decades of the sixteenth century, the writings of Giovanni Pontano had a profound impact.[1] These discussions, led by Bernardo Rucellai (who had met Pontano in Naples in 1486) often focused on Livy – a Livy read from an aristocratic perspective, widely different from the republican Livy later advocated by Machiavelli and his young followers. Yet a link between these two phases in the Orti Oricellari debates might be found in Pontano's *De prudentia*. The humanist Giovanni Corsi brought a copy made from the original manuscript to Florence, possibly in the year of Pontano's death (1503), and published it in 1508. The same year, a slightly different version, edited (and sometimes modified) by Pietro Summonte, came out in Naples.[2]

---

1 See Felix Gilbert, 'Bernardo Rucellai and the Orti Oricellari: A Study on the Origin of Modern Political Thought', *Journal of the Warburg and Courtauld Institutes* 12 (1949), pp. 101–31, esp. pp. 105, 110, 118. A recent bibliography on Pontano is cited in the entry devoted to him by B. Figliuolo in the *Dizionario biografico degli Italiani*. And see now Claudio Finzi, 'Pontano, Gioviano' in *Enciclopedia machiavelliana*, vol. II, pp. 341–5. I am grateful to Maria Luisa Catoni for her valuable comments.

2 All subsequent quotations are from Giovanni Pontano, *De prudentia* (Florence: Philippi Giuntae, 1508) (Biblioteca dell'Archiginnasio, Bologna, shelf mark: 16.i.I.10). I also consulted a copy of the Neapolitan edition: Biblioteca Universitaria, Bologna, shelf mark: Raro. D. 34/1). The Florentine edition is closer to Pontano's lost

In dedicating Pontano's *De prudentia* to Cosimo de' Pazzi, archbishop of Florence, Giovanni Corsi, who declared himself a 'pupil of Bernardo Rucellai', nostalgically evoked Florence's glorious past under the government of Lorenzo de' Medici. Carlo Dionisotti imagined Machiavelli 'enjoying Pontano's *De prudentia*, smiling at Corsi's provocative preface'.[3] In fact, as Brian Richardson demonstrated (in an essay curiously unmentioned by Dionisotti), Pontano's *De prudentia* was an important precedent, in form and content alike, for Machiavelli's *Discourses*.[4] In the fourth and fifth books of his treatise, Pontano boldly juxtaposed ancient (mostly Livian) and contemporary examples of prudence – Numa Pompilius and Giovanni Caracciolo, Archaelaus and Lorenzo de' Medici, and so forth – as well as examples of lack of prudence, like Ludovico Sforza. We might regard this heterogeneous series as anticipating Machiavelli's *Discourses*, a work that does not seem to belong to any pre-existing genre.[5]

---

manuscript: see Liliana Monti Sabia, 'Per l'edizione critica del *De prudentia* di Giovanni Pontano', in *Tradizione classica e letteratura umanistica. Per Alessandro Perosa*, vol. II , ed. Roberto Cardini et al. (Rome: Bulzoni, 1985), pp. 595–615 (on p. 600 the copy commissioned by Corsi is dated between the spring and autumn 1503). See also Paul Oskar Kristeller, 'Un uomo di stato e umanista fiorentino: Giovanni Corsi' (1936), in *Studies in Renaissance Thought and Letters* (Rome: Edizioni di Storia e Letteratura, 1956), pp. 242–57 (with an appendix), as well as the entry 'Corsi, Giovanni' in *Dizionario biografico degli Italiani* (by Paolo Malanima).

3 Carlo Dionisotti, *Machiavellerie. Storia e fortuna di Machiavelli* (Turin: Einaudi, 1980), p. 142.

4 Brian Richardson, 'Pontano's *De Prudentia* and Machiavelli's *Discorsi*', *Bibliothèque d'Humanisme et Renaissance* 33/2 (1971), pp. 353–7. There are no references to this essay in recent literature on prudence: cf. Victoria Kahn, *Rhetoric, Prudence, and Skepticism in the Renaissance* (Ithaca, NY: Cornell University Press, 1985), with some superficial comments on Pontano's *De prudentia*, pp. 69–75; Eugene Garver, *Machiavelli and the History of Prudence* (Madison: University of Wisconsin Press, 1987), does not mention Pontano.

5 On Machiavelli's *Discourses* from the standpoint of literary genre, see Carlo Ginzburg, 'Ein Plädoyer für den Kasus', in *Fallstudien: Theorie – Geschichte – Methode*, ed. Johannes Süßmann, Susanne Scholz and Gisela Engel (Berlin: Trafo, 2007), pp. 29–48.

2. Richardson stressed 'the practical (both ethical and political) application which Pontano wanted his writing to have': something Machiavelli will have been sympathetic to. More debatable, as we shall see, is the 'scholarly approach' Richardson attributes to *De prudentia*.[6]

Prudence, Pontano wrote, is 'neither a science nor an art: it refers to actions'.[7] This definition echoes Aristotle's *Nicomachean Ethics*, as well as Aquinas's commentary on the latter, where politics and prudence were defined as 'right reason with respect to possible actions, good or bad' (*recta ratio rerum agibilium circa humana bona vel mala*).[8] The verb ἄγειν (and its derivatives) alluded to the Aristotelian distinction between prudence and art, ἄγειν and ποιεῖν: two verbs usually translated into Latin as *agere* and *facere*, the first pertaining to politics and prudence, the second to arts (τέχναι). Pursuing this line, Pontano observed that all arts use hands and are based on making (*facere*) and specified that 'prudence, on the contrary, refrains not only from making, but also from acting; it prefers to direct actions' (*non modo non faciat, sed ne agat ipsa quidem, quin potius dirigat actiones*).[9]

Having distinguished prudence from science and the arts alike, Pontano introduced a set of reflections that proceeded in a different, more innovative direction. His linguistic sensitivity, reinforced by his humanist education, suggested to him a polemical allusion to some recent philosophers, who, despite their intelligence, had employed Aristotle's terminology, 'without taking sufficient account of the particularities of the Latin tongue': possibly an oblique reference to Leonardo Bruni's translation of the

---

6 Richardson, 'Pontano's *De prudentia*', pp. 353–4, 357.

7 Pontano, *De prudentia*, fols LVIIIv–LIXr: 'Prudentiam neque scientiam esse, neque artem, sed in actionibus versari.'

8 Thomas Aquinas, *In decem libros Ethicorum Aristotelis profundissima commentaria, cum triplici textus translatione, antiqua videlicet Leonardi Aretini, necnon Joannis Argyropili suis locis inserta* (Venice: Lucantonium de Giunta, 1519), fol 95v. In *Secunda Secundae* (quaestio XLVII, art. 11) politics is defined as prudence 'quae ordinatur ad bonum commune'.

9 Pontano, *De prudentia*, fol LIXv.

Nicomachean Ethics.[10] '*Nam neque actio est factio, neque factio est actio*' (literally, for neither is acting making, nor is making acting), Bruni had written, following an established medieval tradition.[11] In *De prudentia* Pontano refrained from using the word *factio*. Pointing out that Greek and Latin words are not always equivalents, he stressed that the verb *facere*, for instance, has a very wide (*latissimus*) range of meanings. In fact, we say '*pacem fecit et bellum* [made peace and war], *indutias fecit et foedera* [arranged a truce and made an alliance], *fortiter fecit ac constanter* [acted firmly and consistently], *filia me avum fecit* [my daughter made me a grandfather], *sororque avunculum* [my sister made me an uncle], *verba fecit in Senatu* [made a speech in the Senate]', just as we say '*Apelles fecit Alexandri imaginem et aeneum Phalaridi Perilaus taurum* [Apelles made an image of Alexander and Perilaus made a bronze bull for Phalarides]'.[12]

Facere, then, is not a verb exclusively associated with the arts (τέχναι). But the comparison between Greek and Latin paved the way for a comparison with the vernacular and with the present. We find it in the longest chapter of Pontano's treatise, devoted to the difference between *sapientia* and *prudentia* (and between both of them with *ars*).[13] In a passage in the *Nicomachean Ethics* (1141a9–1149a12), Aristotle had observed that artists (*artifices*)

---

10 Ibid., fol VIIIr: 'Recentiores enim philosophi, quamquam praestantissimi quidem, maximeque acuti viri, dum Graeco tamen modo, quibusque ab Aristotele traditum est verbis, philosophantur, parum curaverunt videre, quid Latine etiam dici, et quonam modo, quaque etiam ratione ac via, au possit, aut etiam debeat.'

11 Aristotle, *Libri Ethicorum decem de moribus per clarissimum virum Leonardum Aretinum e Graeco in Latinum traducti* (Rome: Conrad Sweynheym and Arnold Pannartz, 1473), fols unnumbered. And see *Aristoteles Latinus, XXVI*, 1–3: *Ethica Nicomachea translatio Roberti Grosseteste Lincolnensis, Recensio pura*, ed. René Antoine Gauthier (Leiden and Brussels: Brill-Desclée De Brouwer, 1972), p. 256 (VI, 3): 'Alterum autem est faccio et accio . . . et neque continentur sub invicem accio et faccio. Neque enim accio faccio, neque faccio accio est.' And see also ibid., p. 257 (VI, 4).

12 Pontano, *De prudentia*, fol LXVr.

13 Ibid., fols LXIIr–LXVIIr: 'Quae sit differentia inter sapientiam et prudentiam.'

like Phidias and Polycletus were called *sapientes*, not *prudentes*. Pontano changed Polycletus into Praxiteles and registered a symmetrical slippage not between *ars* and *sapientia*, but between *prudentia* and *sapientia*. Often, he observed, jurists are called *sapientes*, although they usually employ prudence when dealing with private and public issues. And he added: when I was a child, I heard older people saying that Francesco Foscari and Cosimo de' Medici were *sapientes*, on account of their 'excellent and very prudent' government of Venice and Florence, respectively. It is true that (unlike Phidias and Praxiteles) 'neither Giotto, nor Gentile da Fabriano, nor Jean of Burgundy, highly praised as painters, were ever called *sapientes*, although they painted excellently'.[14] But our contemporaries (*nostri*) usually describe as 'experts' (*peritos*) those who achieve prominence in a specific domain: in jurisprudence, like Bartolo, Baldo and Ludovico (Bolognini); in warfare, like Niccolò Piccinino and Francesco Sforza; in oratory, like Leonardo Bruni; in painting, like Giotto; in sculpture, like Donatello. In Latin, observed Pontano, expertise is sometimes defined as *sapientia*.[15] Perhaps he also had in mind the opposite course, which emerges in Aquinas's comment on the passage in the *Nicomachean Ethics* on the term *sapientes* applied to Phidias and Polycletus: 'what we call wisdom simply signifies excellence in the arts' (*nihil aliud dicimus sapientiam, quam virtutem artis*).[16]

Hence, Pontano observed, in contemporary usage expertise

---

14 Ibid., fol LXIIIv: 'At neque Ioctium neque Gentilem Fabrianensem aut Ioannem Burgundionem laudatissimos pictores e nostris quisquam appellaverit sapientes, licet egregie pinxerint.'

15 Ibid., fol LXIIIv: 'Nam et Bartholum et Baldum et Lodovicum iuris ac civilium legum peritos vocant, et Nicolaum Picininum et Franciscum Sfortiam rei militaris atque administrandi belli peritissimos, et Leonardum Aretinum dicendi, Ioctium autem pingendi, Donatellum vero formandarum statuarum maxime peritos fuisse, ut peritiam, quae sapientiam Romana in lingua appellare hanc videri possit, magis idoneum ac proprium. Plura tamen usui concedenda sunt, sed ita quidem concedenda, ne rei tamen ipsius ratio ignoretur.'

16 Thomas Aquinas, *Sententia libri Ethicorum*, bk. VI, lectio 5, no. 6 (in *Corpus Thomisticum*, ed. Enrique Alarcón, corpusthomisticum.org/iopera.html).

– a term derived from the morally neutral sphere of the arts – tends to erase the traditional distinction between *sapientia*, *prudentia* and *ars*. And he continued: 'We should make large concessions to usage, but we must also concede that the nature of the issue [literally: the nature of the thing] should not be ignored.' What reemerged was the traditional distinction, Aristotelian in origin, between *prudentes* and *sapientes*: the former devote their actions to domestic and public life; the latter confine themselves to knowledge and contemplation of natural and celestial things, and examination of human matters.[17]

3. A subsequent revision of *De prudentia* (which, as has been noted, appeared posthumously) might have erased these oscillations. But what impelled Pontano to distance himself from Aristotelian categories, relying on the concept of *ars*?

The section of *De prudentia* devoted to painting is striking for the self-confidence and scope of the choices made in it. Probably, these were the result of direct experience: Giotto (like Donatello, mentioned later) was conspicuously present in Naples.[18] As regards Gentile da Fabriano, perhaps Pontano saw his paintings in Rome. Bartolomeo Facio, a historian from the court of Aragon, had recorded them with warm praise in his *De viris illustribus*, written in Naples between 1455 and 1457.[19] And yet Pontano (whom Facio characterized as *'familiaris noster'*, very close friend[20]) would have searched in vain for the

---

17 Pontano, *De prudentia*, fol LXIVr: 'Sapientes vero qui cognitionem rerum tantum modo ipsi quidem habeant ab usu vero tum domestico tum civili omnino aversi, civilibusque ab actionibus, ac domesticis compendiis, sola cognitione, ac coelestium, naturaliumque contemplatione, humanarumque indagatione rerum contenti.'

18 See Fausto Nicolini, *L'arte napoletana del Rinascimento e la lettera di P. Summonte a M. A. Michiel* (Naples: Ricciardi, 1925), pp. 159–60, 166, 181–90.

19 See the entry 'Facio, Bartolomeo' by Paolo Viti in *Dizionario biografico degli Italiani*.

20 Berthold Louis Ullman, 'Pontano's Handwriting and the Leiden Manuscript of Tacitus and Suetonius', *Italia medioevale e umanistica* 2 (1959), pp. 309–35: here p. 309.

name of Jean of Burgundy (*Ioannem Burgundionem*), perhaps identifiable with Jean Fouquet (who was born in Tours; but Facio had called the Flemish Jan van Eyck 'Ioannes Gallicus'). One is tempted to detect in Pontano's words a trace of Fouquet's hypothetical stay in Naples.[21]

But in addition to guiding Pontano's taste and preferences, Facio may have inspired his reflection more generally. Introducing the section on painting, Facio called it 'an art which requires greater prudence (*majorem prudentiam desiderat*)' than other arts, because it represents not only the external features of a face or body, but also 'inner feelings and emotions (*interiores sensus, ac motus*)'.[22] A humanist like Facio was, of course, aware that to connect an art like painting to prudence (*prudentia*) implied a distantiation from Aristotelian categories, which were consciously used by him in characterizing Francesco Foscari and Cosimo de' Medici as examples of prudence.[23]

Reading Facio may have reinforced Pontano's tendency to

---

21 Roberto Longhi, 'Ancora sulla cultura di Fouquet' (1952), now in *'Arte italiana e arte tedesca' con altre congiunture fra Italia ed Europa* (Florence: Sansoni, 1979), vol. IX of the *Opere complete di Roberto Longhi*, pp. 39–40; Pierluigi Leone de Castris, ed., *Quattrocento Aragonese. La pittura a Napoli al tempo di Alfonso e Ferrante d'Aragona* (Naples: Electa, 1997), pp. 36–48; Gennaro Toscano, *El Renacimiento Mediterráneo*, ed. Mauro Natale (Madrid: Thyssen-Bornemisza Museum, 2001), pp. 353–6. Fouquet's name does not appear in the letter on the arts in Naples that Pietro Summonte, a disciple and literary executor of Pontano, sent to Marcantonio Michiel: cf. Nicolini, *L'arte napoletana del Rinascimento*, p. 144ff.

22 The section on painting in Bartolomeo Facio, *De viris illustribus*, was published by Michael Baxandall in the appendix to his *Giotto and the Orators* (Oxford: Clarendon, 1971), pp. 163–68, and is illuminatingly discussed by him at pp. 98–111. Baxandall translates '*prudentia*' as 'discretion' (p. 104). '*Prudentia*' does not figure in the index of humanistic terms.

23 Baxandall refers to Guarino (whose disciple Facio was) and his 'Aristotelian insistence on the inability of the painter to show moral quality' (*Giotto*, p. 90; see also p. 88). I am grateful to Silvia Ginzburg for directing me to this passage. See also Bartolomeo Facio, *De viris illustribus*, ed. L. Mehus (Florence: Ex typographia Joannis Pauli Giovannelli, 1745), pp. 56–7.

blur the boundaries between art and prudence in the name of expertise. In the chapter of book IV entitled 'De experientibus et peritis', Pontano observed that the ancients called legal experts *prudentes* (in another passage he had called them *sapientes*).[24] Usually, he added, *peritia* and *solertia* are synonymous. 'And these words, as you know, are taken from art and then referred to actions (*ab arte primum, ut videtis, traducta, post translata sunt ad actiones*)'. The role played by example (*exemplum*) in the domain of action (*in agendo*), Pontano concluded, is comparable to the role played by norm (*norma*) in the domain of art.[25]

Once again, Pontano's argument was based on everyday language, on craft jargon: 'the norm, as it is called by artists' (*ea ipsa quae ab artificibus vocata est norma*).[26] He realized that contemporary realities did not easily fit into Aristotelian categories. Τέχνη and *ars* (a word which in Pontano's *De prudentia* indicates the vernacular *arte*) were not wholly identical terms. Pontano subscribed to the traditional view that arts (*artes*) originated in scarcity (*inopia*) and that all of them involved the use of hands.[27] But he appreciated the importance of a factor bound up with a notion of art that was then emerging. Implicitly relying on Alberti, Pontano noted that a statue is not praised for the material it is made from, like bronze or marble, but for 'the artist's work' (*artificis opera*).[28] Perfection derives from the individual who imparts form (*ab informante*). In the same way, Homer's poetry is praised for its form, not its subject: the account of the Trojan War is full of fabulous details, and the war itself possibly never occurred. The subject of Lucan's poem (*Pharsalia*) is excellent, but the execution is uneven.[29]

---

24 Pontano, *De prudentia*, fol LXXXVIIIv: 'Ipsi illi igitur periti sunt, quos non multo ante diximus vocatos ab antiquis iuris prudentes.'

25 Ibid., fol LXXXIXr–v.

26 Ibid., fol LXXXIXv.

27 Ibid., fol VIIIv: 'Inopiam esse unum e principiis'; fols Ixr–v: 'Hominem natum esse ad agendum, agendoque informari.'

28 On possible echoes of Alberti in Pontano's work, see Stefano Borsi, *Leon Battista Alberti e Napoli* (Florence: Polistampa, 2006), pp. 278–95.

29 Pontano, *De prudentia*, fol XVIIv.

Behind Pontano's idea of transferring competence from the sphere of art to that of action, we glimpse Facio's remark on painting being informed by prudence on the one hand and Alberti's emphasis on the crucial role of *disegno* on the other. But Pontano's reflections (and Alberti's) cannot be examined in isolation. They must be placed in a protracted, underground history that unfolded in streets and workshops and which has left traces (as Pontano understood) in the language. Linguistic innovations, constraints and compromises created cognitive possibilities. A word like *disegno*, with its manifold meanings (artistic and political), is exemplary in this regard.[30]

4. Transferring into the sphere of politics terms derived from the morally ambiguous domain of the arts betokens tacitly subverting Aristotelian distinctions from within. In ancient writers like Sallust or Livy, Pontano noted, the word 'arts' (*artes*) could refer to acts that were good or heinous.[31]

An example will serve to clarify the implications of this terminological transfer. In commenting upon the rape of the Sabine women, Pontano recalled that his disciple Pietro Summonte wondered whether Romulus's decision could be ascribed to prudence. Was it not an evil gesture, since it violated the laws of hospitality? Pontano came to a different conclusion: 'If Romulus played art with art (*si artem arte lusit*), he does not need to be pardoned for a crime ... The result of his plan and action, and the greatness of the empire, attest to the prudence of his action.'[32]

---

30   See David Summers, *Michelangelo and the Language of Art* (Princeton, NJ: Princeton University Press, 1981), pp. 250–61; Michael Baxandall, 'English *Disegno*', in *Words for Pictures: Seven Papers on Renaissance Art and Criticism* (New Haven, CT: Yale University Press, 2003), pp. 83–97.

31   Pontano, *De prudentia*, fol LXv (with reference to Sallust, *Bellum Catilinae*, I, 34; Livy, *Ab urbe condita*, II, ii, 20): 'Cum historici alii dixerunt artes Hannibalis et comici, servorum artes ac lenonum. Itaque ad actiones referri artes ipsas etiam videntur ac mores, unde in proverbii fere locum concessit.'

32   Ibid., fols CIIv–CIIIr: 'Si artem arte lusit Romulus, non iniuria quidem videtur excusandus ... Quae vero prudenter ab illo [Romulo]

In a passage of the *Discourses* (I, 9) devoted to Romulus's murders of Remus and Titus Tatius, Machiavelli ventured a similar judgement: 'It is truly appropriate that while the act accuses him, the result excuses him, and when the result is good, like that of Romulus, it will always excuse him.'[33] As Brian Richardson has pointed out, the two passages are, if not 'identical', very similar.[34] But this specific convergence must be seen in a larger framework: the transfer, effected by Pontano, of prudence from the sphere of morality to the morally neutral domain of art.

5. This transfer was at the heart of a splendid, largely unnoticed essay on Machiavelli, written by Charles Singleton many years ago.[35] Singleton's dense, elegant, almost reticent demonstration began by quoting Aquinas's definition of prudence: *recta ratio rerum agibilium*. Singleton did not care to mention that it recurs in a sermon by Savonarola that Machiavelli summarized for Ricciardo Becchi, in a letter dated 9 March 1498.[36]

The trajectory that led Machiavelli to deliberately distance himself from Aristotle's (and Aquinas's) notion of prudence can

---

excogitatum sit et actum, exitus ipse ac tanti magnitudo imperii declaravit.'

33 Niccolò Machiavelli, *Discourses on Livy*, tr. Julia Conaway Bondanella and Peter Bondanella (Oxford: Oxford University Press, 2008), p. 45. (*Discorsi*, ed. Corrado Vivanti [Turin: Einaudi, 1997], p. 223: 'Conviene bene che, accusandolo il fatto, lo effetto lo scusi; e quando sia buono come quello di Romolo, sempre lo scuserà.')

34 Richardson, 'Pontano's *De prudentia*', p. 355.

35 Charles S. Singleton, 'The Perspective of Art', *Kenyon Review* 15/2 (Spring 1953), pp. 169–89. My debt to this essay is evident in chapters 1 and 2 above.

36 'Prudentia est recta cognitio [correctly: "ratio"] agibilium': Niccolò Machiavelli, *Lettere*, *Opere*, vol. II, ed. Corrado Vivanti (Turin: Einaudi, 1999), pp. 6, 1457. Christian Lazzeri, 'Prudence, éthique et politique de Thomas d'Aquin à Machiavel', in *De la prudence des anciens comparée à celle des modernes. Sémantique d'un concept, déplacement des problématiques*, ed. André Tosel (Paris: Les Belles Lettres, 1995), p. 105 n. 2, mentions the letter but fails to mention that Machiavelli is quoting from Savonarola's sermon.

only be partially reconstructed. But Pontano's *De prudentia* must have played an important role in it, at a stage which preceded the *Discourses*. It will suffice to recall an expression that recurs in the letters to Francesco Vettori accompanying the conception and composition of *De principatibus*: politics as *arte dello stato*.[37]

---

37 On *arte dello stato*, see above, chapter 2, pp. 42–6.

4

Intricate Readings:
Machiavelli, Aristotle,
Thomas Aquinas

1. Machiavelli's work must be distinguished from its reception: on this issue scholars have long been in agreement. Machiavellianism and anti-Machiavellianism are important subjects for research, but Machiavelli must be analysed aside from the stereotypes, positive or negative, bound up with his contrasting fortunes. Machiavelli may be regarded as an especially relevant instance of a general hermeneutic perspective, based on analysis of the context in which the text (in the broadest sense of the term) took shape.[1]

This perspective has proved very fertile. And yet, urged on by Old Nick (an Elizabethan nickname for the devil), I feel tempted to play the devil's advocate and ask, to what extent does the clear-cut distinction between the reception of a text and analysis of it help us to reach a better understanding of its meaning?[2]

For the avoidance of any doubt, let me stress right away that I strongly reject (as I have for many years) neo-sceptical

---

1 Quentin Skinner, 'Meaning and Understanding in the History of Ideas', *History and Theory*, 8/1 (1969), pp. 3–53. (For an abbreviated and revised version, see Skinner, *Visions of Politics*, vol. 1, *Regarding Method* [Cambridge: Cambridge University Press, 2002], pp. 57–89.)

2 Claude Lefort posed a question that is similar in some respects in his *Le travail de l'oeuvre. Machiavel* (Paris: Gallimard, 1972). But the road followed here, and the destination, are very different.

approaches arguing that all readings are equally permissible. I likewise reject the idea that the history of a text's reception can be regarded, even implicitly, as an alternative to textual philology. In some fine pages, Roberto Longhi showed how historical (i.e., contextual) analysis of the reception of a painting can pave the way for the judgement of the connoisseur.[3] Following Longhi's example, we can try to rework the well-known distinction between etic and emic levels advanced by the anthropologist and linguist Kenneth Pike. Faced with a text (or a work of art, a ritual, etc.), philologists, historians and anthropologists start from questions formulated in the unavoidably anachronistic and ethnocentric categories of the observer. Through these etic questions, bit by bit duly corrected, it is possible to arrive at an understanding of the emic answers, articulated in the inevitably different language of the actors.[4] Translated into the language of reception theory, the etic level refers to the readers, the emic level to the text and its meaning. But in the sphere of history or philology (the case of anthropology is often different), the reactions recorded by observers can be multiple, diffused in time and space: and here we encounter reception history. As I shall try to show in the following pages, Machiavelli's reception can throw light on a little-known (and possibly unknown) aspect of his work. The experiment will be guided by the history of the reception, duly assessed, even if it will require independent confirmation.

---

3   Roberto Longhi, 'Due dipinti inediti di Giovan Gerolamo Savoldo' (1927), in *Saggi e ricerche: 1925–1928*, vol. I (Florence: Sansoni, 1967), pp. 148–55. On reception, see at any rate Giuliano Procacci, *Machiavelli nella cultura europea dell'età moderna* (Rome and Bari: Laterza, 1995) and Sydney Anglo, *Machiavelli: The First Century: Studies in Enthusiasm, Hostility, and Irrelevance* (Oxford: Oxford University Press, 2005).

4   Carlo Ginzburg, 'Our Words, and Theirs: A Reflection on the Historian's Craft, Today', in *Historical Knowledge: In Quest of Theory, Method and Evidence*, ed. Susanna Feldman and Marjatta Rahikainen (Cambridge: Cambridge University Press, 2012), pp. 97–119.

2. In his *Dictionnaire* (see above, chapter 1), Bayle referred to two accusations levelled at Machiavelli: having plagiarized Aristotle and having plagiarized Thomas Aquinas. Both accusations dated back to Kaspar Schoppe (known as Scioppius), who in his *Paedia politices* (1623) had defended Machiavelli, without naming him, maintaining that the sinister arguments ascribed to some unnamed 'writers about politics' had been already advanced by Aristotle and Aquinas (see below, pp. 80–1).[5] Albeit rooted in a specific context – Counter-Reformation Rome – Scioppius's interpretation can help us read Machiavelli's works, written in Florence one hundred years before.

The experiment will begin with a question: Had Machiavelli read Aristotle's *Politics*? An affirmative answer seems obvious, since Aristotle is explicitly mentioned in Machiavelli's *Discourses on Livy*, book III, chapter 26.[6] Further, though debatable, evidence emerges from correspondence between Francesco Vettori and Machiavelli. In a letter of 20 August 1513, invoking Aristotle as an authority, Vettori argued that the Swiss could not expand very far because they formed part of a confederal republic: 'Because, if you read the book on *Politics* attentively and [look at] the republics of the past, you will find that a divided republic, like that one [the Swiss], cannot expand itself.'[7]

On 26 August, Machiavelli replied irritably: 'I don't know what Aristotle says about divided [i.e., confederate] republics; but I do think carefully about what reasonably could be, what is and what has been . . .'[8]

---

5 See the entry 'Schoppe (Scioppio), Kaspar' (by P. Carta), in *Enciclopedia machiavelliana*, vol. II, pp. 498–9.

6 Niccolò Machiavelli, *Discourses on Livy*, tr. Julia Conaway Bondanella and Peter Bondanella (Oxford: Oxford University Press, 2008), p. 319.

7 Vettori to Machiavelli, 20 August 1513, in Niccolò Machiavelli, *Opere*, vol. II, ed. Corrado Vivanti (Turin: Einaudi, 1999), p. 285: 'perché, se voi leggerete bene la *Politica* et le republiche che sono state, non troverete che una republica, come quella, divulsa possa fare progresso.'

8 Machiavelli to Vettori, 26 August 1513, in ibid., p. 289 (and cf.

Machiavelli was reacting impatiently against what he deemed to be a bookish analysis of political reality. Later, in the *Discourses* (II, 4), he tacitly accepted Vettori's argument about the inherent limits to Swiss power.[9] In any event, Vettori took it for granted that Machiavelli was familiar with the *Politics*, and did not bother to mention its author.[10] A few months later, on 13 December, Machiavelli announced to Vettori the composition of *The Prince*:

> I have … composed a little book *On Principalities*, in which I delve as deeply as I can into this subject, and discuss what a principality is, how many different types there are, how they are gained, how they are held and why they are lost.[11]

As has been observed, this résumé of the first eleven chapters of *The Prince* summarizes a series of topics from Aristotle's *Politics*.[12] Obviously, this does not mean that Machiavelli was a follower of Aristotle (he wasn't). In general, his relationship to reality was anything but bookish. But in the dedicatory letter to

---

p. 1567): 'Né so quello si dica Aristotile delle republiche divulse; ma io penso bene quello che ragionevolmente potrebbe essere, quello che è, e quello che è stato'.

9 Machiavelli, *Discourses*, pp. 166–7.

10 This knowledge is excluded by M. Martelli, 'Machiavelli e i classici', in *Cultura e scrittura di Machiavelli*, Proceedings of the Florence–Pisa Conference, 27–30 October 1997 (Rome: Salerno Editrice, 1998), pp. 279–309, esp. pp. 291–2; and see also Martelli, 'I dettagli della filologia', in ibid., pp. 306–9). What follows shows the groundlessness of this conjecture.

11 Niccolò Machiavelli, *The Prince*, ed. Quentin Skinner and Russell Price, tr. Russell Price (Cambridge: Cambridge University Press, 2016), appendix A, pp. 93–4. (*Opere*, vol. II, p. 296: 'io ho … composto uno opuscolo *De principatibus*, dove io mi profondo quanto io posso nelle cogitazioni di questo subbietto, disputando che cosa è principato, di quale spezie sono, come e' si acquistono, come e' si mantengono, perché e' si perdono'.)

12 The chasm between those chapters and the following ones was pointed out by Friedrich Meinecke in his introduction to Niccolò Machiavelli, *Der Fürst und kleinere Schriften*, tr. E. Merian-Genast (Berlin: Hobbing, 1923), pp. 38–47.

The Prince he wrote that he wished to offer Lorenzo de' Medici 'knowledge of the conduct of great men, learned through long experience of modern affairs and continual study of ancient history'.[13] Reading Aristotle's *Politics* unquestionably formed part of this 'study' – but in which edition?

3. This question is less obvious than the previous one. The scholarly debate on Machiavelli's sources has sometimes involved references to editions he could not have consulted, or to texts written in languages (e.g., Greek) he was unable to read.[14] To avoid those anachronistic slips, it would be best to circumscribe our enquiry, listing two possibilities:[15]

(1) The edition of Aristotle's writings (including his *Politics*) in three volumes, with commentaries by Averroes, Venice 1483;

(2) Leonardo Bruni's Latin translation of the *Politics*, with Thomas Aquinas's commentary, Rome 1492.

---

13 Machiavelli, *The Prince*, p. 3 (*Il principe*, p. 58: 'la cognizione delle azioni delli òmini grandi, imparata con una lunga esperienzia delle cose moderne e una continua lezione delle antique'.)

14 In a recent book on Machiavelli's *Discourses*, all the quotations from Aristotle's *Politics* are taken from an edition of Leonardo Bruni's translation, published in Venice in 1542, fifteen years after Machiavelli's death: cf. Gabriele Pedullà, *Machiavelli in tumulto. Conquista, cittadinanza e conflitto nei 'Discorsi sulla prima deca di Tito Livio'* (Rome: Bulzoni, 2011), p. 22 n. and passim, which refers to 'Aristotele, *Politicorum libri*, a cura di Raffaele Volterrano, traduzione di Leonardo Bruni, Venice, Hieronymus Scotus, 1542'. In fact, Raffaele Maffei, known as Volterrano (1451–1522), was not the editor of the volume but the author of the short résumés introducing each book. A more precise reference would cite *Aristotelis Stagiritae Politicorum ad Nicomachum lib. primus Raphaelis Volaterrani argumenta in eosdem. Leonardo Aretino interprete* (Venetiis: apud Hieronymum Scottum, 1542 [= 1543]).

15 For these sources I have used the invaluable list provided in an appendix to Niccolò Machiavelli, *The Discourses*, tr. and ed. L. J. Walker, vol. II (New Haven: Yale University Press, 1950), pp. 273–7 (on Aristotle).

The second (or the reprint of it, published in Venice in 1500) is, in my view, the edition Machiavelli read.[16]

This hypothesis, if proven, would involve a series of Chinese boxes, which might be described in reverse chronological order as follows:

(a) the twofold accusation made against Machiavelli that he plagiarized both Aristotle and Thomas Aquinas is a caricature

(b) of the argument put forward by Scioppius, in which Machiavelli is presented implicitly as a follower of both Aristotle and Aquinas. This, in turn, is a simplified description of

(c) the profound impact on Machiavelli of his reading Aristotle's *Politics* as glossed by Thomas Aquinas. (To the best of my knowledge only one, earlier edition, published in 1478 in Barcelona, pointed out that the commentary's second part had been written by a follower 'and imitator' of Aquinas, Auvergne.)[17]

---

16 For the Rome 1492 edition see below, pp. 135–6. The reprint is Thomas Aquinas, *In octo Politicorum Aristotelis libros cum textu eiusdem. Leonardo Aretino interprete*, Venetiis, 1500 (colophon: 'Venetiis, impensis domini Andree Torresani de Asula arte vero Simonis de Luere ultimo mensis Octobris MD. feliciter'). Another edition was published in Venice in 1514, 'mandato et impensis heredum ... Octaviani Scoti ciuis Modoetiensis et sotiorum summa diligentia impressis Venetijs per Georgium Arrivabenum'; there is a copy in Florence, Biblioteca Nazionale Centrale, MAGL. 5.2.338./b. On these editions, C. Martin, 'The Vulgate Text of Aquinas's Commentary on Aristotle's *Politics*', *Dominican Studies* 5 (1952), pp. 35–64, remains fundamental.

17 Lidia Lanza, 'Aspetti della ricezione della *Politica* aristotelica nel XIII secolo: Pietro d'Alvernia', *Studi medievali*, 3rd ser, 35/2 (1994), pp. 643–94. See Thomas Aquinas, *In libros polithicorum Ar[istotelis] comentum foeliciter incipit*, Barcelona 1478, colophon: 'Comentum in Ar[istotelis] polythicorum libros per sanctum Thomam fratrem sacri ordinis predicatorum initum per venerabilem vero Petrum Aluerniensem eiusdem ordinis fratrem illius doctrine studiosum ac solertem imitatorem. Absolutum foeliciter explicit ab Ioanne Ferrario cive barchin[onensi] humanitatis studiorum amantissimo accuratissime emendatum qui ut legentibus Ar[istotelis] commemoratos poliythicorum libros facilior sit aditus textui antiquae traductionis huius nove Leonardi Arethini textum

The possibility that Machiavelli had read Aristotle's *Politics* along with Aquinas's commentary has been suggested in the past, notably by Leslie J. Walker. In his discussion of Aquinas as a source of Machiavelli, however, Walker dwelled primarily on *De regimine principum*. I shall focus, instead, on Aristotle's *Politics* as translated by Leonardo Bruni, and especially on the fifth book, as well as the commentary attributed to Thomas Aquinas (in fact partly written by his follower, Peter of Auvergne).[18]

4. But first we shall have to describe the book that (as I shall argue) was read by Machiavelli. It is a folio volume, printed in Rome by Eucharius Silber, alias Franck, in 1492.[19] The copy I consulted, today held by the Biblioteca Comunale degli Intronati, Siena, possesses particular value, since it was originally owned by the man who initiated the editorial project: Agostino Piccolomini (1470–1496), a nephew of Cardinal Francesco Todeschini Piccolomini (subsequently Pope Pius III).[20] In a dedicatory letter addressed to Ludovico Valenza – a learned

---

subiungere non praetermisit', Barcelona, Pedro Bruno and Nicola Spindeler, December 18, 1478'. I consulted a reproduction of the copy owned by the Biblioteca Universitaria, Sassari.

18 See *The Discourses*, ed. Walker, vol. II, pp. 293–8, esp. p. 298. He refrained from mentioning (let alone commenting on) the fifth book of the *Politics*. The possibility that Machiavelli had read Thomas Aquinas's *Summa* was mentioned, in a paradoxical tone, by Charles Singleton, 'The Perspective of Art', *Kenyon Review* 15, (1953), pp. 169–89, esp. p. 188.

19 Thomas Aquinas, *Commentarii ... in octo Politicorum Aristotelis libros cum textu eiusdem. Interprete Leonardo Aretino*, Romae, 1492. The colophon reads: 'impressum est hoc opus Romae per magistrum Eucharium Silber alias Franck, xiiii kal. Aug. 1492'. On this edition (IGI 841; ISTC ia01024000), see Martin, 'The Vulgate Text of Aquinas's Commentary', pp. 41–3 (but the reference to Ludovico Valenza's criticisms is rather cursory).

20 Biblioteca Comunale degli Intronati, Siena, a-z8 A-I8. This Agostino Piccolomini is not to be confused with Agostino Patrizi Piccolomini: see R. Avesani, 'Per la biblioteca di Agostino Patrizi Piccolomini vescovo di Pienza', in *Mélanges Eugène Tisserant*, 7 vols (Vatican City: Biblioteca Apostolica Vaticana, 1964), vol. VI, p. 2 n. 4.

Dominican friar and professor of theology, who had been his teacher – Agostino explained that the previous summer, in Tuscany, he had come across a manuscript containing Thomas Aquinas's commentary on Aristotle. Publication had taken time, because the text, written by an incompetent copyist, was full of mistakes and blunders. Having searched in vain for other manuscripts in Rome to compare with the one he had found, Agostino had entrusted the editorial work to Fra Ludovico Valenza 'to help those men, involved in public life (*civiles viri*), who endeavour to understand Aristotle'. A cleaned-up, unblemished edition, Agostino went on, would be invaluable for 'city governors and state administrators', for 'when they read Aristotle only in order to put his precepts into practice, they have to struggle with the interpretation of words; therefore they reject and ignore Aristotle.' But if Fra Ludovico would accept this editorial task, 'they will praise you, they will put Aristotle's precepts into practice, they will venerate him'. You should put aside your theological studies for a while, Agostino insisted, to devote yourself to the correction and emendation of this commentary, tidying it up as one would a vegetable garden. If you want to include Leonardo Bruni's translation of the *Politics*, do so, even though (Agostino stated emphatically) it was published in such a confusing way that not a word by Bruni survives.[21] Your edition will provide an unblemished Aristotle and 'will bring Thomas Aquinas, previously buried in darkness, back to the light'.[22]

---

21 This was probably a reference to the edition published in Barcelona in 1478 (see above, n. 16). Another possibility would be Aristotle, *Ethica, Politica et Oeconomica, Leonardo Aretino interprete* (Strasbourg: Johann Mentelin, *ante* 10 April 1469). See K. Schorbach, *Der Strassburger Frühdrucker Johann Mentelin (1458–1478). Studien zu seinem Leben und Werke* (Mainz: Gutenberg-Gesellschaft, 1932, p. 10*.

22 Thomas Aquinas, *Commentarii ... in octo Politicorum Aristotelis libros*, 1492 edn, fol a1v: 'Quod si (ut spero) expolitum candidumve librum praestabis, quantam ab his qui civitatibus praesunt qui ve una respublicas administrant sis consequuturus tu qui prudentissimus es considera. Hi enim cum Aristotelem legunt ut praecepta solum exequantur, dum in verborum interpretatione immorari

Another dedicatory letter follows, from the editor, Fra Ludovico, to Agostino's uncle: the cardinal, who, a decade later, would become Pope Pius III for a few months (Francesco Piccolomini was himself nephew of Pope Pius II, Enea Silvio Piccolomini). Those names speak for themselves: the project to publish Aquinas's commentary on Aristotle's *Politics* was conceived in Siena, at the highest level of the ecclesiastical hierarchy, in a humanist ambience. Aquinas's commentary was regarded as an indispensable tool for putting Aristotle's precepts to practical use. But then (Ludovico explained) an obstacle emerged. There were those who thought that the old translation of the *Politics* commented on by Aquinas (this was William of Moerbeke's) did not correspond to Aristotle's text.[23] Ludovico did not agree, though he acknowledged that Bruni's translation was certainly 'more transparent' and its Latin 'more accurate'. But ultimately, he realized that 'St Thomas had commented on the old translation, but it was as if he had interpreted the new one'.[24] The obstacle had been overcome.

---

eos necesse est et Aristotelem damnant et negligunt. Quod si laborem hunc dempseris et summopere te laudabunt et philosophi praecepta exequentes Aristotelem maxime venerabuntur. Quare te rogo ut omissis paulum sacris studiis, ad hos commentarios corrigendos emendandosque tanquam in hortulum, cum tibi per maximas curas licebit, descendas, ut si forte eos Leonardi Arretini translationi, que ita confuse impressa est, ut ne verbum quidem Arretini contineat, adnectere velimus, possimus uno tempore Aristotelem mendis vacuum, Divumque Thomam in tenebris latitantem in lucem emittere.'

23 Aristotle, *Politicorum libri octo cum vetusta translatione Guillelmo de Moerbeka*, ed. F. Susemihl (Leipzig: Teubner, 1872).

24 Thomas Aquinas, *Commentarii ... in octo Politicorum Aristotelis libros*, 1492 edn, fol a2r: 'Sed cum Leonardi Aretini translatio aperta magis et latina sit, que tamen impressa nec Aretini verbum continere videatur, suasit et Thomae interpretationem ei coaptare translationi et expurgare depravatum Aristotelis librum. Hoc certe satis mihi difficile visum est, eos recte sentire existimans, qui veterem translationem, quam tamen Thomas commentatus fuit, non consentire Aristoteli censent. Verum experimento didici eiusmodi viros quod non intelligant temere iudicare. Nihil enim magis consonum et consentaneum et coaptatum esse potest quam vetus novaque Politicorum Aristotelis translatio. Nam etsi Divus Thomas

5. Better, more faithful texts, written in a better Latin, in the service of a better politics: just what we would expect from a Renaissance edition of Aristotle. But the juxtaposition of Aristotle's text in Bruni's translation and Aquinas's commentary – an ancient palace, framed by a medieval building, made accessible by a humanist – generated an underlying tension. We can see it emerging from Agostino Piccolomini's dedicatory letter to Fra Ludovico. The letter's conclusion was unequivocal: the 'dreadful and dirty' (*horridum immundumque*) manuscript on which the edition was based must be drastically cleaned up. No additions, no omissions introduced by the copyist were to be allowed; anything unrefined, barbarous or uncouth must go.[25] The assumption of an intrinsic convergence between truth and classical Latin paved the way for rejection (not fully shared, as we have seen, by the editor, Fra Ludovico) of the old translation commented on by Aquinas. But what about Thomas's commentary itself? Could it not also be characterized as 'unrefined' and 'barbarous'?

We can read these bold questions between the lines of a passage in Ludovico Valenza's dedicatory letter, attacking 'contemporary rhetoricians who despise all writers who either do not deal with history or do not discuss rhetoric. These kind of people refuse to read or know anything else.'[26] A polemical blow followed by a defensive statement, in which Fra Ludovico declared his veneration for Plato, Theophrastus and their translators, like Theodore Gaza. Then came a further attack, against 'those who, although they know nothing about nature, as soon

---

veterem exposuerit, novam tamen interpretari videtur.' See on this issue F. E. Cranz, 'The Publishing History of the Aristotle Commentaries of Thomas Aquinas', *Traditio* 34 (1978), pp. 157–92, esp. pp. 171–2.

25 Thomas Aquinas, *Commentarii ... in octo Politicorum Aristotelis libros*, 1492 edn, fol 1v: 'Ne quid in eo quod a scriptore additum diminutumve sit, inconcinnum, barbarum incultumque legatur'.

26 Ibid., fol a2r: 'sed culpa vestra est o rhetores nostrae aetatis qui contemnitis omnes scriptores qui vel historiam non tradunt vel de oratoria non disserunt. Omnes alios legere et scire recusatis.'

as they can say something about *de Urbe condita* [by Livy] or the tasks of the orator, begin to criticize any type of knowledge'.[27]

Who were Fra Ludovico's unnamed adversaries? Humanists, for sure.[28] His polemical words reveal the underlying polemic of the Renaissance – understood as a movement, not a period, according to Ernst Gombrich's indispensable distinction.[29]

6. Machiavelli has long been regarded as an emblem of the Renaissance – or of 'modernity', an emic category devoid of analytical value. But the Middle Ages/Renaissance dichotomy does not help us to understand Machiavelli's intellectual development. As argued above (chapter 1), the considerations on the rule and the exception in *Mandrake* and *The Prince* derived from the profound impact of his reading of *Quaestiones mercuriales* by Giovanni d'Andrea, a professor of canon law who died in Bologna in 1348. A copy of *Quaestiones mercuriales* formed part of the library of Niccolò's father, Bernardo Machiavelli.[30]

The commentary on Aristotle's *Politics* begun by Thomas Aquinas and completed by Peter of Auvergne implied something else: the complex relationship between the scholastic tradition and the legacy of antiquity. Whether Machiavelli read the commentary, we do not know for sure. But we can try to perform a thought experiment, imagining his reactions to a section of it, taken from the fifth book.

---

27   Ibid., fol a2r: 'Sed in illos dico qui totius naturae ignari cum aliquid de Urbe condita aut de rhetoris officio possunt dicere omnium se artium censores faciant.'

28   Augusto Campana, 'The Origin of the Word "Humanist"', *Journal of the Warburg and the Courtauld Institutes* 9 (1946), pp. 60–73; reprinted in Campana, *Scritti*, vol. I, *Ricerche medievali e umanistiche*, ed. R. Avesani, M. Feo and E. Pruccoli (Rome: Edizioni di Storia e Letteratura, 2008), pp. 263–81.

29   E. H. Gombrich, 'The Renaissance: Period or Movement?', in *Background to the English Renaissance: Introductory Lectures*, ed. J. B. Trapp (London: Gray-Mills, London 1974), pp. 9–30.

30   See chapter 1, p. 7.

7. Aristotle had remarked that tyranny is 'a compound of both oligarchy and democracy in their most extreme forms: it is therefore most injurious to its subjects, being made up of two evil forms of government, and having the perversions and errors of both' (1310 b 1–9).[31] Then he moved on to a consideration of the ways in which tyrannical governments can be preserved. I shall cite the passage from a modern translation of the *Politics*:

> As to tyrannies, they are preserved in two quite opposite ways. One of them is the old traditional way in which most tyrants administer their government. Of such arts Periander of Corinth is said to have been the great master, and many similar devices may be gathered from the Persians in the administration of their government. There are firstly the prescriptions mentioned some distance back, for the preservation of a tyranny, in as far as this is possible; viz. that the tyrant should lop off those who are too high; he must put to death men of spirit; he must not allow common meals, clubs, education, and the like; he must be upon his guard against anything which is likely to inspire either courage or confidence among his subjects; he must prohibit schools or other meetings for discussion, and he must take every means to prevent people from knowing one another (for acquaintance begets mutual confidence).[32] (1313a 35-b 7)

In Leonardo Bruni's Latin translation (republished, as we have seen, in the 1492 edition of Aquinas's commentary), the sentence 'there are firstly the prescriptions mentioned some distance back' contained one more word – an adjective identifying those prescriptions as *perniciosa* (pernicious): '*Sunt autem hec illa perniciosa quae supra retulimus.*'[33] Bruni's

---

31   Aristotle, *Politics*, in *Complete Works: The Revised Oxford Translation*, ed. Jonathan Barnes, 2 vols (Princeton NJ: Princeton University Press, 1984), vol. II, p. 2080.

32   Ibid., p. 2085.

33   Aristotle, *Ethica, Politica et Oeconomica, Leonardo Bruni interprete, ante* 10 Apr. 1469 edn, fol 156v. On this basis it is possible to

intervention may seem irrelevant: after all, Aristotle was listing a series of measures that he unquestionably considered to be cruel and violent. Bruni merely inserted an adjective to reinforce the description. We may recall that in the past he had defended his own translation of the *Nicomachean Ethics*, comparing the old translators of Aristotle to those who disfigured the paintings of Apelles, and good translators to faithful copyists.[34]

Might Bruni have been trying with his insertion to avert a possible misunderstanding – hence a distortion – of Aristotle's remarks? Certainly, the dry paraphrase provided by Aquinas's continuator, Peter of Auvergne, which Bruni might have seen, and which framed his translation of Aristotle in the 1492 Roman edition, betrayed no trace of moral disapproval. One of the methods for preserving tyranny, the commentary reads, is to murder, to kill (*spegnere*, as Machiavelli used to say) the most powerful, the richest and wisest people: '*Fuit excellentes in potentia vel divitiis interimere ... Iterum interficere sapientes ...*'[35] The second method was more ambiguous, because it implied an imitation of monarchical government. Here is Aristotle once again:

> And there is another [method] which proceeds upon an almost opposite principle of action ... for as one mode of destroying kingly

---

confirm that the word *perniciosa* was not added by Fra Ludovico; cf. Thomas Aquinas, *Commentarii ... in octo Politicorum Aristotelis libros*, 1492 edn, fol 160v.

34 Carlo Ginzburg, *History, Rhetoric, and Proof* (Hanover NH: New England University Press, 1999), p. 65. Cf. the entry 'Bruni, Leonardo' (by C. Vasoli), in *Dizionario biografico degli Italiani*; Leonardo Bruni, *Sulla perfetta traduzione*, ed. Paolo Viti (Naples: Liguori, 2004). According to Eugenio Garin, Bruni's translation of the *Nicomachean Ethics* was 'a systematic re-working and correction' ('Le traduzioni umanistiche di Aristotele nel secolo XV', *Atti e memorie dell'Accademia fiorentina di scienze morali 'La Colombaria'*, 2nd ser., 16 (1947–50), pp. 55–104, esp. p. 67).

35 Thomas Aquinas, *Commentarii ... in octo Politicorum Aristotelis libros*, 1492 edn, fols 160r–v.

power is to make the office of king more tyrannical, so the salvation of a tyranny is to make it more like the rule of a king. But of one thing the tyrant must be careful; he must keep power enough to rule over his subjects, whether they like him or not, for if he once gives this up he gives up his tyranny ... In the first place he should pretend concern for the public revenues, and not waste money in making presents of a sort at which the common people get excited when they see their hard-won earnings snatched from them and lavished on courtesans and foreigners and artists ... Also he should appear to be particularly earnest in the service of the gods; for if men think that a ruler is religious and has a reverence for the gods, they are less afraid of suffering injustice at his hands, and they are less disposed to conspire against him, because they believe him to have the very gods fighting on his side.[36] (1314 a 30–1315 a2)

Aquinas's (i.e., Peter of Auvergne's) commentary on this shocking page sometimes reads more like an expansion than a literal paraphrase. Take, for example, the passage about the tyrant's attitude towards religion:

He says that to preserve tyranny, the tyrant must behave very carefully and reverentially in matters related to religion and worship, differently from everyone else given that he is more powerful than everyone else. And the reason is this: if his subjects regard their prince as a religious and pious man, they will not be afraid of receiving evil from him. From a divine being no one expects any evil.[37]

---

36 Aristotle, *Politics*, ed. Barnes, pp. 2086–7.

37 Thomas Aquinas, *Commentarii ... in octo Politicorum Aristotelis libros*, 1492 edn, fol 164r: 'et dicit quod ad salvationem tyrannidis, tyrannus in his quae ad religionem et cultum divinum pertinent studiose et reverenter se debet habere et tanto magis differenter ab aliis quanto magis excellit. Cuius ratio est: quia si subditi existiment principantem religiosum et deicolam esse non timebunt male pati ab ipso. A divino enim nullus expectat malum per se.'

Three points:

(1) The commentator's gloss – 'From a divine being [*A divino*] no one expects any evil' – suggests an admixture of religious and secular power, introducing a note absent from Aristotle's text.

(2) The commentator characterizes the tyrant's actions as '*contra iustitiam*' (Bruni's translation of τι παράνομον), using the abstract noun *male* (evil), giving a moral overtone to the Greek word νόμος and its violation.

(3) Echoing the medieval translator William of Moerbeke, who had used the word *princeps* (prince), the commentator chose a neutral word – *principans* (prince) – instead of *tyrannus* (tyrant).[38]

We may try to imagine Machiavelli reacting to both Aristotle's text (as translated by Bruni) and the commentary attributed to Aquinas, endeavouring to distinguish between them.

8. The Machiavellian flavour of book V of Aristotle's *Politics* has repeatedly been highlighted, from the sixteenth century onwards. In his *Les Politiques d'Aristote* (1576), Louis Le Roy, professor at the Collège de France, commented on the methods used by tyrants to preserve their government, starting with *perniciosa* – the adjective inserted by Bruni into his translation: 'Et estans tres pernicieux . . .'[39] Antonio Brucioli had inserted the same adjective in his Italian translation of the *Politics* (1547).[40] Le Roy makes the implications of Bruni's addition clear:

---

38 See, e.g., Aristotle, *Politica: (libri I–II.11). Translatio prior imperfecta interprete Guillelmo de Moerbeka*, ed. P. Michaud-Quantin (Bruges and Paris: Desclée de Brouwer, 1961), 1252 a30: 'Principans autem natura et subiectum propter salutem'. See also Nicolai Rubinstein, 'The History of the Word *Politicus*', in *The Languages of Political Theory in Early-Modern Europe*, ed. Anthony Pagden (Cambridge: Cambridge University Press, 1990), pp. 41–56 (*principans* as an adjective).

39 See Procacci, *Machiavelli nella cultura europea dell'èta moderna*, pp. 143–50.

40 *Gli otto libri della republica, che chiamono Politica di Aristotile, nuovamente tradotti di Greco in vulgare Italiano per Antonio Brucioli*, Alessandro Brucioli e fratelli, in Venetia, 1547, fol 121v: 'Et sono queste, quelle perniciose che io ho dette di sopra.'

And given that these methods are highly pernicious, Aristotle did not list them to approve or teach them to men, but because they are to be avoided, knowing the misery of tyrants, who are compelled to use these evil means to protect their own persons and states. The Florentine Machiavelli, writing on the Prince, derived from this passage the majority of his precepts, adding to them examples referring to Rome and Italy.[41]

Le Roy's attempt to tone down the most disturbing passages of Aristotle's *Politics* implied that even *The Prince* could be read in a non-Machiavellian perspective. This was a way of distancing himself from the stereotype of Machiavelli prevalent in France during the Wars of Religion.[42]

It has been argued that Aristotelianism and Machiavellianism were incompatible, since their respective mottoes were *in medio stat virtus*, 'virtue lies in the middle', and *in medio stat corruptio*, 'corruption lies in the middle'.[43] This is an unacceptable thesis, not only because it is based on broad and vague categories like Aristotelianism and Machiavellianism.

---

41 Aristotle, *Les Politiques . . ., esquelles est montree la science de gouverner le genre humain en toutes espèces d'estats publiques, traduittes de grec en françois, avec expositions prises des meilleurs Autheurs*, tr. Louis Le Roy (Paris: Michel de Vascosan, 1576), p. 372: 'Et estans tres pernicieux [these methods] n'ont été recueillis par Aristote pour les approuver ou enseigner aux hommes ains plustot à fin de s'en garder, en cognoissant la misere des tyrans, qui sont contraincts venir à tels maux pour asseurer leurs personnes et estats. Machiavel Florentin escrivant du Prince, a tiré de ce passage la pluspart de ses instructions, en y adioustant exemples Romains et Italiens.' On the basis of this passage, L. A. Burd's claim that the similarity between Aristotle's *Politics* and *The Prince* was first signalled in 1599 (Machiavelli, *The Prince*, Burd edn, p. xi) will have to be backdated.

42 Innocent Gentillet, *Discours, sur les moyens de bien gouverner et maintenir en bonne paix un royaume ou autre principauté . . . Contre Nicolas Machiavel florentin* [Geneva], 1576; for a modern edition, see *Anti-Machiavel*, ed. C. Edward Rathé (Geneva: Librairie Droz, 1968).

43 Bernard Guillemain, 'Machiavel, lecteur d'Aristote', in *Platon et Aristote à la Renaissance*, XVI Tours International Conference (Paris: Vrin, 1976), pp. 163–73, esp. p. 169.

Machiavelli's undoubted preference for extreme solutions could have found validation in Aristotle's *Politics*, as well as in the commentaries by Thomas Aquinas and Peter of Auvergne. It is enough to think of the passages quoted above, describing the 'opposite' method that may be used to preserve tyrannies. But things become more complicated if we bear in mind the distinction between ἁπλῶς and κατὰ χρόνον advanced by Aristotle at the beginning of his *Peri hermeneias* (16a18–19). In that text, translated by Boethius as *De interpretatione*, countless generations of students learned the difference between an absolute atemporal dimension (ἁπλῶς) and a dimension related to a specific time (κατὰ χρόνον) – a contrast translated by Boethius as *simpliciter* and *secundum quid* (the latter expression being much more comprehensive than Aristotle's reference to time).[44] The impersonal question 'how are tyrannical regimes preserved (σῴζονται)?' implied neither a judgement about tyrannical regimes *simpliciter* – that is, in absolute terms – nor a moral choice inspired by the 'virtue lies in the middle' principle. It was a question requiring an answer *secundum quid*, bound up with specific circumstances.[45] This approach inspired the distinction between legitimate and illegitimate conspiracies against tyrants ventured by Aquinas in his *Summa theologiae* (*Secunda secundae*, quaestio XLII). Machiavelli, imprisoned and tortured for his alleged involvement in the anti-Medicean conspiracy of Pietro Paolo Boscoli, (this is the customary spelling) was certainly familiar with Aquinas's distinction, subsequently adopted by Savonarola's followers. It is recalled, for example, at the end of Luca della Robbia's *Recitazione del caso di Pietro Pagolo Boscoli e di Agostino Capponi*, composed around 1513.[46] Giovanni

---

44 Carlo Ginzburg, 'Myth: Distance and Deceit', in *Wooden Eyes: Nine Reflections on Distance*, tr. Martin Ryle and Kate Soper (New York: Columbia University Press, 2001), pp. 25–61, esp. pp. 29–35.

45 I am indebted to Maria Luisa Catoni for clarifying this point for me.

46 See Luca della Robbia, *La morte di Pietro Paolo Boscoli*,

Folchi, interrogated following the discovery of the conspiracy, said that 'sometimes Pietropagolo [Boscoli] and he read Aristotle's *Politics* which spoke about the government of the city'.[47]

9. The distinction between *simpliciter* and *secundum quid* brings us back once again to Scioppius, one of the most perceptive readers of Machiavelli's writings. In his *Paedia politices*, Scioppius argued that both Aristotle in his *Politics*, and Thomas Aquinas, in his commentary on it, divided their subject matter into four parts:[48]

(1) 'knowing which form of state is absolutely (*simpliciter*) the best, and the most desirable';
(2) 'knowing which is the best according to specific circumstances (*pro conditione*) ... since the character of some populations does not adapt itself to the best form of state' – for example, inhabitants of Asia who, as Agesilaos said according to Plutarch, are incapable of living in liberty, but make excellent slaves;[49]

---

ed. Riccardo Bacchelli (Florence: Le Monnier, 1943), pp. 146–7: the Dominican Fra Cipriano, then at the convent of San Marco, said, correcting his previous remark (see pp. 111–12): 'sappi che San Tommaso fa questa distinzione: o che il tiranno i popoli sel sono addossato, o che a forza in un tratto a dispetto del popolo e' reggono. Nel primo modo non è lecito far congiura contro al tiranno, nel secondo è merito. E questo io l'ho poi letto.' Cf. Adriano Prosperi, 'Machiavelli e la "tirannide". Note sui "Discorsi", *Quaderni di storia* 71 (January–June 2010), pp. 5–28, esp. pp. 21–3.

47 Cf. J. N. Stephens and H. C. Butters, 'New Light on Machiavelli', *English Historical Review* 97/382 (1982), pp. 54–69, esp. p. 67. I have 'lui' refer to Folchi himself, unlike Sandro Landi, *Lo sguardo di Machiavelli. Une nuova storia intellettuale* (Bologna: Il Mulino, 2017), p. 187 n. 18, for whom it refers to Machiavelli (named a little earlier).

48 Kaspar Schoppe, *Paedia politices* (Romae: ex typographia Andreae Phaei, 1623), p. 17.

49 See Plutarch, *Sayings of the Spartans* (*Moralia*, 213C), in his *Moralia*, vol. III, ed. and tr. F. Cole Babbitt, Loeb Classical Library (Cambridge, MA: Harvard University Press, 1989), p. 275.

(3) knowing how to reform and preserve the state, whatever it is: Aristotle had spoken in this connection of '*res publica ex hypothesi*' (a 'hypothetical state');

(4) and knowing which state form 'is most widespread and fitting to most people'.[50]

'*Politia est ars*', Scioppius concluded: politics is an art that deals with a very wide range of phenomena. (The word *ars*, which translated Aristotle's τέχνη, can be glimpsed behind the expression *arte dello stato*, used by Machiavelli in his famous letter to Francesco Vettori of 10 December 1513.[51]) Therefore, all forms of state will have to be analysed: not only the one that is absolutely the best (*simpliciter optima*), but also that which is best 'according to the specific conditions' (*pro conditione rerum*), and in general all extant forms.

10. Scioppius's argument was based on the beginning of book IV of Aristotle's *Politics*, filtered through the commentary ascribed to Aquinas (but actually written by Peter of Auvergne). 'The true legislator and statesman', Aristotle wrote,

---

50 In the UCLA library copy I consulted, this fourth point has a marginal note in a seventeenth-century hand: 'De tali forma Principatus agit Machiavellus'.

51 Schoppe, *Paedia politices*, Notice to the reader, p. 3: 'qui artem ipsam civilem sive Politicam non didicerint nec rerum civilium usum habeant'. See Machiavelli to Vettori, 10 December 1513, in *The Prince*, appendix A, pp. 94–5: 'This work . . . will reveal that I have not been asleep or wasted my time during the fifteen years that I have been engaged in studying statecraft.' (*Opere*, vol. II, p. 297: 'si vedrebbe che quindici anni che io sono stato a studio all'arte dello stato, non gl'ho né dormiti né giuocati'.) On this letter see Ezio Raimondi, 'Il sasso del politico', in his *Politica e commedia. Il centauro disarmato* (Bologna: Il Mulino, 1998), pp. 3–43; and J. M. Najemy, *Between Friends: Discourses of Power and Desire in the Machiavelli-Vettori Letters of 1513–1515* (Princeton: Princeton University Press, 1993), esp. pp. 215–40 (but the alleged implications of Machiavelli's passing reference to the story of *Geta e Birria* seem forced). On *arte dello stato*, see above, chapters 1 and 2 (with references to Singleton, 'The Perspective of Art').

ought to be acquainted, not only with that [government] which is best in the abstract (ἁπλῶς) but also with that which is best relatively to circumstances. We should be able further to say how a state may be constituted under any given conditions (ἐξ ὑποθέσεως) ... We should consider, not only what form of government is best, but also what is possible and what is easily attainable by all.[52] (1288b 25–37)

But Aristotle insisted that his aim was the practical one of convincing people to act in the existing circumstances:

Since there is quite as much trouble in the reformation of an old constitution (πολιτείαν) as in the establishment of a new one ... And therefore, in addition to the qualifications of the statesman already mentioned, he should be able to find remedies for the defects of existing constitutions, as has been said before.[53] (1289a 4–7)

This passage, in Leonardo Bruni's translation and Peter of Auvergne's commentary on it, left a profound mark on Machiavelli's mind. First, the commentary: 'Therefore, those who wish to correct a constitution must first remove its discordant features, and then introduce a new order' (*Oportet enim qui vult corrigere aliquam policiam prius amovere inordinationes quae sunt in illa policia et deinde inducere novum ordinem*).[54]

To introduce a new order ('inducere novum ordinem'): this expression, which today sounds typically Machiavellian, followed the commentary by Peter of Auvergne, not Bruni's translation of the passage in *Politics* quoted above: '*Nam est non minus difficile corrigere remp[ublicam] iam institutam quam ab initio instituere: quemadmodum et post discere quam ab initio didicisse.*'[55]

---

52 Aristotle, *Politics*, ed. Barnes, p. 2045.

53 Ibid., pp. 2045–6.

54 Thomas Aquinas, *Commentarii ... in octo Politicorum Aristotelis libros*, 1492 edn, fol 97r.

55 Ibid. See Machiavelli, *The Prince*, chapter 6, pp. 20–1: 'Those who ... become rulers through their own abilities, experience

But it must be noted that Bruni had once again altered Aristotle's phrase ('the qualifications of the statesman already mentioned'), inserting a contrast between states that only exist in books and states that exist in reality. A citizen (*civilis homo*) must know how to reform both: 'It is therefore appropriate for a citizen, as we said, to be able to reform not only republics that are written in books, but also those that exist in reality' (*Quapropter non solum his quae libris scriptae sunt resp[ublicae], verumetiam illis quae revera existunt auxiliari posse oportet civilem hominem ut diximus*).[56]

In a famous remark in chapter 15 of *The Prince*, Machiavelli reworked the opposition between states that exist in books and states that exist in reality. His words echo the anti-Platonic overtones of the passage from Aristotle he had read in Bruni's translation:

> But because I want to write what will be useful to anyone who understands, it seems to me better to concentrate on what really happens rather than on theories or speculations. For many have

difficulty in attaining power, but once that is achieved, they keep it easily. The difficulties encountered in attaining power arise partly from the new institutions and laws they are forced to introduce in order to establish their power and make it secure. And it should be realised that taking the initiative in introducing a new form of government is very difficult and dangerous, and unlikely to succeed. The reason is that all those who profit from the old order will be opposed to the innovator, whereas all those who might benefit from the new order are, at best, tepid supporters of him.' (*Il principe*, pp. 117–18: 'Quelli li quali per vie virtuose simili a costoro diventono principi, acquistono el principato con difficultà, ma con facilità lo tengano; e le dificultà che hanno in acquistare el principato nascono in parte da' nuovi ordini e modi che sono forzati introdurre per fondare lo stato loro e la loro securtà. E debbasi considerare come non è cosa più dificile a trattare, né più dubbia a riuscire, né più pericolosa a maneggiare che farsi capo a introdurre nuovi ordini, perché lo introduttore ha per nimico tutti quegli che delli ordini vecchi fanno bene, e ha tepidi defensori tutti quelli che delli ordini nuovi farebbano bene.') See John H. Whitfield, 'On Machiavelli's Use of *Ordini* ', *Italian Studies* 10 (1955), pp. 19–39.

56 Thomas Aquinas *Commentarii ... in octo Politicorum Aristotelis libros*, 1492 edn, fol 97r.

imagined republics and principalities that have never been seen or known to exist.[57]

11. In *Paedia politices* Scioppius defended unnamed political thinkers who, following the example of Aristotle and Thomas Aquinas, wrote *ex hypothesi*, from a hypothetical perspective. To say that a tyrant, in order to preserve his power, must murder wise and excellent men, was 'not an absolute, simple, categorical discourse', but a hypothetical one, bound up with specific exceptions and conditions.[58] This example, taken from Aristotle and his commentator, was introduced by a more general remark. Some people complain, Scioppius observed, that writers on politics describe tyrannical governments, without saying how horrendous they are. But a true philosopher knows that such judgements 'are completely foreign to reflection about politics [*schola politica*], since they belong to the domain of ethics and moral philosophy'.[59] (Three centuries later, without referring to Scioppius's *Paedia politices*, Benedetto Croce would write that, as was 'well known', Machiavelli had discovered 'the autonomy of politics, of politics which is beyond, or rather beneath, moral good and evil'.[60])

But Scioppius also advanced a very different argument in defence of Machiavelli. An explanation may be 'either straightforward and more open, or oblique and more covert'. If a politician (i.e., Machiavelli) says 'that the tyrant is half-man and half-animal, part

---

57 Machiavelli, *The Prince*, p. 54. (*Il principe*, p. 215: 'Ma, sendo l'intento mio, scrivere cosa utile a chi la intende, mi è parso più conveniente andare drieto alla verità effettuale della cosa che alla immaginazione di essa. E molti si sono immaginati republiche e principati, che non si sono mai visti né conosciuti essere in vero.')

58 Scioppius, *Paedia politices*, p. 30: 'est loquendi modus non absolutus, simplex, aut categoricus, sed hypotheticus, sive cum exceptione aut conditione'.

59 Ibid., p. 20: 'Hoc autem a schola politica alienissimum esse, et ad ethicam vel moralem pertinere'.

60 Benedetto Croce, 'Machiavelli e Vico. La politica e l'etica', in *Elementi di politica* (Bari: Laterza, 1925) p. 60. Cf. J. H. Whitfield, 'The Politics of Machiavelli', *The Modern Language Review* 50/4 (October 1955), pp. 433–43, esp. p. 433.

lion and part fox', and so forth, we may conclude, Scioppius wrote, that tyrannical governments are to be avoided.[61]

The image of *The Prince* as an anti-tyrannical text – indirectly suggested, as we have seen, by Louis Le Roy – enjoyed remarkable success. Today, no one would accept it as such. But can we accept Scioppius's less conventional idea that Machiavelli wrote *ex hypothesi*, in a hypothetical perspective?

12. In the context I am talking about, the word 'perspective' is not a mere metaphor. In the dedicatory letter of *The Prince* to Lorenzo de Medici (later Duke of Urbino), Machiavelli compared himself to landscape painters ('coloro che disegnono e' paesi'). As it has been conjectured, this was an allusion to Leonardo da Vinci's famous map showing an aerial view of Imola. Leonardo and Machiavelli had met in Imola in 1503, at Cesare Borgia's court.[62] Here is Machiavelli:

> I hope it will not be considered presumptuous for a man of very low and humble condition to dare to discuss princely government, and to lay down rules about it. For those who draw maps place themselves on low ground, in order to understand the character of the mountains and other high points, and climb higher in order to understand the character of the plains. Likewise, one needs to be a ruler to understand properly the character of the people, and to be a man of the people to understand properly the character of rulers.[63]

---

61   Scioppius, *Paedia politices*, pp. 30–1: 'vel directa et apertior, vel obliqua et occultior ... Si ergo dicat politicus, tyrannum esse semi hominem et semibelluam, ex leone puta et vulpe compositum, et vivere in perpetuo metu, ac post obitum aeternam ei paratam esse infamiam, censendus est clare satis fateri, turpem esse tyrannidem meritoque fugiendam'.

62   See Ginzburg, 'Distance and Perspective: Two Metaphors', in *Wooden Eyes*, pp. 139–57.

63   Machiavelli, *The Prince*, p. 4. (*Il principe*, pp. 60–1: 'Né voglio sia reputata presunzione se uno omo di basso e infimo stato ardisce discorrere e regolare e' governi de' principi, perché così come coloro che disegnono e' paesi si pongono bassi nel piano a considerare la natura de' monti e de' luoghi alti, e per considerare

The invention of linear perspective provided Machiavelli with a powerful metaphor – a cognitive equivalent of his approach to politics: a weave of *secundum quid* and *simpliciter*. Only a viewpoint relative to a specific context can give access to *la verità effettuale della cosa*. A momentous discovery, that we are still coming to terms with.

---

quella de' bassi, si pongono alto sopr'a' monti; similmente, a conoscere bene la natura de' populi bisogna esser principe, e a conoscere bene quella de' principi bisogna esser populare.')

5

Moulding the People:
Machiavelli, Michelangelo

1. I will start from a page of a book first published in 1993: *History and Its Images: Art and the Interpretation of the Past*, by Francis Haskell – a great art historian who was also a dear, unforgettable friend.[1] Haskell quoted two passages by Jacob Burckhardt, the Swiss historian, without commenting upon them. In the first passage, from his most famous book, *The Civilization of the Renaissance in Italy*, published in 1860, Burckhardt mentioned the 'appalling' *condottieri* [i.e., leaders of military private armies] who offer us 'some of the earliest instances of criminals deliberately repudiating every moral restraint'.

Andrea del Verrocchio's monument in Venice, dedicated to Bartolomeo Colleoni, the famous *condottiere* (ills. 1, 2, 3) can provide a visual reference to Burckhardt's passage. Burckhardt regarded the Italian Renaissance as the birthplace of modernity, but his attitude towards it was marked by a deep ambivalence: a mixture of fascination and repulsion. 'The fundamental vice [of the Italian character in the age of the Renaissance]', he went on in the same passage, 'was at the same time a condition of its greatness, namely, excessive individualism.'

The implications of this remark emerged from the second quote in Haskell's book, taken from a slightly earlier work by

---

1   I am deeply indebted to Luca Giuliani: to his research on Michelangelo, as well as to his comments on an early draft of this paper.

Burckhardt, *The Cicerone* (1855). This was a comment on Michelangelo's work and personality:

> He [Michelangelo] was like a powerful personification of the *destiny* that lay ahead for art: his work and the successes they enjoyed contain all the elements needed for a definition of the fundamental nature of modern art. What is characteristic of the art of the last three centuries – i.e., subjectivity – makes its appearance in Michelangelo under the guise of a creative force freed from every external constraint – not unwillingly or unconsciously, as in so many of the great movements of the spirit which took place in the sixteenth century, but with weighty intent.[2]

Haskell's juxtaposition of the two passages without a comment implicitly suggested a common element in them: the absence of moral restraint in the *condottieri*, the absence of external constraint in Michelangelo's creative force. In fact, as I recently realized when I double-checked Burckhardt's text, the translation provided by Haskell is slightly incorrect. The original text says that Michelangelo's work and his successes paved the way to 'a definition of the fundamental nature of modern *spirit*', not simply of art; and 'subjectivity' is presented as 'the characteristic of the last three centuries', with no further qualification.[3]

One of the elements of modern spirit was '*césarisme*': a term coined by Auguste Romieu in 1850, one year before Louis Napoleon's coup d'état, and then promptly recorded by Burckhardt, as Maurizio Ghelardi pointed out in commenting on the passage quoted above on Michelangelo in *The*

---

2 Francis Haskell, *History and Its Images: Art and the Interpretation of the Past* (New Haven: Yale University Press 1993), pp. 344–5; Jacob Burckhardt, *The Civilization of the Renaissance in Italy*, tr. S. G. C. Middlemore, intr. Peter Burke, notes by Peter Murray (London: Penguin Classics, 1990), pp. 288–9.

3 Jacob Burckhardt, *Der Cicerone. Eine Anleitung zum Genuss der Kunstwerke Italiens. Architektur und Sculptur*, ed. B. Roeck et al. (München-Basel: C. H. Beck, 2001), p. 539.

Cicerone.[4] In an implicit development of Ghelardi's remark, Haskell put side by side the two passages by Burckhardt: the one on the absence of a moral restraint in the case of *condottieri*, and the one on the absence of an external constraint in the case of Michelangelo.

To give some idea of the lasting impact of Burckhardt's image of the Italian Renaissance, I will mention an unexpected, distorted echo of it – a speech delivered (and suggested) by Orson Welles, impersonating Harry Lime, the villain in *The Third Man* (1949):

> In Italy, for 30 years under the Borgias, they had warfare, terror, murder and bloodshed, but they produced Michelangelo, Leonardo da Vinci and the Renaissance. In Switzerland they had brotherly love, they had 500 years of democracy and peace – and what did that produce? The cuckoo clock.

Orson Welles's oft-quoted, jocular remark may have come to my mind when I first read the two passages quoted by Francis Haskell. I started to make conjectures, which I did not develop until recently, in three different directions.

First of all, I thought that the connection between the aesthetic and the political dimension posited by Burckhardt deserved deeper analysis. Secondly, I asked myself to what extent Burckhardt projected a nineteenth-century perception onto sixteenth-century Italy. Thirdly, I wondered whether the long-term political implications of Burckhardt's vision of the Italian Renaissance should be examined more closely.

2. The first point seems obvious: the first chapter of Burckhardt's *The Civilization of the Renaissance in Italy* is entitled 'The

---

4 Maurizio Ghelardi, *La scoperta del Rinascimento, L'"età di Raffaello" di Jacob Burckhardt* (Torino 1991), p. 185. See Arnaldo Momigliano, 'Contributi a un dizionario storico: J. Burckhardt e la parola "cesarismo"', in *Sui fondamenti della storia antica* (Turin: Einaudi, 1984), pp. 389–92; see also Auguste Romieu, *L'ère des Césars, deuxième édition augmentée d'une preface* (Paris: Ledoyen, 1850).

State as a Work of Art' (*Kunstwerk*). This seems to prove the close connection, in Burckhardt's mind, between art and politics. But this answer would be misleading. Here *Kunst* does not mean 'art', but 'artificiality'.[5] This remark did not prevent Burckhardt from advancing a moral judgement: 'Good and evil lie strangely mixed together in the Italian states of the fifteenth century ... To form an adequate moral judgment [on them] is no easy task.'

A footnote followed, remarking that 'this compound of force and intellect [*Kraft und Talent*] was called by Machiavelli *virtù*, and is quite compatible with *scelleratezza* (wickedness)'.[6]

This is usually the case, insofar as Machiavelli focused on the Latin etymology of *virtù*, from *vir*, 'male'. It must be noted, however, that in a famous passage of *The Prince*, chapter 8, dealing with the case of Agathocles, king of Syracuse, Machiavelli strongly opposed *virtù* and *scelleratezza*:

> Whoever might consider the actions and virtue (*virtù*) of this man [Agathocles], will see nothing or little that can be attributed to fortune. For, as was said above, not through anyone's support but through the ranks of the military, which he had gained for himself with a thousand hardships and dangers, he came to the principate ... Yet one cannot call it virtue (*virtù*) to kill one's citizens, betray one's friends, to be without faith, without mercy, without religion; these modes can enable one to acquire empire, but not glory. For, if one considers the virtue of Agathocles in entering into and escaping from dangers ... one does not see why he has to be judged inferior to any most excellent captain. Nonetheless, his savage cruelty and inhumanity, together with

---

5 Burckhardt, *The Civilization of the Renaissance*, p. 22: on Italian Renaissance states being 'scientifically organized with a view to [their] object'.

6 Ibid., pp. 28, 354 n. 6. A reference follows, to Machiavelli, *Discorsi*, I, 10. The passage is mentioned (mixing up text and footnote) by Lawrence Arthur Burd, in his edition of *Il Principe*, ed. L. A. Burd and introd. Lord Acton (Oxford: Clarendon 1891), p. 178.

his infinite crimes (*sceleratezze*), do not permit him to be celebrated among the most excellent men.[7]

Burckhardt did not mention this passage; but his ambivalence
seems to echo Machiavelli's ambivalence – which leads me to
my second point. The relationship between the observer's categories (in this case, Jacob Burckhardt) and the actors' categories
(in this case, Machiavelli) has intrigued me for many years. At
first, I was inspired by the writings of Kenneth Pike, the American
anthropologist and linguist, who labelled those categories 'etic'
and 'emic' – referring to the observer's and the actors' points of
view, respectively. According to Pike, only etic categories can be
regarded as scientific. I found this conclusion a bit simplistic. In
an essay entitled 'Our Words, and Theirs', I argued that if we
look at this relationship as a process, we realize that historians
inevitably start with etic, anachronistic questions. But this is
only the beginning. Through those etic questions we can try to
grasp emic answers, rescuing the actors' voices. Only this poten-
tially endless dialogue between the two perspectives can open
up the possibility of significant access to the past.[8]

---

7 Niccolò Machiavelli, *The Prince*, tr. with an introduction by
Harvey C. Mansfield (Chicago: University of Chicago Press, 1998), pp.
34–5. (N. Machiavelli, *Il principe*, ed. Giorgio Inglese [Turin: Einaudi,
1995], p. 57: 'Non si può ancora chiamare virtù ammazzare e' suoi
cittadini, tradire gli amici, essere sanza fede, sanza piatà, sanza religione; e' quali modi possono fare acquistare imperio, ma non gloria.
Perché, se si considerassi la virtù di Agatocle nello entrare e nello uscire
de' pericoli e la grandezza dello animo suo nel sopportare e superare
le cose avverse, non si vede perché egli abbia a essere iudicato inferiore
a qualunque eccellentissimo capitano: nondimanco la sua efferata
crudeltà e inumanità con infinite sceleratezze non consentono ch'e sia
in fra gli eccellentissimi uomini celebrato. Non si può adunque
attribuire alla fortuna o alla virtù quello che sanza l'una e l'altra fu da
lui conseguito'). See Victoria Kahn, 'Virtù and the Example of
Agathocles in Machiavelli's *Prince*', in *Machiavelli and the Discourse
of Literature*, ed. Albert Russell Ascoli and Victoria Kahn (Ithaca:
Cornell University Press, 1993), pp. 195–217.
8 C. Ginzburg, 'Our Words, and Theirs: A Reflection on the
Historian's Craft, Today', in *Historical Knowledge: In Quest of*

The case I started from provides a vivid example of the etic/
emic dichotomy and its implications: the word 'subjectivity'
(*Subjectivität*), which, according to Burckhardt, is the distinctive character of the last three centuries (1550–1850), is an etic
category, part of the nineteenth-century intellectual vocabulary.[9]
To project it into Michelangelo's work is far from obvious.
Burckhardt was fully aware of the anachronistic dimension of
this word, since he added a remark (not quoted by Haskell)
introduced by the expression '*als ob*' (as if), which designates a
mental experiment: 'as if' Michelangelo's systematic approach
to art could be compared to 'some philosophies based on the
Ego creating the world' ('*einzelne Philosophien von dem
weltschaffenden Ich*') – an allusion to German idealism, and
especially to Fichte.[10]

Anachronism, mental experiments: as soon as I began to
unfold the implications of the case study I mentioned – the two
passages by Jacob Burckhardt, quoted by Francis Haskell –
some of the basic problems of historical knowledge emerged.
Burckhardt mentioned 'subjectivity' as a fundamental

Theory, Method and Evidence, ed. Susanna Fellman and Marjatta
Rahikainen (Cambridge: Cambridge Scholars Publishing, 2011),
pp. 97–119. See also Antonio D'Andrea, 'Le perplessità di
Machiavelli. Agatocle o della via "scellerata e nefaria" (*Principe*
VIII)', in *Strutture inquiete. Premesse teoriche e verifiche storico-
letterarie* (Florence: Oschki, 1993), pp. 109–28, which I found defi-
nitely unconvincing.

9 Entry 'Sujet' in *Vocabulaire Européeen des philosophies,
Dictionnaire des intraduisibles*, ed. Barbara Cassin (Paris: Seuil, 2004),
pp.1233–54.

10 On the role of mental experiments in historical knowledge see
Carlo Ginzburg, 'Microhistory and World History', in *The Cambridge
World History, VI: The Construction of a Global World, 1400–1800
CE, Part 2, Patterns of Change*, ed. Jerry H. Bentley, Sanjay
Subrahmanyam and Merry E. Wiesner-Hanks (Cambridge : Cambridge
University Press, 2015), pp. 446–73. On Burckhardt's allusion to
Fichte see Vivetta Vivarelli, 'Die Bildner des Übermenschen und der
dithyrambische Künstler: Michelangelo und Wagner in *Also Sprach
Zarathustra*', in *Nietzsche-Studien*, 47 (2018), pp. 326–39, especially
p. 331 n. 18.

characteristic of the last three centuries (in a European perspective, of course). Was he also extending this remark to his own practice of history? I do not think so; but I am inevitably driven to ask myself this question, as a historian of sixteenth-century Italy (and Europe). What would be the counterpart of 'subjectivity', the word used by Burckhardt, in the language of the sixteenth-century actors?

The word 'counterpart', which I have just mentioned, evokes the practice of translation. Now, the Latin word for 'translator' is *interpres*: to translate means to interpret, and the other way round. The historian translates the language of other cultures and other societies, into a language which is the translator's own.

3. As I said, Francis Haskell refrained from commenting on the two passages from Burckhardt. The absence of both moral and artistic constraints, mentioned in them, immediately evokes a standard image of the Italian Renaissance. This image has been analysed by Ernst Gombrich, the great art historian, in an essay entitled 'The Renaissance: Period or Movement?'[11] Renaissance as a period is (as I would say, using a terminology which Gombrich did not use) an etic category; Renaissance as a movement is an emic category. Gombrich insisted on the distinction between them, emphasizing the richness of the category of Renaissance as a movement, and raising doubts about the category of Renaissance as a period, which he found too comprehensive, generic and ideologically biased. A most vivid document of the former is a passage (not quoted by Gombrich) from Niccolò Machiavelli's *Arte della guerra* (The art of war, 1521):

---

11 See Ernst H. Gombrich, 'The Renaissance: Period or Movement?' in *Background to the English Renaissance*, ed. by J. B. Trapp (London: Gray-Mills, 1974), pp. 9–30. See also the Italian translation (with a most helpful introduction): 'Il Rinascimento. Periodo o movimento?' in Ernst H. Gombrich, *Immagini e parole*, ed. Lucio Biasiori (Rome: Carocci, 2019), pp. 127–51.

*Questa provincia pare nata per risuscitare le cose morte, come si
è visto della poesia, della pittura e della scultura* (This province
[i.e., Tuscany] seems born to resuscitate dead things, as has been
seen in poetry, painting and sculpture).[12]

'To resuscitate dead things': the metaphoric use of Renaissance,
to be born again, was already used by one of its main actors,
Niccolò Machiavelli, and referred to the rebirth of the arts after
their decay in the Middle Ages (a category which had not been
invented yet). But a few pages before, in the conclusion of his
Arte della guerra, Machiavelli had used a different metaphor, in
a passage dealing with the difficulty of taking the ancient
Romans as a model in warfare:

For this form can be impressed on simple coarse men of one's
own, not on malicious, badly cared for foreigners. One will never
find any good sculptor who believes he can make a beautiful
statue from a piece of marble badly blocked out; but from one in
the rough he may very well think so.[13]

The words '*imprimere una forma*' (to impress a form) are
used in a metaphorical sense, whose implications are unfolded
immediately afterwards: imposing a habit (in this case, a model

---

12 Somewhat echoing this passage, Michelangelo labelled
Vasari, in a letter addressed to him, 'risuscitatore di uomini morti'
(resuscitator of dead men): Giorgio Vasari, *Le vite*, t. VII, ed.
Gaetano Milanesi (Florence: G. C. Sansoni, 1906), p. 230. See
Martin Warnke, 'Die erste Seite aus den "Viten" Giorgio Vasaris.
Der politische Gehalt seiner Renaissancevorstellung', *Kritische
Berichte*, 5/6 (1977), pp. 5–28.
13 Niccolò Machiavelli, *Arte della guerra e scritti politici minori*,
ed. Sergio Bertelli (Milan: Feltrinelli, 1961), p. 519: 'Perché questa
forma si può imprimere negli uomini semplici, rozzi e proprii, non ne'
maligni, male custoditi e forestieri. Né si troverrà mai alcuno buono
scultore che creda fare una bella statua d'un pezzo di marmo male
abbozzato, ma sì bene d'uno rozzo.' See Christopher Scott McClure,
'Sculpting Modernity: Machiavelli and Michelangelo's *David*',
Interpretation 43 (2016), pp. 111–24, especially p. 122 (quoting from
Christopher Lynch's translation, with minor changes).

inspired by antiquity) on a population is comparable to carving a statue. Several scholars independently detected, in the passage on the sculptor who cannot believe that a beautiful statue may be carved from a badly worked piece of marble, an allusion to Michelangelo and his *David* (ill. 4; ill. 5: detail).[14]

4. Machiavelli and Michelangelo actually knew each other. Biagio Buonaccorsi, one of Machiavelli's closest friends, sent him a letter dated 6 September 1506, saying that he would have received a certain amount of money 'via the hands of the sculptor Michelangelo'.[15] At that moment Michelangelo was in Florence, on his way to the marble quarries of Carrara; his acquaintanceship with Machiavelli, secretary of the Florentine chancery, is unsurprising.[16] Even less surprising is Machiavelli's allusion to the story, familiar to everybody in Florence, concerning the statue of David. For a long time, a huge piece of rough marble had been kept in a courtyard near the city's main church,

14 See N. Machiavelli, *Opere*, ed. by M. Bonfantini, Verona 1954, p. 529, n. 4; Edgar Wind, 'Platonic Tyranny and the Renaissance Fortuna: On Ficino's Reading of Laws IV, 709 A-/12 A', in *De artibus opuscula XL: Essays in Honor of Erwin Panofsky*, vol. I (New York: New York University Press, 1961), pp. 491–6, especially p. 494 n. 14, on the parallel passage in *Discourses* I, XI: 'unmistakable allusion' (see note 16). The same suggestion about the same passage has been put forward, independently, by Corrado Vivanti: see his edition of N. Machiavelli, *Discorsi sopra la prima deca di Tito Livio* (Turin: Einaudi, 1983), p. 68 n. 4. See Franz-Joachim Verspohl, 'Michelangelo und Machiavelli. Der David auf der Piazza della Signoria in Florence', *Städel-Jahrbuch* 8 (1981), pp. 204–46, especially pp. 243–4, n. 147 (for a later, reworked version see *Michelangelo Buonarroti und Niccolò Machiavelli, der David, die Piazza, die Republik* [Bern and Vienna: Wallstein, 2001]).

15 See Christopher Scott McClure, 'Sculpting Modernity', p. 111 (quoting Niccolò Machiavelli, *Opere*, vol. II, ed. Corrado Vivanti (Turin: Einaudi, 1999), p. 30; the entry 'Buonarroti, Michelangelo' in *Enciclopedia machiavelliana*, vol. I, pp. 235–6; Andrea Guidi, 'Due inediti dell'epistolario machiavelliano', in *Annali dell'Istituto Italiano per gli Studi Storici* 20, 2003–2004 (2005) pp. 68–80.

16 Michael Hirst, *Michelangelo: The Achievement of Fame, I, 1475–1534*, (New Haven: Yale University Press, 2011), pp. 64–5.

Santa Maria del Fiore; in 1463–1464 a sculptor, Agostino di Duccio, had started to work on it, but his work was badly received, so he stopped. In 1501 Michelangelo, having been asked to work on a statue of King David, started again to carve the piece of marble; in 1504 the statue was finished.[17] It was nicknamed by contemporary Florentines *Il gigante*, the giant: an allusion to the proportions of the statue, more than five metres high. But the nickname had also a jocular, counter-intuitive point, since in the biblical story the giant was not David, here represented as a young boy with a sling, but his opponent, Goliath.

5. Machiavelli reworked this metaphorical allusion to Michelangelo's *David* in another major work of his: *Discorsi sopra la prima deca di Tito Livio* (Discourses on the first ten books of Titus Livy's *History of Rome*), published only posthumously in 1531. In a chapter devoted to the religion of ancient Romans, Machiavelli described how Numa, one of the Roman kings, 'pretended to be intimate with a nymph who counseled him on what he had to counsel the people'.

'Indeed it is true', Machiavelli went on,

> that since those times were full of religion and the men with whom he had to labor were rough [*grossi*], they made much easier the carrying out of his designs, since he could easily impress any new form whatever on them [*imprimere in loro facilmente qualunque nuova forma*]. Without a doubt, whoever wished to make a republic in the present times would find it easier among mountain men, where there is no civilization, than among those who are used to living in cities, where civilization is corrupt; and a sculptor will carve a beautiful statue more easily from rough marble than from one badly blocked out by another.[18]

---

17   Ibid., pp. 42–8.

18   Niccolò Machiavelli, *Discourses on Livy*, tr. Harvey C. Mansfield and Nathan Tarcov (Chicago: University of Chicago, 1998), p. 35, with slight modifications (*Discorsi sopra la prima deca di Tito Livio*, ed. Corrado Vivanti, p. 68: 'Ben è vero che l'essere quelli tempi pieni di religione, e quegli uomini con i quali egli [Numa] aveva a

Harry Lime, the villain in *The Third Man* played by Orson Welles, would have been intrigued to learn that the 'mountain men' in this passage alluded to the Swiss.[19] But let us look at something more serious. Religion is, Machiavelli points out, 'a thing altogether necessary ... to maintain a civilization' (*una civiltà*): a fundamental political instrument. Machiavelli regarded religion as a very effective instrument, especially in dealing with rough, uncivilized people: but he never regarded religion as a goal in itself. 'To make a republic' implies manipulating the people, like a sculptor manipulates marble (I am using a metaphor which is familiar to us, but echoes Machiavelli's comparison). We are confronted with a sequence based on a double comparison: impressing a new form on rough people, using the instruments of religion/carving a beautiful statue from rough marble. The transition from 'rough people' to 'rough marble', from a new form to a beautiful statue, is smooth. The shift from form to matter is much less obvious, and needs a closer analysis.

6. In sixteenth-century Italy there was a lively debate about *paragone* (i.e., the comparison between painting, sculpture and architecture, and their hierarchy). Michelangelo, who excelled in all of them, argued for the superiority of sculpture.[20] He was not ashamed of the physical effort involved in it (which

---

travagliare grossi, gli dettono facilità grande a conseguire i disegni suoi, potendo imprimere in loro facilmente qualunque nuova forma. E sanza dubbio chi volesse ne' presenti tempi fare una republica, più facilità troverebbe negli uomini montanari, dove non è alcuna civiltà, che in quelli che sono usi a vivere nelle cittadi, dove la civiltà è corrotta: ed uno scultore trarrà più facilmente una bella statua d'uno marmo rozzo, che d'uno male abbozzato da altrui'.)

19   Luigi Zanzi, *Il metodo del Machiavelli* (Bologna: Il Mulino, 2013), p. 503ff.

20   Benedetto Varchi, *Due lezioni ... nella prima delle quali si dichiara un sonetto di m. Michelagnolo Buonarroti. Nella seconda si disputa quale sia più nobile arte la scultura, o la pittura, con una lettera d'esso Michelagnolo* (Florence: Lorenzo Torrentino, 1549). See also Sefy Hendler, *La guerre des arts. Le Paragone peinture-sculpture en Italie XIVe–XVIIe siècle* (Rome: L'Erma di Bretschneider, 2013), pp. 67–9.

Leonardo, on the contrary, regarded as a symptom of the superiority of painting).[21] The French diplomat Blaise de Vigenère, who saw Michelangelo at work on his *Pietà* (today in Florence) (ill. 6), described him in the following terms:

> He was over sixty [in fact, he was seventy-five] and although he was not very strong, in a quarter of an hour he caused more splinters to fall from a very hard block of marble than three young masons in three or four times as much time. No one can believe it who has not seen it with his own eyes. And he attacked the work with such energy and fire that I thought it would fly into pieces.[22]

Leonardo wrote that 'painting was, more than sculpture, the outcome of a mental discourse'; Michelangelo argued for the superiority of sculpture. But both of them were deeply committed to the idea that painting, sculpture and architecture depended on *disegno*: a word which meant (and still means) in Italian 'drawing' as well as 'design' or 'plan'. This ambiguity is significant.[23] In the aforementioned passage by Machiavelli's *Discorsi*, the word 'designs' (*disegni*) plays an important role. Numa, the king who introduced religion to ancient Rome, having to deal with people 'rough [*grossi*], they made much easier the carrying out of his designs, since he could easily impress any new form

---

21 David Summers, *Michelangelo and the Language of Arts* (Princeton: Princeton University Press, 1981), pp. 269–78. 'La pittura è di maggiore discorso mentale e di maggiore artifizio e maraviglia che la scultura' (Leonardo da Vinci, *Scritti artistici e tecnici*, ed. Barbara Agosti [Milan: RCS Libri, 2002], p. 183).

22 Blaise de Vigenère, *La suitte de Philostrate*, Paris 1602, c. 105 *v*. See G. Rèpaci-Courtois, 'Vasari, source de Blaise de Vigenère?', *Revue de l'Art* 80 (1988), pp. 48–51.

23 See Michael Baxandall, 'English *Disegno*' in his *Words for Picture: Seven Papers on Renaissance Art and Criticism*: (New Haven: Yale University Press, 2003), pp. 83–97, as well as the entry 'Disegno' (by Jacqueline Lichtenstein) in *Vocabulaire européen des philosophies, Dictionnaire des intraduisibles*, ed. Barbara Cassin (Paris: Seuil, 2004), pp. 322–5.

whatever on them (*imprimere in loro facilmente qualunque nuova forma*)'. In this context, even the metaphorical sentence 'impress any new form' could have been part of the sculptor's vocabulary. Likewise, in another passage of his *Discorsi* (I, 18) Machiavelli added a pictorial dimension to one of his favourite words, '*disegno*', in the sense of 'plan': '*colorire il disegno loro*', literally 'to colour their plan', in the sense of 'disguising it'.[24]

To sum up: the analogy between the establishment of a republic and the carving of a statue, which Machiavelli put forward while thinking of Michelangelo's *David*, was part of a larger discourse, shared by both.

7. According to Edgar Wind, 'Machiavelli seems to have been impervious to the visual arts.'[25] I will argue the opposite case. The conversations between Machiavelli and Michelangelo are lost forever; but their exchanges left a relevant trace, which has not been identified so far, in one of Michelangelo's most famous works: the statue representing Lorenzo de' Medici, duke of Urbino (ills. 7, 8), which is part of the Medici funerary chapel (Tombe Medicee) in the new sacristy of the Church of San Lorenzo in Florence.

There are no other examples, in the whole of Michelangelo's work, of such an extraordinary interaction of sculpture and architecture. The commission originated in the premature death in 1516 and 1519, respectively, of two young members of the

---

24 Niccolò Machiavelli, *Discorsi*, I, 19 (ed. Vivanti), p. 96 (=*The Discourses*, tr. Mansfield and Tarcov, p. 52). But see the letter he sent on 9 March 1498 to Ricciardo Becchi, about Savonarola: 'viene secondando e tempi e le sue bugie colorendo' (accommodating himself to the times and colouring his lies) (*Lettere*, in *Opere*, vol. II, p. 8). See also, in his legations, the letter sent on 8 January 1503: 'E per dare più colore a questa cosa' (to add colour to this) (*Legazioni*, in *Opere*, II, p. 790) and the letter sent on 23 November 1503: 'sotto colore di quelli nuovi signori' (under the colour of those new lords) [*Legazioni*, in *Opere*, vol. II, p. 888], quoted by Emanuele Cutinelli Rèndina, *Chiesa e religione in Machiavelli* (Pisa–Rome: Istituto Editoriali e Poligrafici Internazionali, 1998), pp. 31, 35.

25 Wind, 'Platonic Tyranny', p. 494, n. 14.

Medici family, Giuliano and Lorenzo.[26] Cardinal Giulio de' Medici, who in 1523 would be elected pope with the name of Clement VII, asked Michelangelo to work on the project. The amount of scholarly work on the Medici funerary chapel is, of course, huge. I will focus on two related essays by Luca Giuliani, a well-known historian of Greek and Roman art. In the first of them he looked very closely at a detail of the statue of Lorenzo de' Medici, which had until then received very little attention (ill. 8).[27]

In fact, most descriptions of the statue did not mention the detail at all. An exception is afforded by John Harford's biography of Michelangelo published in 1857:

> The head, surmounted by a casque of classical form, is gently reclined; the elbow of the left arm reposes upon a casket on the knee of the statue; and the forefinger of the corresponding hand is placed upon the lip in deep meditation.[28]

But is this a casket? And why is there an animal head protruding from it? And which kind of animal is it? The German art historian Anton Springer ignored the so-called casket and identified the animal as a bat, which he connected to the allegorical representations of Night, Day, Dawn and Dusk, placed at the feet of the statues of Lorenzo and Giuliano de' Medici. The bat, along with a 'cash-box', allegedly meaning parsimony, re-emerged in the comments of Erwin Panofsky and Charles de Tolnay. The latter spoke of an 'obolus-box ... decorated with the head of a bat, the bird of the underworld ... evidently a

---

26 Hirst, *Michelangelo*, pp. 189–99.

27 Luca Giuliani, 'Kästchen oder Quader? Zur Sitzstatue des Lorenzo de' Medici in der Sagrestia Nuova und zum Problem der Materialität in den Skulpturen Michelangelos', in *Mitteilungen des Kunsthistorischen Institutes in Florenz* 50 (2013), pp. 334–57.

28 John Scandrett Harford, *The Life of Michael Angelo Buonarroti*, vol. II (London: Longman, Brown, Green, Longmans, and Roberts, 1857), p. 28f. (quoted by Luca Giuliani, 'Kästchen oder Quader?', p. 340).

symbol signifying that he [Lorenzo] is already in the realm of Hades, which is also considered to be the realm of riches'.[29]

Luca Giuliani disagreed with those conclusions and looked once again very closely at the detail of the statue. Here is his detailed description (the ancient Greeks would call it *ekphrasis*).

Lorenzo's left arm is leaning over a block, shaped as a parallelepiped. From one side of it we can see the protruding head of an animal, which at first sight looks like a lion. But its ears are too big, its narrow eyes are too small, its muzzle too pointed, and its huge moustaches do not fit in the lion iconography which was so popular at that time. 'The head', Giuliani commented, 'belongs to a hybrid creature, which does not belong to this world.' It does not look like a bat (*Fledermaus*) but like 'a lion mouse' (*Löwenmaus*).[30]

No less enigmatic is the block. It does not look like a casket: it must be referred, according to Giuliani, not to the person of Lorenzo but to the statue. This is just a piece of stone, in its materiality.[31]

8. Now, my own interpretation. I would like to emphasize that, even if I took a completely different direction, I would have been unable to advance it without Luca Giuliani's path-breaking essay.

Let's start from Michelangelo's statue, representing Lorenzo de' Medici, duke of Urbino (ill. 7). Machiavelli had dedicated *The Prince*, his most famous work, to Lorenzo, presented as the new prince who would be able 'to Seize Italy and to Free Her from the Barbarians', as the title of the last chapter of the treatise reads. Lorenzo died in 1519.[32] *The Prince*, written in 1513,

---

29   Charles de Tolnay, *Michelangelo, III: The Medici Chapel* (Princeton: Princeton University Press, 1970), p. 69 (cfr. Luca Giuliani, 'Kästchen oder Quader?', pp. 341–2).

30   Luca Giuliani, 'Kästchen oder Quader?', pp. 339–40.

31   Ibid., p. 346.

32   See the entry by Gino Benzoni in *Dizionario biografico degli Italiani*.

was not published until 1532, after Machiavelli's death, but it circulated widely in manuscript form in the years before; a plagiarized version by Agostino Nifo, the Aristotelian philosopher, had already come out in 1523.

The Prince was published with a papal privilege but was immediately perceived as a scandalous book. I will comment on a section from its chapter 18, entitled 'In What Mode Faith Should Be Kept by Princes':

> How praiseworthy it is for a prince to keep his faith, and to live with honesty and not by astuteness, everyone understands. Nonetheless, one sees by experience in our times that the princes who have done great things are those who have taken little account of faith and have known how to get around men's brains with their astuteness; and in the end they have overcome those who have founded themselves on loyalty. Thus, you must know that there are two kinds of combat: one with laws, the other with force. The first is proper to man, the second to beasts; but because the first is often not enough, one must have recourse to the second.
>
> Then, since a prince is compelled of necessity to know well how to use the beast, he should pick the fox and the lion, because the lion does not defend itself from snares and the fox does not defend itself from wolves. So one needs to be a fox to recognize snares and a lion to frighten the wolves. Those who stay simply with the lion do not understand this. A prudent lord, therefore, cannot observe faith, nor should he, when such observance turns against him, and the causes that made him promise have been eliminated. And if all men were good, this teaching would not be good; but because they are wicked and do not observe faith with you, you also do not have to observe it with them.[33]

The source (or should we say the target?) of this reference to the lion and the fox is a passage from Cicero's *De officiis* (II, 17) which reads as follows:

---

33 Machiavelli, *The Prince*, tr. Mansfield, pp. 68–9.

There are two ways in which injustice may be done, either through force or through deceit; and deceit seems to belong to a little fox, force to a lion. Both of them seem most alien to a human being; but deceit deserves a greater hatred.[34]

Cicero regarded the lion and the fox as models of injustice (although he remarked that the fox was more hateful); Machiavelli suggested to Lorenzo de' Medici, duke of Urbino, to take the lion and the fox as models for his politics. It would be good if a prince could keep faith – nevertheless, this is impossible. He should lie as a fox and should be able to use force as a lion.[35]

According to an eminent commentator, Lawrence Burd, *The Prince*'s chapter 18 'has given greater offence than any other portion of Machiavelli's writings'.[36] We can understand why.

---

34 J. Jackson Barlow, 'The Fox and the Lion: Machiavelli replies to Cicero', *History of Political Thought* 20 (1999), pp. 627–45; Marcia L. Colish, 'Cicero's *De Officiis* and Machiavelli's *Prince*', *Sixteenth Century Journal* 9 (1978), pp. 80–93; Jerrold E. Seigel, '"Civic Humanism" or Ciceronian Rhetoric?' *Past and Present* 34 (1966), pp. 3–44.

35 Niccolò Machiavelli, *Il principe*, ed. Giorgio Inglese, pp. 115–17: 'Dovete adunque sapere come e' sono dua generazioni di combattere: l'uno, con le leggi; l'altro, con la forza. Quel primo è proprio dello uomo; quel secondo delle bestie. Ma perché el primo molte volte non basta, conviene ricorrere al secondo: pertanto a uno principe è necessario sapere bene usare la bestia e lo uomo. [. . .] Sendo dunque necessitato uno principe sapere bene usare la bestia, debbe di quelle pigliare la golpe e il lione: perché el lione non si difende da' lacci, la golpe non si difende da' lupi; bisogna adunque essere golpe a conoscere e' lacci, e lione a sbigottire e' lupi: coloro che stanno semplicemente in sul lione, non se ne intendono. Non può pertanto uno signore prudente, né debbe, osservare la fede quando tale osservanzia gli torni contro e che sono spente le cagioni che la feciono promettere. E se li uomini fussino tutti buoni, questo precetto non sarebbe buono: ma, perché e' sono tristi e non la osserverebbono a te, tu etiam non l'hai a osservare a loro; né mai a uno principe mancorno cagioni legittime di colorire la inosservanzia.'

36 Machiavelli, *Il principe*, ed. Burd, p. 297.

9. Let's go back to Michelangelo's statue representing Lorenzo de' Medici, duke of Urbino, and, more specifically, to its enigmatic detail: the block of marble with a hybrid animal head (ill. 8). This is not, I will argue, a lion-mouse: it is a lion-fox – an allusion to *The Prince*, chapter 18. All the features which, as Luca Giuliani remarked, do not fit with the image of the lion – the big ears, the small and narrow eyes, the pointed muzzle, the huge moustaches – point at the image of the fox, suggesting a conflation between the two animals.[37] Did Michelangelo consult Machiavelli on this issue? We do not know: in mid-June 1526 Michelangelo sent a letter saying that since one of the two statues was sufficiently advanced (but which one, Lorenzo or Giuliano?) he had begun to work on the other.[38] Machiavelli died in Florence one year later, on 21 June 1527. In any case, Michelangelo's allusion to *The Prince*, chapter 18, in the statue of Lorenzo de' Medici seems irrefutable – even if it might have been a post-mortem, posthumous allusion.

All this casts some additional light upon the meaning of the block of marble. In his essay Luca Giuliani remarked that it should not be referred to Lorenzo: this is just a piece of stone. But as you will recall, in his *Arte della guerra* Machiavelli had compared the impression of a form (i.e., of a behaviour) on a rough population to the act of carving a beautiful statue from a

---

37 In Francisco de Holanda's *Dialoghi Romani* Michelangelo says: 'E si accresce ancora il fascino della decorazione, quando si mette nel dipinto qualche essere chimerico (come novità e riposo dei sensi e come riguardo per gli occhi dei mortali, che talora desiderano contemplare ciò che non avevano mai visto e che sembra non possa esistere': cf. Daniel Sherer, 'Error or Invention? Critical Receptions of Michelangelo's Architecture from Pirro Ligorio to Teofilo Gallaccini,' *Perspecta* 46 (2013), pp. 77–120, esp. p. 87.

38 Michael Hirst, *Michelangelo*, p. 197. Vasari informs us that Fra Giovann'Agnolo Montorsoli worked with Michelangelo in the Medici tombs: 'Condottosi dunque Michelagnolo ed il frate a Firenze, Michelagnolo nel condurre le statue del duca Lorenzo e Giuliano si servì molto del frate nel rinettarle e fare certe difficultà di lavori traforati in sotto squadra; con la quale occasione imparò molte cose il frate da quello uomo veramente divino, standolo con attenzione a vedere lavorare, ed osservando ogni minima cosa' (Vasari, *Le vite*, vol. VI, p. 633).

rough block of marble. Michelangelo must have recalled this allusion to his own *David* while he was carving the statue of Lorenzo de' Medici, with his left arm leaning on a polished (not rough!) block of marble. This was, I guess, a reference to a passage of *The Prince*, chapter 26, which points to Lorenzo as a new leader who could free Italy (a polished, civilized country) from barbarians, introducing a form to it:

> And nothing brings so much honor to a man newly risen as the new laws and the new orders founded by him. When these things have been founded well and have greatness in them, they make him revered and admirable. And in Italy matter is not lacking for introducing every form (*non manca materia da introdurvi ogni forma*); here there is great virtue in the limbs, if it were not lacking in the heads.[39]

According to my own interpretation, Michelangelo's statue of Lorenzo de' Medici, duke of Urbino, to whom Machiavelli dedicated *The Prince*, included a detail – the block of polished marble with the head of a hybrid animal – which alluded to two specific passages of *The Prince* (chapter 18, chapter 26). To explain these references as the result of mere chance would be difficult. It seems more likely to interpret it as an echo either of a reading of *The Prince* (which Michelangelo could have received in a copy by Biagio Buonaccorsi) or of conversations with Machiavelli himself.[40] In any case, we must dismiss the

---

39 Machiavelli, *The Prince*, tr. Mansfield, pp. 103–4; *Il principe*, ed. Inglese, pp. 171–2: 'E veruna cosa fa tanto onore a uno uomo che di nuovo surga, quanto fa le nuove leggi ed e' nuovi ordini trovati da lui: queste cose, quando sono bene fondate e abbino in loro grandezza, lo fanno reverendo e mirabile. E in Italia non manca materia da introdurvi ogni forma: qui è virtù grande nelle membra, quando la non mancassi ne' capi.'

40 See the entry (by Gaspare De Caro) 'Buonaccorsi, Biagio' in *Dizionario biografico degli Italiani*, vol. 15, pp. 76–7 (Buonaccorsi sends a manuscript copy he has made of *The Prince* to Pandolfo Bellacci); Denis Fachard, *Biagio Buonaccorsi. Sa vie, son temps, son oeuvre* (Bologna: M. Boni, 1976).

hypothesis of an allusion inspired by the patron, Giulio de' Medici, who since 1523 had become Pope Clement VII. On 22 November 1524, the latter's secretary, Giovan Francesco Fattucci, informed Michelangelo that the pope had said that, as far as the tombs were concerned, the artist should do whatever he liked: 'The honour and the shame must be yours, and he wouldn't like to be involved in this matter.'[41] One is reminded of the 'creative force freed from every external constraint' that Burckhardt attributed to Michelangelo.

Those subtle allusions to Machiavelli's work in the statue representing Lorenzo de' Medici must have been perceived only by a small circle of friends. In a recent article Luca Giuliani has remarked that the statue representing sculpture, carved by Vincenzo Cioli for Michelangelo's funerary monument, holds a block of marble very much alike the one on which Lorenzo de' Medici is leaning (ills. 9, 10, 11; ill. 12: detail).[42] Giuliani convincingly argues that Cioli attributed to Michelangelo the idea that a block of marble was an appropriate symbol for sculpture. But are we allowed to conclude, following Giuliani, that Cioli's interpretation of the statue representing Lorenzo de' Medici was identical to Michelangelo's? Certainly not, and for a very simple reason: if we compare the two blocks of marble, we immediately see that a crucial detail in Cioli's block is missing – the head of the hybrid animal, which I identified with Machiavelli's lion-fox, *volpe e leone* (ill. 8). This was, we must conclude, a concealed allusion, addressed to the happy few.

---

41 *Il carteggio di Michelangelo*, posthumous edition of Giovanni Poggi, ed. Paola Barocchi and Renzo Ristori, vol. iii (Florence: Sansoni, 1973), letter 674, p. 116: 'Pa[r]lossi con Nostro Signiore dell Sansovino Sua Santità rispose che in tutto et per tutto vole faciate quello che vi pare; non tanto finita questa sepultura, come dite, ma vole faciate ancora l'aultre, solo et aconpagniato et come volete; et vole che l'onore et la vergognia sia tutta vostra, et però non se ne vole inpaciare.'

42 Luca Giuliani, 'Michelangelos Quader. Ein nachtrag', *Mitteilungen des Kunsthistorischen Institutes in Florenz* 58 (2016), pp. 109–16.

10. Jacob Burckhardt thought that the Italian Renaissance was marked by 'excessive individualism' and 'subjectivity'. As I pointed out, these were etic, anachronistic categories, related to the observer's (in this case, Burckhardt's) perception. The next step, after this inevitable beginning, should have implied an attempt to retrieve the emic—that is, the actors' categories. This is what I have tried to do, reconstructing the hypothetical dialogue between Michelangelo and Machiavelli.

Apparently, they shared a common language. May we say 'the language of art'? It would be tempting to say so, since Machiavelli often pointed out, corresponding with his close friends, that his task was *l'arte dello stato*, literally 'the art of the state'. But in this context the word *'arte'* had no connection with aesthetic values. As in the case of its Greek and Latin counterparts, *techne* and *ars*, *'arte'* could refer to a broad range of technical activities: from medicine to commerce, to weaving and so forth. A few years ago I argued that Machiavelli applied the techniques of medieval casuistry, placed at the intersection of medicine, theology and law, to the domain of politics, shifting from norms to exceptions.[43] The shocking remarks I have already mentioned, allowing the prince to lie to his subjects in specific circumstances, were made possible by a casuistic frame of mind.

For centuries, Machiavelli's approach to politics, usually identified with his most popular work, *The Prince*, was rejected as an apology of evil. Machiavelli's awareness of the tragic side of politics was missed, or misunderstood. The complexity of his work was most often turned into a simplified version, ignoring that the author of *The Prince* was also the author of the *Discourses on Livy*: a work celebrating the republican state and the 'common utility that is drawn from a free way of life (*vivere libero*)'.[44] But in both cases Machiavelli stressed the crucial role played by the lawgiver. The title of book I, chapter 8, of *Discourses* reads, 'That It Is Necessary to Be Alone if One Wishes to Order a Republic Anew or to Reform It Altogether outside Its Ancient Orders.' It

---

43 See here, ch. 1 and 2.
44 Machiavelli, *Discourses*, tr. Mansfield, p. 45.

must be noted that the argument concerns 'any republic or kingdom'.[45] 'One could give infinite examples', Machiavelli went on, 'to sustain the things written above, such as Moses, Lycurgus, Solon, and other founders of kingdoms and republics who were able to form laws for the purpose of the common good.'[46] In *The Prince*, chapter 6, Moses is also mentioned with Romulus and others among those 'who became princes by their own virtue and not by fortune'. 'And although', Machiavelli points out, 'one should not reason about Moses, as he was a mere executor of things that had been ordered for him by God, nonetheless he should be admired if only for that grace which made him deserving of speaking with God.'[47] Moses, 'who had so great a teacher' (*che ebbe sì grande precettore*), is mentioned along with Romulus, who killed his brother: a shocking contiguity, which is reinforced in the *Discourses*. Like Romulus, who for the murder of his brother 'deserves excuse, and not blame', Moses is alone. 'To order a republic', Machiavelli concludes, 'it is necessary to be alone (*a ordinare una republica è necessario essere solo*).'[48]

The solitude of the lawmaker and the solitude of the artist: could this parallel be considered as an emic counterpart of Burckhardt's 'subjectivity'? The question sounds immediately marked by anachronism – to the point that I would be tempted to dismiss it on the spot; but I will not refrain from exploring this issue, sooner or later. For the time being, I would prefer to go forward, rather than backward, focusing on a much later link of the long chain I have explored, following Jacob Burckhardt's suggestion. A big leap forward in our historical trajectory will bring us to the early twentieth century.

11. In April 1924 Benito Mussolini, the Fascist dictator, published in *Gerarchia*, the official party journal, an essay entitled 'Prelude to Machiavelli'.[49] Some years later Emil Ludwig, a German

---

45 Ibid., pp. 28–30.
46 Ibid.
47 Ibid., p. 22.
48 Ibid., p. 30.
49 Benito Mussolini, 'Preludio al Machiavelli', *Scritti e Discorsi*,

journalist, published a book based on his conversations with Mussolini. In a flattering tone Ludwig compared Mussolini to a Renaissance *condottiere*, commenting on his alleged physical resemblance with Bartolomeo Colleoni (ill. 3): a standard piece of Fascist propaganda. In their conversations, the 'teacher of dictators' (as Ludwig labelled Machiavelli) surfaced both directly and indirectly. Mussolini told his interlocutor that his own father, a socialist blacksmith, used to read Machiavelli to his children, after dinner. Invented or not, the story underlined Mussolini's appropriation of Machiavelli as part of his public image.

'Once', stated Ludwig, 'you wrote that the masses are not willing to know, but to believe.' Mussolini emphatically agreed:

Modern man's propensity to believe is unbelievable. When I feel the mass in my hands, in the act of believing, or when I mix up with it, and I feel nearly crushed by it, I feel like a piece of this mass. But at the same time, I feel a kind of aversion towards it, like the poet does vis-à-vis the matter he is working with. Does not the sculptor sometimes break the marble in anger, because he feels that he cannot shape it with his hands according to his original vision? Sometimes matter revolts against its shaper.

And then, after a pause: 'The crucial point is to dominate the mass like an artist.'[50]

---

vol. IV, Il 1924 (Milan: Hoepli, 1924), pp. 1–10. See Franco Biasutti, 'Mussolini interprete di Machiavelli', in *Machiavelli: tempo e conflitto*, ed. Riccardo Caporali et al. (Sesto San Giovanni: Mimesis, 2013), pp. 21–33. See also p. 14, above.

50 Benito Mussolini, *Colloqui con Mussolini: Riproduzione della bozze della prima edizione con le correzioni autografe del duce*, ed. Emil Ludwig, tr. Tomaso Gnoli (Milan: Mondadori, 1950), pp. 53, 77, 125: '"La gente oggi ha meno tempo di pensare. La disposizione dell'uomo moderno a credere è incredibile. Quando io sento la massa nelle mie mani, come essa crede, o quando io mi mescolo con essa, ed essa quasi mi schiaccia, allora mi sento un pezzo di questa massa. Eppure rimane nello stesso tempo un po' di avversione, come la sente il poeta contro la materia con la quale lavora. Lo scultore non spezza forse talvolta per ira

The obvious subtext of this tirade was Machiavelli's comparison between imposing a belief on the people and carving a statue from a piece of marble. Once again, this was a gesture of deliberate appropriation: the contexts in which Machiavelli and Mussolini lived and worked were completely different. Mussolini addressed the mass, '*la massa*': a new phenomenon, designated by an ambiguous word, which referred at the same time to physical matter and to humans – an ambiguity which paved the way to the conclusion: 'to dominate the mass like an artist'.

12. 'The logical outcome of fascism is an aestheticizing of political life,' wrote Walter Benjamin, the German philosopher and critic, in his famous essay 'The Work of Art in the Age of Its Reproducibility'.[51] These words sound like a comment on the passage I just quoted from Emil Ludwig's *Conversations with Mussolini*: a book which Benjamin presumably read in German a few years before.[52] It would be tempting to conclude that the last link of the tortuous trajectory I tried to reconstruct belongs to a twentieth-century past, which is now over. However, the long-term potential of the metaphor I have been dealing with – the comparison between controlling society and the carving of a statue – would suggest something else. What about manipulating people through the internet?

But that would be a different story.

---

il marmo, perché questo sotto le sue mani non si plasma precisamente secondo la sua prima visione? Qui talvolta la materia perfino si rivolta contro il suo formatore." Fece una pausa, poi concluse: "Tutto dipende da ciò, dominare la massa come un artista."'

51 Walter Benjamin, 'The Work of Art in the Age of Its Reproducibility', in *Selected Writings, Volume 3 (1935–1938)*, ed. Howard Eiland and Michael W. Jennings, (Cambridge, MA: Belknap, 2002), pp. 101–33, especially p. 121 (second version, written in 1935–1936, published only posthumously).

52 Benito Mussolini, *Mussolinis Gespräche mit Emil Ludwig. Mit 8 Bildtafeln*, ed. Emil Ludwig (Berlin: Zsolnay, 1932).

6

Machiavelli and the Antiquarians

1. In an illuminating essay, the Italian historian Adriano Prosperi has shown how the English cardinal Reginald Pole, an early champion of anti-Machiavellianism, made ample use of Machiavelli in his *De summo Pontifice Christi in terris vicario* (1569).[1] Other cases, involving less famous figures, illustrate the often unpredictable directions of Machiavelli's reception. Yet even the Machiavelli read by antiquarians, of whom we shall speak here, is closely related to the better-known Machiavelli, who ponders 'all the dominions that have held sway over men' (*The Prince*, chapter 1).[2]

2. These pages are a small fragment of a project on the emergence, between the sixteenth and eighteenth centuries, of a comparative approach to religion – a much older phenomenon than the late nineteenth-century codification of the history of religion as an academic discipline. Older, but how much older? Philippe Borgeaud has repeatedly stressed that the

---

1   Adriano Prosperi, 'Il Principe, il Cardinale e il Papa. Reginald Pole lettore di Machiavelli', in *Cultura e scrittura di Machiavelli* (Rome: Salerno, 1998), pp. 241–62. The essay is not cited in Sydney Anglo, *Machiavelli, the First Century: Studies in Enthusiasm, Hostility, and Irrelevance* (Oxford: Oxford University Press, 2005), pp. 115–42.

2   Niccolò Machiavelli, *The Prince*, ed. Quentin Skinner and Russell Price and tr. Russell Price (Cambridge: Cambridge University Press, 2016), p. 5 (*Il principe*, p. 63: 'e' dominii, che hanno avuto e hanno imperio sopra li uomini').

comparative approach has its origins in the Graeco-Roman world.[3] However, this apparent continuity conceals some crucial discontinuities. In a 2010 book, Guy G. Stroumsa has listed four of them: (1) relations between Christians and Jews, and their respective sacred texts; (2) the discovery of New World populations; (3) the Protestant Reformation; and (4) the Renaissance.[4] In each instance religious comparison was utilized in a non-pacific context, marked by polemics, persecutions, forced conversions and massacres. Unlike the *interpretatio romana*, which emerged in the receptive imperial pantheon, the comparative approach to religion established itself in the Christian environment as an instrument of battle. A critically detached attitude towards religions developed in a violent, gory context.

Here we shall dwell on the fourth of these elements listed by Stroumsa, analysing an episode in the reception of Machiavelli's writings.[5] This made a limited, though not negligible, contribution to the elaboration – once again, in a polemical tone – of the comparative approach to religion.[6]

3. To speak of 'Machiavelli's writings' in this context means implicitly evoking some well-known passages, such as the juxtaposition of Moses with Cyrus, Romulus and Theseus in chapter 6 of *The Prince*, or those chapters of the *Discourses* that deal with religion in ancient Rome (book I, chapters 11–15). Less

---

3 Philippe Borgeaud, 'Observe, Describe, Compare: A Small Meditation', *Historia Religionum* 1 (2009), pp. 13–20, esp. p. 15. And see also by the same author, *Aux origines de l'histoire des religions* (Paris: Seuil, 2004).

4 Guy G. Stroumsa, *A New Science: The Discovery of Religion in the Age of Reason* (Cambridge, MA: Harvard University Press, 2010), pp. 5–6 (but the book focuses on the subsequent seventeenth-century phase).

5 Machiavelli's name does not appear in Stroumsa's book, not even in the pages dedicated to 'civil religion' (ibid., p. 45).

6 Here I develop some themes mentioned in my essay 'The Letter Kills: On Some Implications of 2 Corinthians 3, 6', *History and Theory* 49 (2010), pp. 71–89.

well known, in fact escaping (if I am not mistaken) the attention of modern readers, is the incipit of *The Life of Castruccio Castracani*, the biography of the Lucchese *condottiero* (1281–1328):

> Those who consider it, my dearest Zanobi and Luigi, think it wonderful that all, or the larger part, of those who in this world have done very great things, and who have been excellent among the men of their era, have in their birth and origin been humble and obscure, or at least have been beyond all measure afflicted by fortune. Because all of them either have been exposed to wild beasts or have had fathers so humble that, being ashamed of them, they have made themselves out sons of Jove or of some other God.[7]

Machiavelli's readers, beginning with Zanobi Buondelmonti and Luigi Alamanni, to whom *The Life of Castruccio Castracani* is dedicated, as well as their friends, would have caught the impious allusion implicit in the words 'or of some other God'.[8] It was highlighted by the preterition that immediately follows: 'Who these are, since many of them are known to everybody, would be boring to repeat and little acceptable to readers; hence, as superfluous, I omit it.'[9]

---

7   Niccolò Machiavelli, *The Chief Works and Others*, vol. II, tr. Allan Gilbert (Durham, NC: Duke University Press, 1989), p. 533. (*La vita di Castruccio Castracani*, ed. R. Brakkee and introd. Paolo Trovato [Naples: Liguori, 1986], p. 83: 'E' pare, Zanobi et Luigi carissimi, a quegli che la considerano, cosa maravigliosa che tucti coloro, o la maggiore parte di epsi, che hanno in questo mondo operato grandissime cose, et intra gli altri della loro età siano stati excellenti, abbino avuto il principio et il nascimento loro basso et obscuro, o vero dalla fortuna fuora d'ogni modo travagliato; perché tutti o ei sono stati exposti alle fiere o egli hanno avuto sì vil padre che, vergognatisi di quello, si sono fatti figliuoli di Giove o di qualche altro Dio.')

8   Leo Strauss's famous essay, 'Persecution and the Art of Writing' (1941), in his *Persecution and the Art of Writing* (Glencoe, IL: Free Press, 1952), pp. 22–37, should always be borne in mind.

9   Machiavelli, *The Chief Works*, vol. II, p. 533. (*La vita di*

Perhaps, in writing these sarcastic words, Machiavelli was reminded of an equally scandalous passage (which has likewise escaped the attention of modern commentators), from Lorenzo Valla's *Declamatio* (1440) on the alleged 'donation of Constantine'. Among the arguments used to demonstrate the falsity of the document, Valla quotes the passage dealing with its physical location 'on the venerable body of the blessed Peter (sul venerando corpo di San Pietro)'. And he comments,

> When I was a boy, I remember asking someone who had written the *Book of Job*. When he answered, 'Job himself', I asked the further question of how therefore he managed to mention his own death. This can be said of many other books, although it is not appropriate to discuss them here.[10]

Castruccio Castracani, p. 83: 'Quali sieno stati quegli, sendone a ciascheduno noti molti, sarebbe cosa a repricare fastidiosa et poco acepta a chi legiessi; perciò come superflua la obmetteremo.') In the introduction to *La vita di Castruccio Castracani*, pp. 27–8 n. 34, Paolo Trovato comments on the passage, without understanding its implications. Similarly, J. H. Whitfield, 'Machiavelli and Castruccio', *Italian Studies* 8 (1953), pp. 1–28, esp. pp. 12–13; L. Green, 'Machiavelli's *Vita di Castruccio Castracani* and Its Lucchese Model', *Italian Studies* 12 (1987), pp. 37–55, esp. 48–50; M. Palumbo, 'Storia e scrittura della storia: *La vita di Castruccio Castracani*', in *Cultura e scrittura di Machiavell* (Rome: Salerno, 1998), pp. 145–64, esp. pp. 152–3. However, apropos of another passage, which follows shortly after – 'In Castruccio charm increased with the years, and in everything he showed ability and prudence' (Machiavelli, *The Chief Works*, vol. II, p. 535) – Palumbo tentatively wonders (p. 153) if it is not an echo of Luke 2:40: 'And the child grew, waxed strong in spirit, filled with wisdom: and the grace of God was upon him.'

10 Lorenzo Valla, *On the Donation of Constantine*, tr. Glen W. Bowersock (Cambridge, MA: Harvard University Press, 2008), p. 56. (*De falso credita et ementita Constantini donation*, ed. W. Setz, (Weimar: Hermann Böhlaus Nachfolger, 1976), p. 135: 'super venerandum corpus beati Petri posuimus ... Cum essem adolescentulus, interrogasse me quondam memini, quis librum Iob scripsisset, cumque ille respondisset "ipse Iob", tunc me subiunxisse, quo pacto igitur de sua ipsius morte faceret mentionem. Quod de multis aliis libris dici potest, quorum ratio huic loco non convenit.')

By way of an implicit reference to the death of Moses at the end of Deuteronomy (34:5), Valla makes it clear that Moses himself could not have been the author of the Pentateuch. Through the implicit comparison with figures such as Theseus, Cyrus or Romulus, Machiavelli makes a mockery of the divine nature of Christ.

It is a passage that illustrates the aggressive potential of a comparative approach to religion in a Christian context. The roots of this attitude are to be found in the milieu in which Machiavelli was formed: his father Bernardo appears among the interlocutors in the dialogue *De legibus et iudiciis*, composed by the Florentine chancellor Bartolomeo Scala, in which Moses, Zoroaster, Hermes Trismegistus, Numa, Zalmoxis, Mohammed and the like are named.[11] The importance attributed to the religion of the Romans in book I, chapter 11 of the *Discourses*, and elaborated on in subsequent chapters, immediately lays down the premise for a generalization: 'And truly no one who did not have recourse to God ever gave to a people unusual laws, because without that they would not be accepted.'[12]

The reference to 'God', without further qualification, makes it possible, following the rapid evocation of Lycurgus and Solon, to immediately switch the discussion to 'the present'.[13] For Machiavelli the possibility of comparing different religions was absolutely obvious.

4. Machiavelli's comparison was nourished by a variety of readings and reflections, and an extremely powerful imagination – not by scholarly study. Even if Machiavelli was neither a scholar

---

11   Alison Brown, *Bartolomeo Scala, 1430–1497, Chancellor of Florence: The Humanist as Bureaucrat* (Princeton: Princeton University Press, 1979), pp. 288–96; and see above chapter 1. Cf. Robert Fredona, 'Carnival of Law: Bartolomeo Scala's Dialogue *De legibus et iudiciis*', *Viator* 39/2 (2008), pp. 193–214, esp. p. 209ff.

12   Machiavelli, *The Chief Works*, vol. I, p. 225. (*Discorsi*, p. 68: 'E veramente mai fu alcuno ordinatore di leggi straordinarie in uno popolo che non ricorresse a Dio, perché altrimenti non sarebbero accettate.')

13   'tempi presenti' (Ibid.)

nor an antiquarian, his pages on Roman religion attracted the attention of the antiquarians.[14] As Sydney Anglo has noted, two works by the Lyonnais noble Guillaume Du Choul demonstrate this: *Discours sur la castrametation et discipline militaire des Romains … des bains et antiques exercitations Grecques et Romaines* and *Discours de la religion des anciens Romains*, published in Lyon in 1555 and in 1556 respectively, and promptly translated by the Florentine Gabriele Simeoni, a man of letters and antiquarian himself (1556 and 1557).[15] Both works are accompanied by illustrations that enjoyed enduring success (even Poussin used them), some of them inspired by the drawings – now lost – which Jacopo Ripanda had made of Trajan's Column.[16] Du Choul repeatedly drew upon documentation he had collected in 1538–1540 to compose a work of which only a fragment remains, preserved in a splendid manuscript dedicated to Francis

---

14 In the still-fundamental essay by Arnaldo Momigliano, 'Ancient History and the Antiquarian' (1950), in his *Contributo alla storia degli studi classici*, 2nd edn (Rome: Edizioni di Storia e Letteratura, 1979), pp. 67–106, Machiavelli's name is absent.

15 Cf. R. Cooper, 'L'antiquaire Guillaume Du Choul et son cercle lyonnais', in G. Defaux, ed., *Lyon et l'illustration de la langue française à la Renaissance* (Lyon: ENS Éditions, 2003), pp. 261–86 (with an ample bibliography). Other information is provided by J. Guillemain, 'L'antiquaire et le libraire. Du bon usage de la médaille dans les publications lyonnaises de la Renaissance', *Travaux de l'Institut d'Histoire de l'Art de Lyon* 16 (1993), pp. 35–66. (Guillemain is also the author of an unpublished doctoral dissertation on Du Choul.) On Simeoni see T. Renucci, *Un aventurier des lettres au XVIe siècle: Gabriel Symeoni, florentin, 1509–1570?* (Paris: Didier, 1943). A great deal of material is to be found in S. D'Amico and C. Magnien-Simonin, *Gabriele Simeoni (1509–1570?). Un Florentin en France entre princes et libraires* (Geneva: Droz, 2016); see, in particular, A. Villa, 'Gli studi antiquari di Gabriele Simeoni', pp. 323–46 (at p. 344 n. 89 there is a brief mention of Machiavelli; the first version of this chapter is not recorded). On both cf. Anglo, *Machiavelli*, p. 34 and passim, which does not dwell on the passages analysed here.

16 G. Agosti and V. Farinella, 'Calore del marmo. Pratica e tipologia delle deduzioni iconografiche', in *Memoria dell'antico nell'arte italiana*, ed. S. Settis, vol. I (Turin: Einaudi, 1984), p. 418 (the date of the first edition of *Discours de la religion* must be corrected in 'Lione 1556').

I: *Des antiquités Romaines: premier livre* (Ms *Varia*, Royal Library of Turin).[17] Thus the image of two boxers, portrayed in the Turin manuscript (fig. 3) and taken from an engraving by Marco Dente, re-emerges in the illustration that accompanies the *Discours ... des bains et antiques exercitations Grecques et Romaines* ('Combat des cestes entre Dares et Entellus, selon la description de Virgile').[18] Other examples could be offered.[19] But the intention to publish the work *Des antiquités Romaines*, frequently expressed by Du Choul after the death of Francis I, remained unrealized.[20]

---

17 *Varia* 212, Biblioteca Reale, Turin: *Des antiquités Romaines. Premier livre faict par le commandement du Roy par M. Guillaume Choul Lyonnoys, conseiller du dict seigneur et Bailly des Montaignes du Dauphiné*. The importance of this manuscript was pointed out by Francis Haskell, *History and Its Images: Art and the Interpretation of the Past* (New Haven: Yale University Press, 1993), p. 16. On this topic, see the excellent essay by M. Dickman Orth, 'Lyon et Rome à l'antique. Les illustrations des *Antiquités romaines* de Guillaume Du Choul', in *Lyon et l'illustration de la langue française à la Renaissance*, pp. 287–308.

18 Ms *Varia* 212, Biblioteca Reale, Turin; G. Du Choul, *Discours sur la castrametation et discipline militaire des Romains ... des bains et antiques exercitations grecques et romaines. De la religion des anciens Romains* (Lyon: Guillaume Roville, 1555), p. 18v of *Des bains et antiques exercitations grecques et romaines*. Cf. Dickman Orth, 'Lyon et Rome', p. 295, and the entry 'Dente, Marco' (by E. Borea), in *Dizionario biografico degli Italiani*, referring to A. Krug, 'Ein römisches Relief und Raffael', *Städel-Jahrbuch*, new ser., 5 (1975), pp. 31–6.

19 In the *Discours sur la castrametation*, p. 13r, a reference to the battle standard is followed by this comment: 'come l'on verra plus amplement au livre des mes Antiquités de Romme' ('as one will see more fully in my book on Roman antiquities'). The illustration at p. 15r ('Draconarii, et labariferi, Porteinseignes du Dragon et du Labarum, cornette de l'Empereur') is to be compared with Ms *Varia* 212, fol 80r, Biblioteca Reale, Turin.

20 At least three books of the work existed: cf. *Discours de la religion des anciens Romains, escript par Noble Seigneur Guillaume du Choul, Conseiller du Roy, et Bailly des montaignes du Daulphiné, et illustré d'un grand nombre de medailles, et de plusieurs belles figures retirées de marbres antiques, qui se treuvent à Rome, et par nostre Gaule* (Lyon: Guillaume Roville, 1556), p. 248. On the intention to have the work published, see ibid., p. 201.

Fig. 3 *Des antiquités Romaines. Premier livre faict par le commande-*
ment du Roy par M. Guillaume Choul Lyonnoys, conseiller du dict
seigneur et Bailly des Montaignes du Dauphiné (ms *Varia* 212, c. 35r,
Biblioteca Reale, Torino).

In Du Choul's books, the reproductions of medallions, or
other objects of various kinds, alternate with transcriptions of
epitaphs. In a passage from the *Discours de la religion des
anciens Romains*, Du Choul refers to an 'epitaph now in Turin,
which I have drawn from my book *On the epigrams of all Gaul*'
(a book that has not survived).[21] The Italian translation is
slightly different: 'an epitaph which one sees in Turin, already

21   Ibid., p. 142: 'Épitaphe qui se trouve à Turin, que j'ay retiré de
mon livre *Des Epigrammes de toute la Gaule*'.

shown to me by Simeoni'.[22] The translator, Gabriele Simeoni, punctiliously asserted his priority, subsequently reiterated in his *Illustratione de gli epitaffi et medaglie antiche*:

> This epitaph recalled to my mind a greater and nicer one, which, coming back from Piedmont, I showed to the Lord of the mountains of Dauphiné, who used it in his book on the ancient religion of the Romans, printed in French in Lyon by Guillaume Rouillé and translated into Italian by me. I wished to attach this epitaph once again, as it is mine and concerns my argument.[23]

Such insistence is quite unexpected given the social distance separating Simeoni and the noble Du Choul. One catches a glimpse of a close relationship, though one perhaps not free of tensions.[24] Upon closer examination, something emerges that fuelled the antiquarian passions of both men.

In the *Discours sur la castrametation*, after quoting a passage from the *De haruspicum responso* in which Cicero attributes the Romans' military supremacy to their religious piety, Du Choul observed, 'Religion is certainly a necessary thing to maintain an army, a kingdom and a republic, for religion is the cause

22 *Discorso della religione antica de Romani, composto in franzese dal S. Guglielmo Choul Gentilhuomo Lionese e Bagly delle montagne del Delfinato, insieme con un altro simile discorso della castrametatione et bagni antichi de Romani tradotti in Toscano da M. Gabriel Simeoni fiorentino* (Lyon: Gugl. Rovillio, 1559), p. 126: 'Un epitaffio che si vede in Turino, mostratomi già dal Symeone'.

23 G. Simeoni, *Illustratione de gli epitaffi et medaglie antiche* (Lyon: Giovan di Tournes, 1558), p. 8: 'Questo epitaffio mi fece ricordare d'un altro simile, ma più amplo, et più bello, che ritornando di Piamonte io monstrai già al Bagly di Montagna, che se ne servì poi nel suo libro della Religione antica de Romani, stampato in franzese a Lione da Guglielmo Rovilla, et da me ridotto in nostra lingua, il quale epitaffio come cosa mia et a proposito della mia materia io ho voluto di nuovo mettere qui di sotto'. The claim recurs in Simeoni, *Livre premier de Caesar renouvellé ... avec le second de nouveau adiousté par Françoys de S. Thomas* (Lyon: Iean Saugrain, 1570), pp. 78–9.

24 See the warm praise of Du Choul, in ibid., pp. 73–4.

of good order, and good order makes for good fortune, and from good fortune lucky enterprises come.'[25]

In his translation, Simeoni renders the implicit reference to the chapter 'On the Religion of the Romans' in the *Discourses* (book I, chapter 11) with words that are nearly identical to those of Machiavelli: 'This [religion] is a cause of good order, and good order in turn the cause of good fortune, and upon good fortune the happy outcomes of enterprises depend.'[26] At the beginning of the passage just cited, Simeoni inserts a further Machiavellian touch, absent from Du Choul's text: 'Certainly religion is very useful to an army, as a militia of its own soldiers is necessary to safeguard a kingdom or a republic.'[27]

The theme of *armi proprie* ('own arms') was particularly close to the heart of the Florentine exile Simeoni, who discusses it more fully in his *Illustratione de gli epitaffi et medaglie antiche*, contrasting *'legionari'* (legionaries) and *'mercennari'* (mercenaries). Among the examples illustrating the superiority of legionaries – militias of one's own – Simeoni refers to the unfortunate result of the 1530 siege of Florence.[28] From a very young age Simeoni had been connected to Donato Giannotti, one of the major figures in the defence of Florence, who was in France from 1550 in the service of Cardinal de Tournon.[29]

---

25 Du Choul, *Discours sur la castrametation*, p. 24r: 'Certainement c'est une chose tresnecessaire pour maintenir une armee, un Royaume, et une Republicque, que la religion en un exercite: la quelle est cause de bon ordre: le bon ordre fait la bonne fortune; et de la bonne fortune: succedent les heureuses enterprises.'

26 Du Choul, *Discorso della castramentatione*, p. 42: 'Questa [la religione] è causa del buono ordine: et il buono ordine della buona fortuna, et dalla buona fortuna dipendono i felici successi dell' imprese.'

27 Ibid., p. 42: 'Certamente la religione è una cosa molto utile in uno essercito come una militia di soldati proprij è necessaria per guardare un Reame, e una Republica.'

28 Simeoni, *Illustratione de gli epitaffi*, pp. 124–6, esp. p. 125.

29 Renucci, *Un aventurier des lettres au XVIe siècle*, p. 6. See also the entry 'Giannotti, Donato' (by S. Marconi), in *Dizionario biografico degli Italiani*.

5. Du Choul could have reached Machiavelli independently of Simeoni. Nevertheless, some passages from Du Choul's original seem like a faint impression of the Italian translation. Let us take the beginning of the previously mentioned section of *Discours sur la castrametation*:

> We know this from the noblest sentence of Cicero's *On the Response of the Haruspices*, when he told us that the Romans, though they were not as numerous as the Spaniards, as strong as the Gauls, as astute as the Africans, as learned as the Greeks, or as bright as the Latins, with piety and religion, and aided only by their wisdom (through which they had seen that all things are governed by the immortal Gods), have overcome all kinds of people and foreign nations.[30]

And here is Simeoni's Italian translation, which inserts a Machiavellian '*non dimeno*':

> I Romani, benché non fossero di numero eguali a gli Spagnuoli, né di forze a i Franzesi, né d'astutia a gl'Africani, né di scienza a i Greci, né di spirito a i Latini, non dimeno per pietà, religione et singular sapienza ordinando tutte le loro cose sotto la fede et aiuto de gli Dij immortali, soggiogarono tutte le sorti de gl'huomini et strane nationi.[31]

The volume with the translations of Du Choul was preceded by a dedication to Catherine de' Medici, the Florentine noblewoman who had ascended the French throne, signed by the

---

30 Du Choul, *Discours de la castrametation*, p. 24r: 'Ce que nous cognoissons par la tresnoble sentence de Cicero, *De aruspicum responsis:* quand il a dit que les Rommains, encores qu'ils ne fussent de nombre égaux aux Espaignols, de force aux Gaulois, d'astuce aux Africains, de science aux Grecs, d'esprit aux Latins, de piété, religion, et avecques la seule sagesse (par laquelle ils avoyent regardé que toutes choses estoyent gouvernées par l'aide des Dieux immortels) avoyent vaincu toutes manieres de gens et estrangeres nations.'

31 Du Choul, *Discorso della castrametatione*, pp. 41-2.

printer 'Guglielmo Rovillio': 'The purity and sweetness of the Tuscan language seems to be ... held in such esteem that, after Greek and Latin, the Tuscans studying it strive every day to make it more beautiful, foreign men of letters admire it, and (just as Ariosto, Bembo and Sannazzaro have done) try to imitate it in their writings.'[32]

Behind the printer, a transparent figurehead, the recognizable voice of Simeoni emerges once again: the *Discorso della religione* enables us 'to know that the greatness and prosperity of the Roman Empire derived from nothing but the virtue of its own army, its justice, and frequent worship (even though false, as much as ours ordained by the Catholic Church is redeeming and true)'.[33]

For Machiavelli, *armi proprie* should draw inspiration from the merciless religion of the Romans, as opposed to the meek Christian faith. Yet in Du Choul's writings this contraposition paves the way for contrast and comparison:

> After having discussed it at length, I often wondered how the Gentiles dwelt so long in their false, superstitious and erroneous religion, leaving ours which is true and sent by God ... The Romans could as well believe that JESUS CHRIST had made the dead come back to life, like their Asclepius, whom they made rise, full of light, to the heavens and thought was born from a virgin, as they believe that Vesta was a virgin and mother of the Gods. And while they refused to believe that our Lord gave sight to the blind, they were sure that

---

32 'La purità et dolcezza della lingua toscana pare che sia di presente [. . .] salita in tanto pregio, che doppo la greca et la latina, i toscani medesimi studiandola, s'ingegnano ogni giorno di renderla più bella, i letterati stranieri l'ammirano et (come hanno fatto l'Ariosto, il Bembo et il Sennazzaro) ne i loro scritti cercano d'imitarla.'

33 Du Choul, *Discorso della religione antica de Romani*, p. 4: 'Cognoscere che la grandezza et prosperità dell'imperio romano non nacque d'altrove, che dalle virtù dell'armi proprie, dalla giustitia et dal culto frequente (anchora che falso, altretanto che il nostro ordinato dalla Chiesa cattolica, è salutifero et vero).'

Emperor Vespasian had performed the same miracle in Alexandria.[34]

Pagan superstitions are similar to Christian rites, Asclepius and Vespasian are comparable to Christ, and so forth. A poisonous analogy, because reversible.[35] The uniqueness of the Christian religion was being undermined. All of this paved the way for the conclusion of Du Choul's *Discours de la religion des anciens Romains*:

> And if we look with curiosity, we will find that several institutions of our religion have been taken and translated from Egyptian ceremonies and Gentiles, such as tunics and gowns, the crowns of priests, inclinations of the head around the altar, the rite of sacrifice, the music of temples, adorations, prayers and supplications, processions and litanies, and many other things that our priests usurp in our mysteries and refer to an only God IESUSCHRIST, whereas the ignorance of Gentiles, false religion and mad superstition attributed them to their Gods and to mortal men after their consecrations.[36]

---

34 Du Choul, *Discours de la religion des anciens Romains*, p. 263: 'Apres avoir longuement discouru, ie me suis souventesfois esbahi, comme les Gentils demeurerent si longuement en leur religion faulse, superstitieuse et controuvée, laissants la nostre qui est vraye et venue de Dieu. [...] Aussi bien pouvoyent croire les Romains, que JESUS CHRIST avoit resuscité les morts, comme leur Aesculapius, qu'ils firent monter au ciel tout fouldroyé, et de penser qu'il estoit né d'une vierge, comme ils cuyderent que Vesta estoit vierge et mere des Dieux. Et si estoyent bien aveuglez de refuser de croire que nostre Seigneur avoit rendue la veuë aux aveugles, veu qu'ils asseuroyent que Vespasian l'Empereur avoit faict un tel miracle en Alexandrie.'

35 Cooper, 'L'antiquaire Guillaume Du Choul', p. 280, characterizes Du Choul as a 'syncretist': a wholly inappropriate term.

36 Du Choul, *Discours de la religion des anciens Romains*, p. 312: 'Et si nous regardons curieusement, nous congnoistrons que plusieurs institutions de nostre religion ont esté prises et translatées de ceremonies Aegyptienes, et des Gentils: comme sont les tuniques et surpelis, les couronnes que font les prebstres, les inclinations de teste autour de l'autel, la pompe sacrificale, la musique des temples,

Simeoni's translation was slightly different: 'And many other things that a good spirit can easily compare, after having well considered these ceremonies and those.'[37] The 'good spirit' capable of grasping all of this would not have been misled by the predictable sentence which immediately follows: 'Except that those of the Gentiles were false and superstitious, while ours are Christian and Catholic, being performed in honour of God the omnipotent Father, and Jesus Christ his son, to whom be eternal glory.'[38]

6. Direct or indirect echoes of Machiavelli can often be detected in sixteenth-century comparisons between pagan and Christian rites, conducted from a standpoint more or less covertly hostile to the latter.[39] But this antiquarianism, with its vigorously political roots, was open to a much broader comparison, stimulated by the encounter between Europeans and the peoples of the New World.[40] Among the many examples of the slow transformation of antiquarianism into ethnography, one might mention the work

---

adorations, prieres et supplications, processions et letanies: et plusieurs autres choses, que noz prebstres usurpent en noz mysteres, et referent a un seul Dieu IESUSCHRIST, ce que l'ignorance des Gentils, faulse religion et folle superstition representoit à leurs Dieux, et aux hommes mortels apres leurs consecrations.'

37 Du Choul, *Discorso della religione antica de Romani*, p. 248: 'Et molte altre cose, che un buono spirito potrà facilmente raccorre, havendo bene considerato queste cerimonie et quelle.'

38 Ibid., p. 248: 'Eccetto che quelle de Gentili erano false, et superstitiose, ma le nostre sono Christiane et catholiche, essendo fatte in honore di Dio Padre Omnipotente, et di Giesu Cristo suo figliuolo, a cui sia gloria eternalmente.'

39 In this vein, one can read the beautiful essay by Fritz Saxl, 'Pagan Sacrifice in the Italian Renaissance', *Journal of the Warburg and Courtauld Institutes* 2/4 (April 1939), pp. 346–67.

40 Arnold van Gennep, 'Nouvelles recherches sur l'histoire en France de la méthode ethnographique. Claude Guichard, Richard Simon, Claude Fleury', *Revue de l'histoire des religions* 82 (1920), pp. 139–62. And see also Arnaldo Momigliano, 'Prospettiva 1967 della storia greca' (1967), in his *Quarto contributo alla storia degli studi classici e del mondo antico* (Rome: Edizioni di Storia e Letteratura, 1969), pp. 43–58.

of another Lyonnais antiquarian, the jurist Claude Guichard's *Funerailles et diverses manieres d'ensevelir des Rommains, Grecs, et autres nations, tant anciennes que modernes* (1581). Guichard, who had attended the University of Turin, dedicated the book to Duke Charles Emmanuel I of Savoy, remembering that he had offered him a translation of Livy some years earlier. Guichard, too, begins his treatise extolling the 'civility, military art and religion (*police, art militaire et religion*)' of the Romans: 'Furthermore, of these three things not only do the establishment, greatness and safety of every well-ordered republic consist, but on the awareness of them the entire and perfect knowledge of history and antiquities of the Romans also depends.'[41]

The first two books, devoted to the respective funerary rites of the Romans and the Greeks (Guichard states that he is not respecting chronological order), are followed by a journey through the funerary rites of the entire world. Guichard cites his predecessors: Biondo Flavio, Alessandro d'Alessandro, Celio Rodigino, Wolfgang Lazius and Lilio Gregorio Giraldi, author of *De sepulchris et vario sepeliendi ritu* (Basel: Michael Isengrin: Basileae, 1539).[42] But unlike them he devoted a section to funerary rites in the New World: 'We shall find all things new and in the event they will be no less pleasant for their novelty than the previous for their antiquity.'[43]

In Guichard's view the New World is not inferior to the Old. Indeed, the inhabitants of the West Indies, in particular those of

---

41 Claude Guichard (1581), *Funerailles et diverses manieres d'ensevelir des Rommains, Grecs, et autres nations, tant anciennes que modernes* (Lyon: Iean de Tournes, 1581), p. 1: 'Et de vray, outre ce, qu'en ces trois consiste l'establissement, grandeur et asseurance de toute republique bien instituee, de la notice d'iceux depend encore l'entiere et parfaicte congnoissance de l'histoire et antiquité des Rommains.'

42 Ibid., p.12. On Lilio Giraldi, see Giovanni Ricci, *I giovani, i morti. Sfide al Rinascimento* (Bologna: Il Mulino, 2007), pp. 139–60.

43 Guichard, *Funerailles et diverses manieres*, pp. 437–66, esp. p. 437: 'Nous treuverons toutes choses nouvelles, et qui à l'adventure ne seront moins aggreables pour leur nouveauté, que les precedentes pour leur antiquité.'

Peru, 'have done better than all other nations in sumptuousness of tombs and sepulchres (*ont surpassé toutes les autres nations quelles qu'elles soyent en somptuosité de tombeaux et sepulcres*)'. Guichard does not hesitate to compare the funeral chants of the women of Béarn and Gascony with those of the 'poor Americans (*povres Américaines*)'. After concluding his 'universal discourse on funerals (*discours universel des funerailles*)', he moves on to the Egyptians, ancient and modern Jews, and Christians.[44]

7. Here New and Old Worlds are juxtaposed. But in the climate of the Wars of Religion French Protestants and Catholics insistently, and mutually, accused one another of barbarism. We call the Margajas and the Tupinambás 'barbarians, savages', a Protestant pamphlet read: but at least those savages only devoured each other; the Catholics who defiled tombs were far worse than them. The Catholic Henri de Sponde, referring to the 'erudite treatise *Des Funerailles* written by Claude Guichard', objected: cemeteries are sacred places that must be protected from contamination by heretics.[45] The ineradicable hatreds that rage among the 'savages' of Brazil, wrote the Protestant Jean de Léry, are imitated by 'Machiavelli and his disciples (of whom France, to its great misfortune, is now full)'. They were the 'true imitators of barbarous cruelties: for, against Christian doctrine, these Atheists teach, and also practice, that new services must never cause old injuries to be forgotten'.[46] 'Never

---

44 Ibid., pp. 437, 463, 466.

45 Frank Lestringant, 'Anti-funérailles, ou la guerre des cimetières (1594–1598)', in *Les funérailles à la Renaissance. XIIe colloque international de la Société Française d'Etude du Seizième Siècle*, ed. Jean Balsamo (Geneva: Droz, 2002), pp. 295–317.

46 Jean de Léry, *History of a Voyage to the Land of Brazil, Otherwise Called America*, tr. Janet Whatley (Berkeley: University of California Press, 1990), p. 112; trans. modified. Cf. Giuseppe Marcocci, 'Machiavelli, the Iberian Explorations and the Islamic Empire: Tropical Readers from Brazil to India (Sixteenth and Seventeenth Centuries)', in *Machiavelli, Islam and the East: Reorienting the Foundations of Modern Political Thought*, ed. Lucio Biasiori and Giuseppe Marcocci (London: Palgrave Macmillan, 2018), pp. 131–54, esp. p. 143.

have new benefits erased old injuries', wrote Machiavelli (*Discourses*, book III, chapter 4).[47] A cold remark, which Léry turned into a vehemently anti-Christian homily.

The New World was seen through the lens of the Old, and vice versa. A detached approach to religions fed antiquarianism, which in turn fuelled the polemic between them. What we call comparative history of religion emerged, laboriously and painfully, from this bloody tangle.

---

47   Machiavelli, *The Chief Works*, vol. I, p. 426.

7

Machiavelli, Galileo and the Censors

1. Kaspar Schoppe's attempt, at the height of the Counter-Reformation, to rehabilitate the impious Machiavelli by presenting him as a champion of Catholic orthodoxy appears paradoxical today. All the same, it offers valuable cues for interpretation.[1] It is worth examining this bold, failed initiative in a different perspective. Schoppe (in Latin Scioppius, Scioppio in Italian) was born in 1576 in Neumarkt, in the Upper Palatinate, into a Lutheran family. In 1597 he went to Italy, where he spent the greater part of his life. After his conversion to Catholicism in 1599, which he attributed to the experience of reading Cesare Baronio's *Annales ecclesiastici*, Schoppe wrote a large number of learned and polemical works, among them numerous anti-Jesuit tracts published under various pseudonyms. He died in Padua in 1649.[2]

---

1 On the importance of Schoppe's *Paedia politices*, 'an acute and learned book', G. Galeani Napione insisted, in his notes on the life of Giovanni Botero (*Piemontesi illustri*, vol. 1 [Turin: Giammichele Briolo: 1781], pp. 253ff, especially p. 283). Some recent studies ignore Schoppe. See also Giuliano Procacci, who views him, reductively, as an example of the traditional reading of Machiavelli in an Aristotelian-Thomistic register (*Machiavelli nella cultura europea dell'età moderna* [Rome and Bari: Laterza, 1995], pp. 158–61).

2 Besides the entry 'Schoppe (Scioppio), Kaspar' (by P. Carta) in *Enciclopedia machiavelliana*, vol. II, pp. 498–9, see on Schoppe's youth, F. R. Hausmann, *Zwischen Autobiographie und Biographie. Jugend und Ausbildung des Fränkisch-Oberpfälzer Philologen und Kontroverstheologen Kaspar Schoppe (1576–1649)* (Würzburg:

2. In an autobiographical piece, Schoppe recalled that in 1619, in the Carthusian monastery in Milan where he was then living, he had for some months subjected Cardinal Alessandro Ludovisi (later Pope Gregory XV) to his 'elucubrations' in Machiavelli's defence. The future pope's reaction was encouraging: rehabilitation of an author who was at the time on the Index would have allowed the Church to see off the recurring accusation of having published his writings with the approval of Clement VII.[3]

Schoppe's plan was not new. When, in 1620, he spoke of it to a group of Florentines, the poet Pietro Strozzi recounted how, fourteen years earlier, Roberto Bellarmine, who was already a cardinal, had urged him to work 'pro Machiavello', providing commentary on his writings. Strozzi had given up in the end, consigning the fruits of his reflections to the flames.[4] Machiavelli continued to circulate under the table, in variously disguised formats.[5]

The long apologia that Schoppe wrote in Latin in 1618–1619 remained unpublished. It survived in various copies, most of them under the title *Machiavellica*.[6] It is an extremely repetitious work.

Königshausen & Neumann, 1995); G. Almási, 'Rehabilitating Machiavelli: Kaspar Schoppe with and against Rome', in *History of European Ideas* 42/8 (2016), pp. 981–1004 (many thanks to Marcelo Barbuto for having brought this article to my attention).

3   Mario D'Addio, *Il pensiero politico di Gaspare Scioppio* (Milan: Giuffrè, 1962), p. 40.

4   Schoppe quotes Pietro Strozzi's words: 'tardipedi Deo daturum / Infelicibus ustulanda lignis' (an allusion to Catullus, poem 36). Bellarmino had at that time characterized Machiavelli as an 'arch-heretic': see the entry 'Index librorum prohibitorum' (by V. Frajese) in *Enciclopedia machiavelliana*, vol. II, pp. 12–17, esp. p. 14.

5   Procacci, *Machiavelli nella cultura europea dell'età moderna*, pp. 85–121.

6   See Carlo Morandi, 'L'"Apologia" del Machiavelli di Gaspare Scioppio', *Nuova Rivista Storica* 17 (1933), pp. 277–94. See also Schoppe's letters to Johannes Faber published by O. Tommasini, *La vita e gli scritti di Niccolò Machiavelli nella loro relazione col machiavellismo* [1883] (Bologna: il Mulino, 1994), pp. 613–16; D'Addio, *Il*

Illustration 1. Andrea del Verrocchio, *Bartolomeo
Colleoni* (Campo San Zanipolo, Venice)

Illustrations 2, 3. Andrea del Verrocchio, *Bartolomeo Colleoni* (Campo San Zanipolo, Venice)

Illustrations 4, 5. Michelangelo, *David*
(Galleria dell'Accademia, Florence)

Illustration 6. Michelangelo, *Pietà Bandini* (Museo dell'Opera del Duomo, Florence)

Illustration 7. Michelangelo, *Lorenzo de' Medici*
(Sagrestia Nuova, San Lorenzo, Florence)

Illustration 8. Michelangelo, *Lorenzo de' Medici*
(Sagrestia Nuova, San Lorenzo, Florence)

Illustration 9. Giorgio Vasari et al., *Monument to Michelangelo* (Santa Croce, Florence)

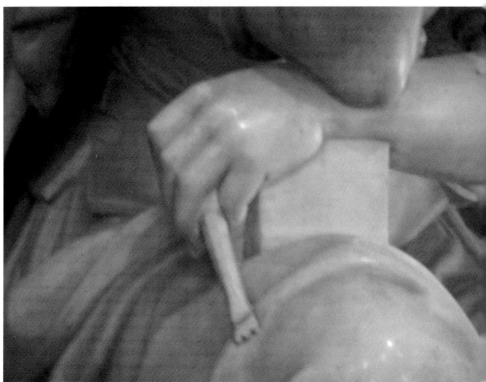

Illustrations 10, 11. Vincenzo Cioli, *Sculpture* (Santa Croce, Florence)

Schoppe's argumentation turns essentially on the adjective *lubricum* (literally 'slippery', and by extension 'ambiguous') and its meanings. In order to distinguish between what is *lubricum* in the mind of the reader and what is *lubricum* in Machiavelli's text, Schoppe argues, the reader must remain aware of four criteria: first, the general intention and scope of the book; second, the author's intention in any given part of it; third, the type of discourse – absolute or hypothetical? – employed by the author at a given stage; and fourth, the sense in which the author has understood his own work. If, read in keeping with these criteria, the text remains ambiguous, it is necessary to conclude that the ambiguity resides in the mind of the reader.

The third of these criteria, the author's discursive strategy, is particularly relevant; it is based on the distinction between discourse formulated in an absolute perspective (*simpliciter*) and that formulated hypothetically (*sub conditione*). This scholastic distinction opens the way to an extremely detailed comparison between the most scandalous pages of *The Prince* and certain parts of Aquinas's commentary (in fact, redacted by Peter of Auvergne) on Aristotle's *Politics*, book V.[7] Here is a sample of its role in Schoppe's reasoning:

> In order to safeguard his own rule the tyrant must kill the richest and most powerful, considering that they can act against him. Then he must kill the wisest, since they can use their intelligence to destroy tyranny . . . His subjects must be reduced to penury, to weaken any attempt at revolt against the tyranny.[8]

---

pensiero politico di Gaspare Scioppio, p. 133cf. On the manuscripts of the 'Apologia', see ibid., pp. 416–17ff. I consulted ms 958 in Biblioteca Casanatense, Rome.

7   See here, chapters 1, 3, 4.

8   Schoppe, *Machiavellica*, fol 33r (ms 958, Biblioteca Casanatense, Rome); see also Codice Scioppiano 206, fols 163ff, Biblioteca Laurenziana, Florence. See D'Addio, *Il pensiero politico di Gaspare Scioppio*, p. 424ff; Lidia Lanza, 'Aspetti della ricezione della *Politica* aristotelica nel XIII secolo: Pietro d'Alvernia', *Studi Medievali*, 3rd ser., 35/2 (1994), pp. 643–94.

And so on. All this is indubitably ambiguous (*lubricum*), Schoppe commented. But it is not proposed in an absolute manner (*simpliciter*). These are counsels proposed hypothetically, *sub conditione*: if a tyrant wishes to defend his rule, he must act in this way. *The Prince* too was written hypothetically, and that is why, in 1532, Pope Clement VII authorized its publication.

Given the state of the Church before the Council of Trent, Schoppe continued, the criticisms that Machiavelli levelled at the clergy were not groundless. His fundamentally Catholic allegiance was proven by the furious attack launched against him by the Calvinist Innocent Gentillet's *Anti-Machiavel*. Hence Schoppe's conclusion that Machiavelli's writings, on the Index since 1599, were in reality faithful not only to Aristotle's thought, but also to that of Aquinas and as such should not be banned, merely expurgated.[9]

3. Schoppe sought permission from the Sacred Congregation of the Index to publish his wordy defence of Machiavelli, without success. Then, thanks to the mediation of Cardinal Ludovico Ludovisi, the nephew of Gregory XV, a compromise was reached. Schoppe wrote a short text giving the gist of his arguments but without mentioning Machiavelli's name, and submitted it to the Dominican theologian Niccolò Riccardi, the rector of Santa Maria sopra Minerva and a consultant to the Congregation, known as Father Monster as much for his obesity as for his astonishing memory.[10] Father Riccardi's initial doubts about the wisdom of circulating such audacious theses were dispelled in the face of Schoppe's insistent argumentation, and in 1623 in Rome there appeared a booklet

---

9 See the entry 'Index librorum prohibitorum' in *Enciclopedia machiavelliana*.

10 D'Addio, *Il pensiero politico*, p. 160ff. See *Philotheca Scioppiana*, an autobiographical text written by Schoppe in Padua in 1643 (Biblioteca Medicea Laurenziana, Florence, Codice Scioppiano 243, which is a partial reproduction of it; see also D'Addio, *Il pensiero*, pp. 609ff, esp. p. 650).

of forty-two pages entitled *Paedia politices sive suppetiae logi-cae scriptoribus politicis latae* (Political instructions, or logical resources for political writers), dedicated to Cardinal Ludovisi.[11] In his imprimatur, Father Riccardi declared that, on the advice of Niccolò Ridolfi, Master of the Holy Apostolic Palace, the highest authority in matters of literary censorship, he had read and reread Schoppe's hugely learned text with great pleasure, and found nothing in it contrary to faith or morals.[12]

Schoppe's argument, in a nutshell, was this. Politics is an art and therefore, as Aristotle taught, morally neutral. As such, it includes all the varieties of its kind. The study of politics must follow Aristotle and Aquinas in examining all forms of polity, not only the best, 'which may never have existed and perhaps never will'.[13] Following this polemical allusion to Plato and his successors came a parallel between political writers and physicians. The latter treat the body in any condition, from the best to the worst, from perfect health to grave illnesses. This wasn't a new argument: it had been put forward in similar terms by Agostino Nifo in his plagiarism of *The Prince* and by Bernardo Giunti in a letter to Giovanni Gaddi prefacing his own edition of Machiavelli's work, published in Florence in 1532.[14] Basing himself again on Aristotle's *Politics* and on the comment traditionally attributed to Aquinas, Schoppe cited the latter

---

11 See the correspondence between Schoppe and Riccardi, recounted with ample quotation by D'Addio, pp. 500–12 (Biblioteca Medicea Laurenziana, Florence, Codice Scioppiano 217, cc. 159r–v, 154r–158v; Codice Scioppiano 223, cc. 84r–85r, 86r–88v [autographs]).

12 From the imprimatur: 'Vacat omni censura, et nihil continet dissonans moribus sive adversarium pietati.' *Paedia politices* was republished with a vast commentary, along with Gabriel Naudé's *Bibliographia Politica*, by Hermann Conring (Helmstadt: H. Müller, 1663): see D'Addio, p. 555ff.

13 Schoppe, *Paedia politices*, p. 17.

14 See Luigi Firpo, 'Le origini dell'anti-machiavellismo', in *Scritti sul pensiero politico del Rinascimento e della Controriforma* (Turin: UTET, 2005), pp. 24–56, esp. pp. 39, 55.

discussing 'means evil in themselves [*mala secundum seipsa*] but good for escaping tyranny', and so not to be employed absolutely (*simpliciter*) but only against tyranny, which is evil in itself (*quae secundum se mala est*).[15] Some criticize political writers for abstaining from condemnation of tyrannical government, but that kind of criticism belongs to the sphere of ethics and morals, not politics.[16]

Schoppe had wanted the *Paedia* to include an appendix setting out 'a method of evaluating political writers and the writings of Niccolò Machiavelli in particular', followed by a résumé of *The Prince*.[17] These requests were denied. However, the *Paedia*'s readers did not overlook the transparent allusions to Machiavelli.[18] The publication was bound to cause a scandal. In the reprint that came a year later in Milan, with the imprimatur of the local Church authorities, the dedication to Ludovisi had disappeared.

4. At the end of 1621, in his capacity as adviser to the Index, Father Riccardi received the manuscript of *Atheismus triumphatus*: the book that another Dominican, Tommaso Campanella, had sent to the Inquisition from the Neapolitan prison in which he had been rotting for more than twenty years, having been found guilty of conspiring against Spanish rule. The first Italian edition of this work (dating from 1615 and rediscovered not long ago) bore the long title *L'ateismo trionfato overo riconoscimento filosofico della religione universale contra l'antichristianesimo macchiavellesco* and opened with a long dedication expressing the author's deep gratitude to Kaspar

---

15   *Paedia politices*, p. 36. (See also, with minimal variations, Thomas Aquinas, *Commentarii* ... *in octo Politicorum Aristotelis libros cum textus eiusdem, Interprete Leonardo Aretino* [Romae, 1492], f. 88v.)

16   Ibid., p. 20.

17   Biblioteca Medicea Laurenziana, Florence, Codice Scioppiano 216, ff. 209r–213v; cfr. D'Addio, *Il pensiero politico*, pp. 500–1.

18   See ch. 4, n. 50.

Schoppe, styled 'the Dawn of our century'.[19] In 1607, Schoppe had visited Campanella in prison and promised to fight for his release and the publication of his books – which he then proceeded to loot and pass off as his own. Campanella took dryly bitter note of the plagiarism years later, in giving his *Atheismus triumphatus* to the printers (1631).[20]

The path to that edition was long and difficult. In 1621 and again in 1626–1627, Father Riccardi, who was now Master of the Apostolic Palace, discussed the manuscript of *Atheismus triumphatus* with other theologians in the most unrestrained terms: the author was an 'eel', the book a 'sewer full of every heresy'.[21] The others concurred with Riccardi in finding Campanella – who by this time had been released from prison – guilty of Pelagianism for his idea of a natural religion based on reason. A judgement of censure in extremis led to the withdrawal of the first edition, which survives in a single copy containing Campanella's final handwritten corrections. In the first Italian version, the subtitle *antichristianesimo macchiavellesco* became *antichristianismum achitophellisticum* – after Achitophel, adviser to David and Absalom in the Second Book of Samuel and eventually a suicide.[22] Machiavelli's name had

---

19 Campanella, *L'ateismo trionfato*, ed. Germana Elisa Ernst (Pisa: Scuola Normale Superiore, 2004), vol. 1, p. 5. On relations between Schoppe and Campanella, see Ernst, '"Oscurato è il secolo". Il Proemio allo Schoppe del ritrovato "Ateismo trionfato" italiano', *Bruniana & Campanelliana* 2/1–2, (1996), pp. 11–32.

20 T. Campanella, *Atheismus triumphatus seu reductio ad religionem per scientiarum veritates ... contra antichristianismum achitophellisticum* (Romae: apud Haeredem Barthomaei Zannetti, 1631), at the end of the introduction: 'Misi hunc libellum amico, ut proficeret in Germania, anno Domini M. DC.VII, multosque libros meos, quibus ad suorum compositionem profecit'. See Ernst's introduction to Campanella, *L'ateismo trionfato*, vol. I, p. 37, n. 60; and also D'Addio, p. 211ff.

21 Ernst, 'Cristianesimo e religione naturale. Le censure all'*Atheismus triumphatus* di Tommaso Campanella', *Nouvelles de la République des Lettres* 1–2 (1989), pp. 137–200, esp. pp. 174, 187.

22 In the copy of *Atheismus triumphatus* owned by Biblioteca dell'Archiginnasio (shelf mark: 16.c.I.44) Campanella erased from the

disappeared, but his presence was unmistakable nevertheless, in strongly polemical contexts throughout the work. Its nineteenth and final part, certainly dating from after 1627, engaged with an unnamed admirer of Machiavelli identifiable as Kaspar Schoppe, whose *Paedia* comes in for detailed discussion.[23]

'Now', Campanella began, this author maintains that 'those who accuse Machiavelli do not understand art. They debate the prince's honesty and reprove his misdeeds, and this has nothing to do with art.'[24] This admirer 'contradicts himself in many ways'. He continued:

First he says that the politician [that is, Machiavelli] describes the arts of tyranny without approving of them; he goes on then from description to approval of a strictly hypothetical kind, teaching the arts he has described in case tyrannical rule should have need of them. Finally, switching from a hypothetical to an absolute mode, he teaches good arts, as opposed to what he calls evil, and which we call good; and so comes the accusation raised against us of not understanding what is an art and of asserting the contrary of the truth, and he confirms this, adding [*inertiae, et falsitatis nos accusavit, et hoc confirmat, subdens*] that in certain cases a political reign can be corrupted by virtues, such as clemency, piety or trust.[25]

Nos accusavit, et hoc confirmat: the present-tense *confirmat* refers to the *Paedia*, but what is the past-perfect *accusavit* alluding to? Could it be to the discussions Campanella had had with Schoppe in Naples twenty years earlier? It is not a far-fetched

---

imprimatur the words '*machiavellisticarum*' and '*machiavellizantes*'. On this copy see L. Firpo, 'Appunti campanelliani. XXI. Le censure all' *Atheismus triumphatus*', in *Giornale critico della filosofia italiana*, 3rd ser., 5 (1951), pp. 509–24.

23 D'Addio supposes that Campanella had been able to read the *Paedia* thanks to Father Riccardi (p. 535). But this is a needless hypothesis, given that Campanella had regained his freedom in 1626.

24 *Atheismus triumphatus*, p. 173.

25 Ibid., p. 179. An allusion to Schoppe, *Paedia politices*, p. 39.

hypothesis: Schoppe had begun writing about Machiavelli in 1618, but his interest went farther back. Visiting Campanella in prison, he suggested the title (*Atheismus triumphatus*) of the work then in progress and also criticized the anti-Machiavellianism of his interlocutor, using the arguments later developed in the *Paedia*. Among these, the distinction between *simpliciter* and *secundum quid*, which Campanella, in his stubborn opposition to Aristotle (sharply attacked by Schoppe), may have rejected prejudicially, before doing so in a reasoned manner many years later.[26] 'But since he *machiavellizes* Aristotle', we read in *Atheismus*: words with which Campanella implicitly underwrites the interpretation of Machiavelli's unnamed admirer – and at the same time disagrees with both of them.[27]

5. A few days before authorizing the printing of the *Paedia*, Father Riccardi had entered an enthusiastic judgement on Galileo's *Il Saggiatore*, saying that he considered himself 'lucky to have been born in his time'.[28] With this eulogy, which was

26 See Domenico Berti, 'Nuovi documenti su Tommaso Campanella', in his *Scritti varii* (Turin: Editori Roux, 1892) (a letter to Campanella, undated but likely from 1607–1608, in which Schoppe defends Saint Thomas's peripatetic philosophy inasmuch as it is God's will).

27 Campanella, *Atheismus triumphatus*, p. 176, and see D'Addio, *Il pensiero*, p. 543.

28 G. Galilei, *Il Saggiatore nel quale con bilancia esquisita e giusta si ponderano le cose contenute nella Libra astronomica e filosofica di Lotario Sarsi Sigensano* (Rome: Giacomo Mascardi, 1623), imprimatur: 'ci ho avvertite tante belle considerazioni appartenenti alla filosofia nostrale, ch'io non credo che 'l nostro secolo sia per gloriarsi ne' futuri, di erede solamente delle fatiche de' passati filosofi, ma d'inventore di molti segreti della natura, ch'eglino non poterono scoprire, mercé della sottile, e soda speculazione dell'autore, nel cui tempo mi reputo felice d'esser nato' (cfr. *Il Saggiatore*, ed. L. Sosio [Milan: Feltrinelli, 1965], p. 2). Father Riccardi's evaluation was subordinated to the final judgement delivered by Maestro del Sacro Palazzo, who later conceded the imprimatur: see *I documenti vaticani del processo di Galileo Galilei (1611–1741)*, new edition expanded, revised and annotated by Sergio Pagano (Vatican City: Vatican Secret Archive, 2009) (hereafter *Documenti*), p. LXXVII.

hardly to be expected, there began a tortuous relationship that was destined to become profoundly ambiguous. The course of events is well known; here, then, a brief recall will suffice.

On 24 February 1616 the advisers to the Holy Office, responding to an inquiry from the Congregation of the Index of Forbidden Books, had declared the assertion of an unmoving sun philosophically foolish and absurd, and formally heretical inasmuch as contrary to many passages of scripture and their interpretation; the assertion of a moving Earth was pronounced 'erroneous with regard to faith'.[29] It was not for the Congregation to issue a condemnation for heresy; there had never been such a papal pronouncement on the Copernican theory at any time.[30] However, the next day Paul V, having seen the advisers' responses, instructed Cardinal Bellarmine to summon Galileo and warn him to abandon the Copernican view. The minutes of the Congregation for the Holy Office for 3 March record that Bellarmine conveyed the warning to Galileo, who had accepted it (*acquievit*).[31] Two days later, the Congregation banned a book by the Carmelite Paolo Antonio Foscarini concerning the opinions of Pythagoras and Copernicus and the new Pythagorean world system, and decreed that Copernicus's *De revolutionibus orbium coelestium* and Diego de Zúñiga's commentary on the book of Job be expurgated.

In April the previous year, Bellarmine had sent Foscarini (and thereby Galileo) a gentle but plain warning: 'It appears to me

---

29   Ibid., p. 7. See also Galileo's *Lettera a Cristina di Lorena,* ed. Franco Motta with an introduction by Mauro Pesce (Genoa: Marietti, 2000), for the editor's comments, pp. 167–70.

30   Descartes insisted on this point in 1634, in a letter to Mersenne cited by Giorgio de Santillana, *Processo a Galileo: studio storico-critico* (Milan: Mondadori, 1960), p. 580 (and see also pp. 651–2 n. 16). See V. Frajese, 'Il decreto anticopernicano del 5 marzo 1616', in *Il 'caso Galileo'. Una rilettura storica, filosofica, teologica, Convegno internazionale di studi, Firenze 26–30 maggio 2009,* ed. M. Bucciantini, M. Camerota and F. Giudice (Florence: Olschki, 2011), pp. 75–89; V. Frajese, *Il processo a Galileo Galilei. Il falso e la sua prova* (Brescia: Morcelliana, 2010).

31   *Documenti*, p. 177, n. 124.

that the Reverend Father and Signor Galileo would do well to rest content with speaking *ex suppositione* rather than in an absolute way, as I have always taken Copernicus to have done.'[32]

Here Bellarmine took over the reasoning of the theologian Andreas Osiander, who, in an unsigned preface to *De revolutionibus*, had presented the work as a purely hypothetical model of the universe.[33] He continued:

> To say that the supposition of a moving Earth and a stationary Sun saves the phenomena more effectively than the epicycles can is apt indeed and in no way dangerous – and that's enough for mathematics. But to claim that the Sun is in reality the centre of the universe, revolving only in itself without crossing from east to west, and that the Earth is in the third heaven travelling at full speed around the Sun – that is very dangerous, not only as an irritant to the scholastic philosophers and theologians but also because it undermines Holy Faith by imputing error to Sacred Scripture.[34]

---

32 Galileo Galilei, *Opere*, ed. Antonio Favaro in 20 volumes (Florence: Edizione Nazionale, 1890–1909 [hereafter *OG*], vol. XII, pp. 171–2; and Galileo, *Scienza e religione: scritti copernicani*, ed. Massimo Bucciantini and Michele Camerota (Rome: Donzelli, 2009), pp. 157–9.

33 See A. Damanti, *Libertas philosophandi. Teologia e filosofia nella Lettera alla Granduchessa Cristina di Lorena di Galileo Galilei* (Rome: Edizioni di Storia e Letteratura, 2010), pp. 89–93, esp. pp. 89–90, n. 2, rejecting the interpretation put forward by U. Baldini, 'L'astronomia del cardinale', in *Legem impone subactis. Studi su filosofia e scienza dei gesuiti in Italia 1540–1632* (Rome: Bulzoni, 1992), p. 330, n. 18, who connects 'io ho sempre creduto' and 'assolutamente'. See, in the same perspective, G. Galilei, *Scienza e religione. Scritti copernicani*, p. 157, n. 2. On the epistemological foresight attributed, anachronistically, to Bellarmino by many interpreters, see de Santillana, *Processo a Galileo*, p. 238.

34 *OG*, vol. XII, p. 171; *Scienza e religione*, pp. 157–8. See also, in the same direction, Federico Cesi's letter to Galileo (Acquasparta, 12 January 1615): 'Quant'all'opinione di Copernico, Bellarmino istesso, ch'è de' capi nelle congregatione di queste cose, m'ha detto che l'ha per heretica, e che il moto della terra, senza dubio alcuno, è contro la Scrittura' (Damanti, *Libertas philosophandi*, p. 65).

Supposition ... reality. Deferring to Bellarmine, Galileo accepted the first alternative. This was an imposition sorrowfully borne, as is clear from the letter he had written in March 1615 to the papal referendary Piero Dini: 'The attempt to show that Copernicus didn't truly believe in a mobile Earth will find no support, in my view, unless among those who haven't read him.'[35]

As for Osiander's preface, in a text written at the end of 1615 or the beginning of 1616, Galileo dismissed it as 'the vain product of the printer's shop', no substitute for 'the entire work of the author himself, the indubitable proof that Copernicus was convinced of the reality of a stationary Sun and a mobile Earth'.[36]

The warning issued by the Congregation of the Index on 15 May 1620 in prescribing an expurgated edition of *De revolutionibus* used terms other than Bellarmine's. Without a doubt, it went, 'this work is not argued hypothetically; it offers its assertions as certain truth. However, since it contains elements of the greatest public utility [Copernicus's calculations were used in the construction of the Gregorian calendar], we have decided unanimously that it may be published, on condition that the passages speaking of a mobile Earth assertively, not only as a hypothesis [*non ex hypothesi, sed asserendo*], have been corrected'.[37]

6. Thus, the discussions of Machiavelli and Copernicus that unfolded in Rome at this time invoked terms that were partly shared (*simpliciter* and *secundum quid*, or *ex suppositione*) and involved the same individuals: above all, Father Riccardi, the interlocutor and censor of Schoppe and Galileo, as well as Campanella, author of the anti-Machiavellian *Atheismus triumphatus* and the *Apologia di Galileo*. An obvious terminological convergence, we may say, fruit of the Aristotelian-Thomistic vocabulary employed by anyone who exercised the censor's power – or who, like Schoppe, endured it. But this general

---

35   *Scienza e religione*, p. 20 (and see the whole letter, pp. 17–32).
36   *Considerazioni circa l'opinione copernicana*, pp. 85–110, at pp. 101–2 (and see *OG*, vol. V, p. 363).
37   *OG*, vol. XIX, p. 400.

observation is insufficient. What resources did this language offer in the face of entirely new situations?

On 8 June 1624 Galileo wrote to his friend Federico Cesi, founder of the Lincei Academy in Rome, saying that he had had six meetings with Pope Urban VIII (Maffeo Barberini), who had received him benignly. Cardinal Zoller, before leaving for Germany, had informed the pope that all the heretics shared the view of Copernicus. The pope replied: 'The Holy Church has not and is not about to condemn it for heresy, only for temerity; and no one should fear that it could ever be proved to be necessarily true.' Yet another warning to Galileo, who communicated it to his friend without comment. The letter goes on to mention two other participants in the meeting:

Father Monster and Signor Schoppe, although far from being capable of absorbing the essentials of such astronomical speculations, nevertheless are firmly of the opinion that the matter isn't one of faith, or something calling for reference to Scripture. As for what is true or not true, Father Monster sides with neither Ptolemy nor Copernicus, but is happy, in his way, with the thought that angels move the heavenly bodies as they go, without difficulty or special complication, and that should be enough.[38]

Galileo's irony was justified. Father Riccardi knew little about astronomy, although it was said of him that he leaned 'very strongly' towards Tycho Brahe's system; but his opinion as a theologian was not of no account.[39] Some years later, in the face of mounting attacks on Galileo as a supporter of the Copernican theory, the Benedictine Benedetto Castelli, who was close to him, met with Riccardi to try to make out his attitude. On 26 February 1628 Castelli informed Galileo of the upshot of the conversation: 'Father Monster said that Your Lordship's

---

38   OG, vol. XIII, pp. 182–3. See also Johannes Faber's letter to Cesi, sent a few days earlier (p. 181).

39   Letter from Filippo Magalotti to Mario Guiducci, 4 September 1632 (*OG*, vol. XIV, p. 381).

opinions are not in any way contrary to Faith, being *simply philosophical*.'[40]

So, the Aristotelian-Thomistic distinction between *simpliciter* and *secundum quid* lent itself, at least in theory, to unscrupulous uses, turned to unconventional ends: re-evaluating Machiavelli, protecting Bible interpretation from the novelties of astronomy. In both cases, Schoppe and Riccardi, from opposite beginnings, had found themselves in agreement. With Galileo, things went differently.[41]

7. In the approach to the publication of the *Dialogo sopra i due massimi sistemi del mondo, tolemaico e copernicano*, relations between Galileo and Riccardi – who in the meantime had become Master of the Holy Apostolic Palace – became closer. On 7 March 1631 Galileo informed Andrea Cioli, the secretary to Cristina di Lorena, Grand Duchess of Tuscany, that he had sent Riccardi, at his request, 'the preface and conclusion of the book, where higher authorities will be able to add, remove and enter protests as they see fit, not refraining from calling these thoughts of mine chimeras, dreams, paralogisms and vain fantasies, entrusting and submitting the whole thing to the absolute wisdom and inerrant teaching of the higher sciences etc'.[42]

An emphatic declaration, which Father Riccardi acknowledged, returning to Galileo on 19 July the text of what would become the preface to the *Dialogo*, reviewed by Friar Giacinto Stefani for the Holy Office, together with a suggestion for the conclusion.[43] The text, which was then published with minimum

---

40   *OG*, vol. XIII, p. 393 (my emphasis).

41   See Richard J. Blackwell, *Galileo, Bellarmine and the Bible* (Notre Dame, IN: Notre Dame Press, 1991) (the chapter on 'Reflections on Truth in Science and in Religion').

42   *OG*, vol. XIV, p. 216.

43   *OG*, vol. XIX, p. 330. Libero Sosio comments: 'Today it is impossible to establish what is Galileo's and what is owed to Riccardi. In any case it is noteworthy that a good deal of the accompanying argumentation had already been set out in a letter to Francesco Ingoli in 1624, a general sketch of the *Two Great Systems*

revision and a double imprimatur (Florentine and Roman), gave immediate prominence to the term 'hypothesis': a tactical move, which may not have been exclusively Riccardi's work.[44] 'As for the Copernican hypothesis', Galileo had already written in *Il Saggiatore*, 'when through the benefit of paramount wisdom we Catholics are saved from error and our blindness is illuminated . . .'[45] The letter to Francesco Ingoli, revised by Galileo in 1624 and then circulated in manuscript, likewise begins by taking its distance from 'the Copernican hypothesis', even though this preliminary concession is followed by the most stringent criticism of the Ptolemaic theory.[46] Equally, the opening notice to 'the judicious reader' of the *Dialogo* advises,

To this end, I take here the Copernican side, following a purely mathematical hypothesis, seeking by every possible artifice to

anticipating and prefiguring the principal theses of the book': Galileo Galilei, *Dialogo*, ed. Libero Sosio (Turin: Einaudi, 1970), p. 7 n. 1. See also E. Festa, *Galileo. La lotta per la scienza* (Rome: Laterza, 2007), pp. 264–71.

44 On the ambiguity of the term 'hypothesis' in this context, see Guido Morpurgo-Tagliabue, *I processi di Galileo e l'epistemologia* (Milan: Edizioni di Comunità, 1963), p. 118ff (for Father Riccardi) and throughout, for useful reflections even if they are vitiated by anachronism.

45 Galileo Galilei, *Il Saggiatore*, p. 39. Thus, Mauro Pesce's rather hasty statement must be corrected: 'the term "hypothesis", referred to the Copernican theory, does not seem to be Galileian' ('Una nuova versione della lettera di G. Galilei a Benedetto Castelli', in *Nouvelles de la République des Lettres* 2 [1991] pp. 89–122, esp. pp. 101, 120, n. 112). But dissimulation was part of Galileo's history. On the opposite side, it must be rejected, as anachronistic, the interpretation put forward by Morpurgo-Tagliabue: 'Here [in the *Dialogue*] mathematical hypothesis means rational hypothesis, i.e. scientific hypothesis: reality. Scientific reality, experimental and rational, as opposed to absolute and metaphysical reality' (*I processi di Galileo*, p. 82). This interpretation is justified in the following terms: 'Although we would like to avoid all kind of anachronism, we must point out that we are confronted with an epistemological problem which has been articulated by contemporary epistemology' (a quote from Max Planck follows) (ibid., p. 100).

46 OG, vol. VI, pp. 501–61, esp. pp. 510–11.

establish its superiority, not *absolutely* in relation to the affirmation of a stationary Earth but *according to the way in which* it is defended by those who are Peripatetics only in name.[47]

'Seeking by every possible artifice ...' – it is the author who speaks here, but the context has been framed by Father Riccardi. The distinction between 'absolutely' (*simpliciter*) and 'according to the way in which' (*secundum quid*) seems to echo that between *ex suppositione* and 'absolutely', formulated by Bellarmine in connection with heliocentrism. But in the notice to the 'judicious reader', the distinction, first Aristotelian, then Thomistic, between *simpliciter* and *secundum quid* comes to refer to the relation between the Copernicans and the Ptolemaians. The superiority of the first, proposed hypothetically and via the artifice of the dialogue form, is a superiority *secundum quid*: a move in which it is tempting to see the fruit of a compromise between Galileo and his censor. Kaspar Schoppe made use of the distinction to defend Machiavelli, first in an apologia that went unpublished, then in the *Paedia politices*, which Riccardi spoke of having 'read and reread' before conceding his imprimatur. In the notice to the judicious reader, the situation is turned upside down: the Ptolemaic system is discredited, yes, but *secundum quid*. Here again is Schoppe's strategy in the *Paedia*. Whether on Riccardi's advice or at his dictation, Galileo pursued it by introducing a work of a quite different genre.

8. The *Dialogo* closes by reaffirming the inscrutable power and wisdom of God, which puts an end to the confrontation between the two astronomical systems.[48] This conclusion, suggested by Pope Urban VIII via Father Riccardi, is spoken by a bookish follower of Aristotle called Simplicio.[49] A huge error,

---

47 *Dialogo*, pp. 8–9; my emphasis.
48 See Jules Speller, *Galileo's Inquisition Trial Revisited* (Frankfurt: Peter Lang, 2008), p. 375ff.
49 *Dialogo*, p. 548.

or, as we would say today, a parapraxis revealing the uncon-
scious aggression of someone who had been constrained to
hide his own ideas. The pope was enraged. He felt he had been
tricked, as Riccardi himself had been tricked, he said.[50] But the
friar felt endangered: evidently, the control he had exercised
over the publication of the *Dialogo*, to which he had granted
his imprimatur, was deemed to have been insufficient. Riccardi's
disquiet emerges in a letter from Francesco Niccolini, the
Tuscan diplomat and a friend of Galileo, to Andrea Cioli, sent
on 11 September 1632.[51] In an exchange with Niccolini, Father
Monster had alternated between lies and threats. On the one
hand, he claimed to have called for the Jesuit Melchior Inchofer
to be included in the special commission charged with
pronouncing on the *Dialogo*, assuring Niccolini that he acted
in an impartial spirit (when the reality was that Melchior was
very hostile to the Copernican view). On the other hand,
Riccardi, with the usual confidence and secrecy, confided to
Niccolini (whose wife was a relation) that 'the records of the
Holy Office have it that Galileo has held this opinion for
around 12 years and disseminated it in Florence, and, being
summoned to Rome on this account, he was forbidden by
Cardinal Bellarmine, in the name of the Pope and the Holy
Office, to hold this opinion, and that alone was enough to ruin
him for ever'.[52]

9. The compromising document found in the records of the Holy
Office was identified as the so-called Seghizzi protocol.[53] In the
file of the proceedings against Galileo this occupies two sheets,
both only half full, and containing not one but two documents

---

50 Letter from Filippo Magalotti to Mario Guiducci, 4 September
1632 (*OG*, vol. XIV, pp. 379–82).

51 See de Santillana, *Processo a Galileo*, pp. 416–18. Annibale
Fantoli, *Galileo per il copernicanesimo e per la Chiesa*, 2nd edn revised and corrected (Vatican City: Libreria Editrice Vaticana, 1997), pp.
431–2 n. 6, speaks of a 'double game'; likewise *Documenti*, p. clxv.

52 *OG*, vol. XIV, p. 389.

53 The spelling varies: Seghizzi, Segizzi, Seghezzi.

dated, respectively, 25 and 26 February 1616.[54] In the first, Cardinal Mellini reported to the reverend fathers of the Holy Office and to the commissary, Michelangelo Seghizzi from Lodi, that, in accordance with papal disposition, Cardinal Bellarmine would have summoned Galileo Galilei into his presence to admonish him to abandon the Copernican view. 'If he refuses to obey, the father commissary will, in the presence of a notary and witnesses, establish a protocol requiring him to abstain entirely [omnino] from teaching, defending or discussing that doctrine; if he disobeys, he will go to prison.'[55] In the second document, it is stated that Galileo has been summoned to Bellarmine's palace by the commissary, who has announced, 'with immediate effect' (successive et incontinenti) and on pain of prosecution by the Holy Office, the prohibition of 'espousing, teaching or defending, in whatever form [quovis modo], spoken or written', the thesis that the sun is the centre of the universe and that Earth moves. Galileo has consented to this protocol and promises to obey it.[56]

The relationship between Mellini's report and the Seghizzi protocol is unclear. We learn from the minutes of the meeting of the Congregation for the Holy Office, held on 3 March 1616, that Bellarmine had admonished Galileo to abandon the Copernican view, and he, Galileo, had consented (acquievit).[57] But how then to explain the summons of 26 February, and the protocol communicated to Galileo by Commissary Seghizzi? And why didn't Bellarmine say anything about the protocol at the meeting of 3 March? In the face of these and other difficulties, various doubts have been expressed about 'the Seghizzi protocol'.[58] On the one hand, it is maintained that the protocol had no legal standing, since it lacked the signatures of Bellarmine,

54 Documenti, p. clxvii and n. 1, pp. 45–6. (Archivio Segreto Vaticano, Misc., Arm. X 204, modern numbering: cc. 43v–44r).

55 Documenti, n. 21, p. 45.

56 Ibid., n. 21, pp. 45–6.

57 Ibid., n. 124, p. 177.

58 The bibliography on the matter is vast. For a partial recapitulation, see Maurice A. Finocchiaro, Retrying Galileo, 1633–1992 (Berkeley University of California Press, 2007), pp. 241–58.

Seghizzi, the notary who drew up the document and the witnesses (whose names were listed).[59] On the other hand, there is the hypothesis that the protocol is a forgery. Many scholars, foremost among them Giorgio de Santillana, have insisted on both points.[60] Still, they remain distinct.

With regard to the first point, it has been objected that the protocol is a digest (*imbreviatura*), a legal document not requiring the signatures of witnesses or a notary – although Commissary Seghizzi's presence, in this context, is anomalous.[61] Discussion of the second point has been more intricate, beginning in the mid-nineteenth century and continuing, livelier than ever, to the present day.[62] The stakes could hardly be higher: in the trial of 1633 the Seghizzi protocol had a decisive importance.[63] In the opening session, responding to the judges who had asked him to describe his coming to Rome in 1616, Galileo produced a copy, included in

---

59   Fantoli, *Galileo per il copernicanesimo e per la Chiesa*, pp. 208–9.

60   See *Processo a Galileo,* chapters 8 ('The Audience with Bellarmine') and 16 ('The Problem of the Fake Protocol').

61   Francesco Beretta, 'Le procès de Galilée et les archives du Saint-Office. Aspects judiciaires et théologiques d'une condamnation célèbre', *Revue des Sciences philosophiques et théologiques* 83/3 (1999), pp. 447, 476–7.

62   For a summary see S. Pagano, 'Il precetto del cardinale Bellarmino a Galileo: un "falso"? Con una parentesi sul radio, Madame Curie e i documenti galileiani', *Galilaeana* 8 (2010), pp. 143–203, rejects the hypothesis of a forgery. The essay by Scartazzini, mentioned on p. 153, n. 51, and hastily dismissed, includes five sections, rather than one: G.A. Scartazzini, 'Il processo di Galileo Galilei e la moderna critica tedesca', in *Rivista Europea* 8/4 (1877), pp. 829–61; 9/5, (1878), pp. 1–15, 221–49; 6, (1878) pp. 401–23; 10 (1878), pp. 417–53.

63   This is denied by Annibale Fantoli ('The Disputed Injunction and Its Role in Galileo's Trial', in *The Church and Galileo,* ed. Ernan McMullin [Notre Dame, IN: Notre Dame Press, 2005] pp. 117–49), who rejects the hypothesis of a fabrication and upholds the legality of the Seghizzi protocol – and therefore that of the trial. Reaching the same conclusions with different arguments is Thomas F. Mayer, *The Roman Inquisition: Trying Galileo* (Philadelphia: University of Pennsylvania Press, 2015), pp. 53–120.

the record of the trial, of an autograph document given to him by Bellarmine.[64] Here was evidence refuting the prevailing belief that Galileo had been constrained to recant and confirming that he had agreed to espouse Copernican theory in a strictly hypothetical vein. To this the judges responded by reminding Galileo that the protocol ordered him not to 'espouse, teach or defend' the Copernican view in any form (*quovis modo*). Galileo replied:

I don't remember that this protocol was conveyed to me by anyone other than Lord Cardinal Bellarmine in spoken form, and I do remember that the undertaking was that I could not maintain or defend [the Copernican view]. It may be that teaching [*docere*] was included too. I don't remember either that that particular item, *quovis modo*, was there, but it may have been – I haven't reflected on that, or I've formed another recollection, since a few months later, on 26 May, I received from the Lord Cardinal Bellarmine the document I have exhibited, forbidding me to hold or defend the view in question. I have no recollection of the two particulars that have now been pointed out to me in that protocol, namely the ban on teaching and the stipulation *quovis modo*, because, I believe, they were not made clear in the statement I relied upon and kept for my recollection.[65]

It didn't escape Galileo that the absent 'particular' *quovis modo* in the autograph document received from Bellarmine opened the way to the incrimination of the *Dialogo*. In the concluding sentence of the trial, the Seghizzi protocol was quoted to the letter:

And in execution of this Decree on the following day in the Palace, in the presence of the said Most Eminent Cardinal

---

64   *Documenti*, n. 41, p. 76 (copy) and n. 43, pp. 78–9 (autograph).

65   *Documenti*, deposition 12 April 1633, pp. 66–72, esp. 69–70. The verb *docere*, absent from the note of 'undertaking' made available by Bellarmine, appears in both the Mellini report and (along with *quovis modo*) the Seghizzi protocol (*Documenti*, nn. 20 and 21, pp. 45–6).

Bellarmine, the same Lord Cardinal who benignly advised and admonished you, the then father commissary of the Holy Office, with a notary and witnesses, summoned you to renounce this false [Copernican] opinion altogether, in future not holding or defending or teaching it, *in whatever form*, in speech or in writing, and having promised to obey, you are released.[66]

10. The Seghizzi protocol was first invoked in a memorandum drafted at the request of Urban VIII and concerning the printing of Galileo's book in Florence – therefore after 21 February 1632.[67] The memorandum reconstructed in great detail the contact between Father Riccardi and Galileo before the publication of the *Dialogo*; there followed a letter from Riccardi to the Florentine inquisitor (24 May 1631) and the latter's response (31 May), plus a nearly final version of the notice 'To the judicious reader' accompanied by a second letter from Riccardi to the inquisitor, dated 19 July 1631. The dossier has been attributed, quite plausibly, to Riccardi.[68]

'It is claimed', went the memorandum, that Galileo 'has fraudulently covered up a protocol issued to him by the Holy Office in 1616 in these terms' (there followed the text of the Seghizzi protocol, cited again in the closing summary under the title 'In facto'). 'It is necessary now to decide how to proceed against the person as well as the book already published.'[69] The sentence addressing the offender conceded benignly that his 'concealment of the protocol at the time of his requesting permission to give the book [the *Dialogo*] to the printer' was owing to a lapse of memory, 'since in the document [received from Bellarmine] the two particulars, *docere* and *quovis modo*, were not mentioned'.[70]

---

66 Ibid., n. 114, pp. 161–2 (my emphasis).

67 Ibid., n. 5, pp. 49–57.

68 According to Jules Speller, the summary can be attributed to Riccardi, while the text preceding it emerged from the commission of inquiry: 'Deception at the Origin of Galileo's Trial', *Revue d'histoire ecclésiastique* 109/3–4 (2014), pp. 698–727.

69 *Documenti*, n. 5, p. 50.

70 Ibid., n. 114, p. 163.

11. There is no need to insist on the importance of the Seghizzi protocol in the Galileo trial. But the hypothesis put forward by some scholars that the protocol was a fabrication dating from 1632 has been undermined by palaeographical evidence identifying the hand as that of the notary who recorded the decrees of the Holy Office in 1616: Andrea Pettini da Forlì, who died in 1624.[71] Was it then a forgery concocted in 1616? The case remains open. Certainly, the author would not have been Father Riccardi, who, however, very ably exploited the protocol to extricate himself from the tangle he had got into in granting the *Dialogo* an imprimatur.

12. Galileo was condemned and obliged to recant; Machiavelli's writings remained on the Index. In both cases, the distinction between *simpliciter* and *secundum quid*, which Riccardi had embraced as his own, be it only for the occasion, proved inadequate to its purpose. With hindsight, the juxtaposition may seem affected: the Index of Forbidden Books was abolished in 1966, and the condemnation of Galileo remains for the Catholic Church, today more than ever, an open wound. Nevertheless the analogy so proposed between two distinctions – that between politics and morality, at the heart of the *Paedia politices*, and that between theology and science, in the *Lettera a Cristina di Lorena* – is worth further reflection.[72]

---

71 See Beretta, p. 477; Vittorio Frajese, *Il processo a Galileo Galilei* (Brescia: Morcelliana, 2010), p. 57ff; appendix edited by E. Condello, pp. 103–6. On the basis of a detailed analysis, Stefano Zamponi (whom I thank) concluded that the transcription of the Holy Office Congregation meeting held on 3 March 1616, written by notary Andrea Pettini, and the Seghizzi protocol, have been executed by the same hand.

72 D'Addio, p. 174. In the same study (pp. 511–12), D'Addio compares Schoppe's unpublished treatise *De zeli natura et usu* (1622) with Galileo's *Lettera a Cristina di Lorena* – which Father Riccardi judged superior to the *Dialogo*: see Filippo Magalotti's letter to Mario Guiducci, 4 September 1632, in *OG*, vol. XIV, pp. 380–2. On the circulation of the *Lettera* before its publication see Damanti, *Libertas philosophandi*; G. Galilei, *Lettera a Cristina di Lorena*, critical edition by O. Besomi, with the help of D. Besomi (Rome-Padua: Antenore, 2012), pp. 15–21.

Schoppe and Galileo knew one another and had a friend in common: Johannes Faber, the secretary of the Lincei Academy. But the supposition that Schoppe could have read the *Lettera* prior to its publication, thanks to Faber, would be gratuitous, and pointless at that. It will be more useful to compare the two texts, so revealing the gulf between the Aristotelianism of the *Paedia* and Galileo's position.

The *Lettera*, which was written in 1615 but published only in 1636, reiterates at many points, and often word for word, Galileo's letter to Benedetto Castelli, from December 1613.[73] Both make use of the metaphor, medieval in origin, of the two books, Holy Scripture and the Book of Nature.[74] They are 'equal as expressions of the divine Word ... one as it is dictated by the Holy Spirit, and the other as the strictest operation of God's laws'. But there is a substantial difference: 'In the Scriptures, in order to facilitate understanding of the universe, many things are said that differ in appearance and literal meaning from absolute truth.' The scriptures speak a human language adapted to the rough condition of the people they are addressing.[75] So often, in many passages in scripture, it is necessary to depart from a literal interpretation, which would imply 'grave heresies and blasphemies too', such as when God is said to have feet, hands, eyes or human feelings such as anger and hatred. In the case of nature, this difficulty doesn't arise, nature being 'inexorable, immutable and not caring whether her obscure laws and modes of operation are explained in terms that men can understand: therefore she would never transgress the terms of the

---

73 OG, vol. V, pp. 279–88, and reproduced in full in Galileo's *Scienza e religione*, pp. 3–16.

74 See E. R. Curtius, *European Literature and the Latin Middle Ages*, tr. W. R. Trask (London: Routledge & Kegan Paul, 1979).

75 OG, vol. V, pp. 282–3. On the idea of *accommodatio* or adaptation, see Amos Funkenstein, *Theology and the Scientific Imagination* (Princeton: Princeton University Press, 1986), p. 213ff, and also Stephen D. Benin, *The Footprints of God: Divine Accommodation in Jewish and Christian Thought* (Albany: State University of New York Press, 1993).

laws imposed on her'.[76] Some years later, Galileo restated his thesis concerning the asymmetry of scripture and nature in a famous page of *Il Saggiatore*, pre-announced by the two female figures who flanked its frontispiece, Natural Philosophy and Mathematics (the latter wearing a crown, as befits a queen):

> Philosophy is written in this great book – I mean the Universe – that stands ever open to our eyes but cannot be understood if first we do not learn the language, recognize the characters, in which it is written. That language is mathematics, and its characters are triangles, circles and other geometrical figures, without which it is humanly impossible to understand any of it; without this we wander vainly in a dark labyrinth.[77]

Nature does not speak the language of men, reveal herself to them, or concern herself with them: she is 'inexorable and immutable'. Whenever there appears a divergence between scripture and nature, the latter should prevail. Here Galileo effectively took a distance from the Jesuit Benito Pereyra, who had been cited as an authority in the *Lettera a Cristina di Lorena*. A correct reading of scripture cannot 'contradict the reasonings and experiments of honest human inquiry', he had declared in his commentary on Genesis.[78] But Galileo's letter

---

76 *OG*, vol. V, pp. 282–3; with minimal variations, Galilei, *Lettera a Cristina di Lorena*, ed. Besomi, p. 49. See G. Stabile, 'Lo statuto di "inesorabile" in Galileo Galilei', in *Lexiques et glossaires philosophiques de la Renaissance*, ed. J. Hamesse and M. Fattori (Louvain-La-Neuve: FIDEM, 2003), pp. 269–85; M. Torrini, 'La natura della nuova scienza', *Nuncius* 17 (2002), pp. 409–22; Ph. Hamou, "La nature est inexorable". Pour une reconsidération de la contribution de Galilée au problème de la connaissance', *Galilaeana* 5 (2008), pp. 149–77.

77 *Il Saggiatore*, p. 25 [ed. Sosio, p. 38]. On the front-page see Damanti, *Libertas philosophandi*, pp. 321–5, who corrects P. Redondi, 'Teologia ed epistemologia nella rivoluzione scientifica', *Belfagor* 45/6 (1990), pp. 613–36; but see also *Il Saggiatore*, critical ed. O. Besomi and M. Helbing (Rome: Antenore, 2005), pp. 437–40.

78 Pereyra, *Prior tomus commentariorum et disputationum in Genesim*, Rome 1589, pp. 10ff. See F. Motta's commentary in Galilei,

was proposing a very clear hierarchy within the domain of human inquiry:

> I entreat those wise and prudent Fathers to consider with great care the difference that exists between doctrines subject to opinion and those subject to proof. Considering the force exerted by necessary inferences, they may ascertain that it is not in the power of the professors of demonstrative sciences to change their opinions at will and apply themselves first to one side and then to the other. There is a great difference between commanding a mathematician, or a philosopher, and influencing a lawyer or a merchant, for demonstrated conclusions about things in nature or in the heavens cannot be changed with the same facility as opinions about what is or is not lawful in a contract, bargain, or bill of exchange.[79]

13. The political world is different from that of morals, Schoppe maintained, even if moral values are not affected by it: tyranny is evil in and of itself (*quae secundum se mala est*).[80] Galileo too inhabited a world of compromise and adaptation: that of court life and the tribunals of the Inquisition.[81] But beyond that world, for Galileo, was the order of 'inexorable and immutable' nature, which, as he wrote to Elia Diodati on 15 January 1633, 'has

---

Lettera a Cristina di Lorena, pp. 102–4, n. 45, and Damanti, *Libertas philosophandi*, cit., pp. 203–4, 211–23, 328; on p. 221 he rejects (perhaps too drastically) the hypothesis of Pereyra having been read by Galileo. M. Pesce, 'Le redazioni originali della lettera "copernicana" di G. Galilei a B. Castelli', *Filologia e Critica* 17/3 (September–December 1992), pp. 394–417, identified echoes of Pereyra's commentary in the letter to Castelli.

79 *Lettera a Cristina di Lorena*, p. 71. On the averroistic roots of this distinction see B. Nardi, 'Riflessioni sul processo di Galileo in occasione del IV centenario della sua nascita', *De homine* 13–14 (1965), pp. 111–42. Helpful remarks on this passage in Damanti, *Libertas philosophandi*, pp. 288–93.

80 Schoppe, *Paedia politices*, p. 36.

81 See Mario Biagioli, *Galileo, Courtier: The Practice of Science in the Culture of Absolutism* (Chicago: University of Chicago Press, 1993).

always maintained, and continues to maintain her style through the movements, patterns and dispositions in every part of the universe'.[82] The possibility of miracles (a theme never mentioned in this context, whether by Galileo or by the ecclesiastical authorities), was by definition excluded. The world of nature does not admit exceptions; the trope of 'nevertheless' is unknown to it. This is a world that human beings are able to know but which neither addresses them nor cares about them.

It was Galileo and the worlds he had discovered that Pascal had in mind when he wrote, 'The eternal silence of these infinite spaces scares me.' (Le silence éternel de ces espaces infinis m'éffraie.)[83]

Postscript

Translating Pascal's fragment into Italian, Leopardi's verb ('*mi spaura*') came to me spontaneously. Then, gradually, I became aware of the problems bound up with this association. 'It has been said', Giovanni Macchia observes, 'that *L'Infinito* retains visible traces of a thought of Pascal's. But not the famous "pensée" ("le silence éternel des ces espaces infinis m'effraie"), which was published for the first time in Faugère's edition (1844). We should speak not of influences from reading, but suggestions, similarities between the thinker and the poet that ripple on the same themes.'[84] We are dealing with truly

---

82 *OG*, vol. XV, pp. 24–5. See S. Garcia, *Élie Diodati et Galilée. Naissance d'un réseau scientifique dans l'Europe du XVIIe siècle*, pref. by I. Pantin (Florence: Olschki, 2004). See also Galileo's letter to Francesco Ingoli: 'ma la natura, Signor mio, si burla delle costituzioni e decreti de i principi, degl'imperatori e de i monarchi, a richiesta de' quali ella non muterebbe un iota delle leggi e statuti suoi' (*OG*, vol. VI p. 538).

83 Blaise Pascal, *Pensées*, ed. Michel Le Guern (Paris: Gallimard, 1977), fr. 187 (Brunschvicg fr. 206), p. 161. The fragment is quoted (with a minimal variation: *des espaces*) by de Santillana, *Processo a Galileo*, p. 45.

84 Giovanni Macchia, 'Leopardi e il viaggiatore immobile' (1980),

astonishing similarities, given that all the words from Pascal's fragment appear in *L'Infinito*: 'silenzio', 'eterno', 'spazi', 'infinito', 'spaura'. But Leopardi projects the infinite beyond the hedge.

A knowledge of the *Pensées* on Leopardi's part is proved by a passage from *Zibaldone*, written two years after *L'Infinito* (12 February 1821): 'Le présent n'est jamais notre but; le passé et le présent sont nos moyens; le seul avenir est notre objet: ainsi nous ne vivons pas, mais nous espérons de vivre, says Pascal' (The present is never our end. The past and the present are our means, the future alone our end. Thus we do not live, but hope to live).[85]

Pascal's verb *effrayer* reappears spontaneously in two French translations of *L'Infinito*, one in prose by Alphonse Aulard (1880) and one in verse by René Char and Franca Roux (1966):

---

in *Saggi italiani* (Milan: Mondadori, 1983), pp. 257–62, esp. p. 259. And see Blaise Pascal, *Pensées fragments et lettres publiés ... pour la première fois conformément aux manuscrits originaux en grande partie inédits*, ed. Prosper Faugère, 2 vols (Paris: Andrieux, 1844), esp. vol. 1, p. 224, fr. 152.

85 Cf. Giacomo Leopardi, *Zibaldone di pensieri*, critical edn annotated by Giuseppe Pacella (Milan: Garzanti, 1991, vol. I, p. 428, notes 648–9, and vol. III, p. 603: the passage is taken from *Pensées de M. Pascal sur la religion* (Amsterdam: Henri Wetstein, 1699) (a copy of this edition is present in Leopardi's library). See, with some variations, Pascal, *Pensées*, ed. Le Guern, fr. 42, pp. 81–82; *Pensées*, tr. Krailsheimer, fr. 47, p. 43. 'Initially', observes Pacella, 'Leopardi remembered only part of the passage (from "ainsi" to "vivre"), attributing it to Montaigne. Subsequently, he completed the quotation and rightly corrected "Montaigne" to "Pascal"' (Leopardi, *Zibaldone*, vol. III, p. 603). Cf. also Giuseppe Pacella, 'Elenchi di letture leopardiane', *Giornale storico della letteratura italiana* 143 (1966), p. 573: 'Let[tres] provinciales'. In a quite different direction, see Marco Arnaudo, 'Su una possibile fonte secentesca dell'*Infinito* di Leopardi', *Italica* 90/4 Winter 2013), pp. 650–4, who refers to Francesco de Lemene, *Dio. Sonetti, ed hinni consagrati al Vicedio Innocenzo Undecimo Pontefice Ottimo Massimo* (Venice: Combi & La Noue, 1685), p. 37: 'Riempie il tutto, e se fingendo io penso, / Oltre al confin de' vasti spazi, e veri, / Deserti imaginati, e spazi novi', and so forth.

Mais, m'asseyant et regardant, au-delà de la haie j'imagine d'interminables espaces, des silences surhumains, un profond repos où peu s'en faut que le coeur ne *s'effraie*. [But, sitting and gazing, beyond the hedge I imagine endless spaces, superhuman silence, a profound calm where my heart is almost terrified.][86]

Mais quand je m'assieds pour la regarder, / Par ma pensée se créent au-delà d'elle / D'interminables espaces, des silences surhumaines, / Une paix très profonde; où peu s'en faut / Que mon coeur ne *s'effraie*.[87]

---

86 Giacomo Leopardi, *Poésies et oeuvres morales … première traduction complète précédé d'un essai sur Leopardi par F.A. Aulard*, 3 vols (Paris: Alphonse Lemerre, 1880), vol. 1, p. 270.

87 Maria Spiridopoulou, 'Translation: Theory and Praxis. Deconstruction and Reconstruction in Giacomo Leopardi', in *Beyond Deconstruction: From Hermeneutics to Reconstruction*, ed. Alberto Martinengo (Berlin: De Gruyter, 2012), pp. 161–78, esp. p. 174.

8

Virtù, Justice, Force: On Machiavelli and Some of His Readers

1. Any analysis of Machiavelli's language which, as often occurs, focuses exclusively on *virtù* and *fortuna* is manifestly insufficient.[1] But both terms do require reflection. Here we shall discuss *virtù*, endeavouring not to repeat things that can be taken for granted.[2]

We may begin with a very well-known passage from Jacob Burckhardt's *The Civilization of the Renaissance in Italy*: 'Good and evil lie strangely mixed together in the Italian states of the fifteenth century. The personality of the ruler is so highly developed, often of such deep significance, and so characteristic of the conditions and needs of the time, that to form an adequate moral judgement on it is not an easy task.' A note followed: 'This compound of force and intellect [*Kraft und Talent*] was called by Machiavelli *virtù*, and is quite compatible with *scelleratezza* (wickedness) – for example, *Discorsi* I, 10 speaking of Septimius Severus.'[3]

---

1 A different version of this essay was presented at the European University Institute on 13 June 2014. I am most grateful to Maria Luisa Catoni and Martin Rueff for their comments.

2 From a very different standpoint, see Quentin Skinner, 'Machiavelli on Misunderstanding Princely *Virtù*', in *From Humanism to Hobbes: Studies in Rhetoric and Politics* (Cambridge: Cambridge University Press, 2018), pp. 45–62 (which I read only after having written these pages).

3 Jacob Burckhardt, *The Civilization of the Renaissance in Italy*, tr. S. G. C. Middlemore and introd. Peter Burke (London: Penguin,

This passage occurs in the first chapter of Burckhardt's *The Civilization of the Renaissance in Italy*, entitled 'The State as a Work of Art' – a famous, frequently misunderstood title. Burckhardt regarded the civilization of the Renaissance in Italy as the dawn of modernity: a phenomenon laden with contradictions.[4] Among them was the intricate relationship between *virtù* and morality illustrated by the passage in the *Discourses*, book I, chapter 10.

Most Roman emperors, writes Machiavelli, suffered a violent death. Among the exceptions was Septimius Severus: 'e se tra quelli che morirono ordinariamente ve ne fu alcuno scelerato, come Severo, nacque da una sua grandissima fortuna e virtù, le quali due cose pochi uomini accompagnano' (*Discorsi*, I, 10).[5]

In Leslie J. Walker's English translation the passage reads thus: 'While, if amongst those who died ordinary deaths, there was a wicked man, like Severus, it must be put down to his great good luck and to his "virtue", two things of which few men enjoy both.'[6]

Father Walker, a Jesuit, put 'virtue' in quotation marks, since (as he explained in a footnote) in this passage *virtù* means 'efficacy' – a notion devoid of moral connotations and therefore (as

---

1990), pp. 28, 354 n. 6. The passage is mentioned (mixing up main text and note) by L. A. Burd, in his edition of *The Prince* (Oxford: Clarendon Press, 1891), p. 178.

4 Burckhardt, *The Civilization of the Renaissance*, p. 289: 'If therefore egotism in its wider as well as narrower sense is the root and fountain of all evil, the more highly developed Italian was for this reason more inclined to wickedness than the members of other nations at that time. But this individual development did not come upon him through any fault of his own, but rather through an historical necessity'. Cf. an illuminating comment by Francis Haskell, *History and Its Images: Art and the Interpretation of the Past* (New Haven: Yale University Press, 1993), pp. 344–5.

5 Niccolò Machiavelli, *Discorsi sopra la prima Deca di Tito Livio*, ed. Corrado Vivanti (Turin: Einaudi 1983), pp. 62–3.

6 *The Discourses of Niccolò Machiavelli*, tr. L. J. Walker (New Haven: Yale University Press, 1950), vol. I, p. 238.

Burckhardt remarked) compatible with wickedness.[7] Hence, according to Walker, *virtù* in Machiavelli's sense is untranslatable into contemporary English (and possibly other contemporary languages as well) – although expressions like 'by virtue of' seem to prove the opposite.

2. The alleged singularity of Machiavelli's use of the term *virtù* vanishes, as another scholar – J. H. Hexter – argues, when it is considered in a broader temporal and spatial perspective: 'Machiavelli does not use the term with any signification different from those of *virtus* in classical Latin. More than this, in the half century before Machiavelli wrote *Il Principe* the English used the cognate term "virtue," and the French used theirs, *vertu*, with every denotation *virtù* has in *Il Principe*.'[8]

In fact, the meanings of the word in Machiavelli are far from univocal. In a passage from chapter 8 of *The Prince* on which Hexter does not comment, they are explicitly counterposed. Machiavelli refers to Agathocles, king of Syracuse, as a man who 'always kept to a life of crime (*tenne sempre per i gradi della sua età vita scelerata*)': 'nevertheless his crimes were accompanied by such virtue of spirit and body (*nondimanco accompagnò le sua sceleratezze con tanta virtù di animo e di corpo*)', and so forth.[9]

---

7   Ibid., vol. II, p. 30.

8   J. H. Hexter, 'The Predatory and the Utopian Vision: Machiavelli and More. The Loom of Language and the Fabric of Imperatives: The Case of *Il Principe* and *Utopia*,' in *The Vision of Politics on the Eve of the Reformation: More, Machiavelli, and Seyssel* (New York: Basic Books, 1973), pp. 179–203, esp. pp. 188–92, 203 (on the occurrences of *virtù* in *The Prince*).

9   Niccolò Machiavelli, *The Prince*, ed. Quentin Skinner and Russell Price and tr. Russell Price (Cambridge: Cambridge University Press, 2016), p. 31; trans. modified. (*Il principe*, pp. 151, 154 [see above, ch. 5]). 'Non si può ancora chiamare virtù amazzare li sua cittadini, tradire li amici, essere sanza fede, sanza pietà, sanza relligione, li quali modi possono fare acquistare imperio, ma non gloria: perché, se si considerassi la virtù di Agatocle nello intrare e nello uscire de' pericoli e la grandezza dello animo suo nel sopportare e superare le cose averse, non si vede perché elli abbia a essere iudicato inferiore a

The word *nondimanco*, which surfaces repeatedly in *The Prince*, points (as we have said) to something that is at the very heart of Machiavelli's oeuvre: the tension between rules and exceptions, inspired by medieval casuistry. In the passage I just quoted, *nondimanco* highlights a tension between *virtù* as energy and *virtù* as moral quality. The second meaning seems to represent the rule to which Machiavelli ostensibly refers, in order to introduce the exception that corresponds to the actual reality. Likewise, in the *Discourses*, book I, chapter 26, we read that a politician must be able to practise 'methods [that] are exceedingly cruel, and are repugnant . . . not only to a Christian but to any human being (modi crudelissimi e nimici d'ogni vivere, non solamente Cristiano, ma umano)': 'nevertheless for the sort of man who is unwilling to take up this first course of behaving well, it is expedient, should he wish to hold what he has, to enter on the path of evil' (Nondimeno, colui che non vuole pigliare quella prima via del bene, quando si voglia mantenere conviene che entri in questo male). This is not lip service paid to conventional morality, but recognition of the tragic dimension of politics.[10]

According to Hexter, in *The Prince* the 'disjunction' between the two meanings of *virtù* 'is sharp and decisive; there is no continuity or overlay' between them.[11] But the first bibliographical reference in support of this claim – the entry *virtus* in

---

qualunque escellentissimo capitano: nondimanco, la sua efferata crudeltà e inumanità con infinite sceleratezze non consentono che sia in fra li escellentissimi òmini celebrato. Non si può adunque attribuire alla fortuna o alla virtù quello che sanza l'una e l'altra fu da lui conseguito.') Chapter 8 of *The Prince* is not mentioned in Alessandro Fontana's entry on 'virtù' in *Vocabulaire européen des philosophies. Dictionnaire des intraduisibles*, ed. Barbara Cassin (Paris: Seuil-Le Robert, 2004, pp. 1368–74). The entry suggests a unilateral, systematic image of Machiavelli, read through his 'true' posterity (Spinoza, Hegel, Nietzsche): see ibid., p. 1373.

10 *Discourses*, vol. I, p. 274 (trans. modified); *Discorsi*, p. 111. And see Adriano Sofri's observations in *Machiavelli, Tupac e la Principessa* (Palermo: Sellerio, 2014), pp. 55–8.

11 Hexter, *The Vision of Politics*, p. 190.

Forcellini's *Totius latinitatis lexicon* (published posthumously in 1771) – confronts us with a different, more intricate semantic history.

3. Forcellini's entry begins with a definition: *virtus*, like the Greek word ἀρετή, refers to 'any kind of human perfection, but especially spiritual perfection'. A series of allegedly equivalent words in several modern European languages follows: in English, for instance, 'virtue, force, power, efficacy'.[12] This is an odd list. Today no one would use 'force, power, efficacy' or their equivalents in other European languages, as synonymous with virtue as moral quality or 'spiritual perfection'. But the alleged synonymity has remote roots: it goes back to Cicero, the creator of Latin philosophical vocabulary. On the one hand, he pointed out the etymology of *virtus* from *vir*, male; on the other, he translated the Greek word ἀρετή, moral virtue, as *virtus*.[13] This choice – typical of a patriarchal society – had unforeseeable consequences.[14] For example, it obscured (without altogether erasing) an earlier meaning of *virtus* that emerges from a

---

12 Egidio Forcellini, *Totius latinitatis lexicon*, apud Joannem Manfrè, Patavii, 1771, vol. IV, p. 1010: 'et dicitur etiam de quacumque hominis perfectione, tam corporis quam animi, sed praecipue animi – *areté* (It. *virtù, forza, valore, capacità, proprietà*; Fr. *vertu, force, propriété, perfection*; Hisp. *virtud, capacidad, valor, propriedad*; Germ. *die Mannheit, Tüchtigkeit, Vorzüglichkeit, Tugend*; Angl. *virtue, force, power, efficacy).*'

13 See Marin O. Liscu, *Étude sur la langue de la philosophie morale chez Cicéron* (Paris: Les Belles Lettres, 1930), esp. pp. 152–61; Claudio Moreschini, 'Osservazioni sul lessico filosofico di Cicerone', *Annali della Scuola Normale Superiore di Pisa. Classe di Lettere e Filosofia*, 3rd ser., 9/1 (1979), pp. 99–178, esp. pp. 141–3; Carlos Lévy, 'Cicéron créateur du vocabulaire latin de la connaissance: essai de synthèse' in *La langue latine, langue de la philosophie, Actes du colloque de Rome (17–19 mai 1990)* (Rome: Publications de l'École française de Rome, 1992), pp. 91–106.

14 'But as is often the case with Cicero, the consequences of his actions far exceeded his intentions': Pierre Vesperini, *La 'philosophia' et ses pratiques d'Ennius à Cicéron* (Rome: Publications de l'École française de Rome, 2012), p. 490.

fragment of Ennius's lost tragedy, *Hectoris lytra* (The ransom of Hector): 'Melius est virtute ius; nam saepe virtutem mali / Nanciscuntur: ius atque aecum se a malis spernit procul' (Justice is better than *virtus*: for bad men often acquire *virtus*: justice and fairness stay far away from bad men).[15]

In his edition of Ennius's fragments (1585), Girolamo Colonna dismissed those lines as 'rather silly'; in 1707 another philologist, Frans Hessel, praised them, noting that in this passage *virtus* means 'physical force'.[16] This interpretation is unconvincing: in the aforementioned passage Ennius (who had three languages: Latin, Greek and Oscan) used *virtus* in a broad sense – not merely physical, although not moral – possibly as an equivalent of a Greek word.[17] This extra-moral meaning surfaces again in some of the evidence listed in Forcellini's *Lexicon*, contradicting his rigid equation of *virtus* with ἀρετή. A passage from Statius's poem the *Thebaid* (XI, 1–2) is eloquent enough: 'Postquam magnanimus furias virtutis iniquae / Consumpsit Capaneus' (When great-souled Capaneus had spent the fury of his unrighteous valour). If *virtus* can be *iniqua* (or opposed to

---

15 *Ennianae Poesis Reliquiae*, ed. J. Vahlen (Leipzig: in aedibus B. G. Teubneri, 1928 [1963]), fr. 188, p. 150; *The Tragedies of Ennius, The Fragments Edited with an Introduction and Commentary by H. D. Jocelyn* (Cambridge: Cambridge University Press, 1969), fr. 71, p. 101; trans. slightly modified. See Myles McDonnell, *Roman Manliness: Virtus and the Roman Republic* (Cambridge: Cambridge University Press, 2006), p. 6.

16 *Q. Ennii poetae vetustissimi fragmenta quae supersunt an Hieron. Columna conquisita disposita et explicata ... accurante Francisco Hesselio* (Amstelaedami: ex Officina Wetsteniana, 1717), p. 227: 'Verum oratio illa apud nostrum videtur personae haud satis intelligentis. Nam et qui justum se, atque aequum una in re praestat, in aliis esse iniquus potest. Et qui aliquo in genere praeclare agit, malus potest esse in caeteris: ut ea quidem ratione inmerito virtus aequo postponatur.' But see ibid., pp. 342–3: 'Aurea plane sententia [...] Virtute intelligit robur et vires corporis.' On Girolamo Colonna (1534–1586), see the entry (by N. Longo) in *Dizionario biografico degli Italiani*.

17 Émile Benveniste, *Il vocabolario delle istituzioni indoeuropee*, tr. Mariantonia Liborio (Turin: Einaudi, 1976), pp. 337–46 (on *kratos*) is, albeit indirectly, very helpful.

aequitas, as Ennius pointed out), it cannot be considered synonymous with 'spiritual perfection'.

4. Is it legitimate to regard this tension between moral and extra-moral dimensions as a prehistory of the notion of *virtù* in Machiavelli? Yes and no. Machiavelli may not have read Statius's passage on Capaneus, although a distinct echo of it resonates in the lines by Petrarch quoted at the very end of *The Prince*: 'Virtù contra furore / prenderà l'arme ...' (Virtue will take up arms against fury). Petrarch, a passionate reader of the *Thebaid*, reworked Statius's lines in a normalizing, Ciceronian direction: on the one hand, suppressing the adjective *iniquus* (unrighteous); on the other, opposing *virtus* to *furia* instead of connecting them. But Statius's fondness for oxymorons, which led him to couple *virtus* with negative adjectives (*horrida, crudelis, tristissima*), had struck another poet whom Machiavelli held dear: Dante.[18]

In the *Commedia* Statius is conspicuously present, first through echoes (implicit and explicit) of the *Thebaid*, and then as a character in *Purgatory*, canto XXV.[19] In Statius's description of the generation of human soul (ll. 32–108), the word *virtù* (and the related adverb *virtualmente*) occurs six times.[20] In his

---

18   Statius, *Thebaid*, V, 172 (*horrida*); VI, 737 (*crudelis*); VII, 51 (*tristissima*). For an echo of *Thebaid*, see Dante, *Inferno*, canto XXXII, ll. 130–2: 'non altrimenti Tidëo si rose / le tempie a Menalippo per disdegno, / che quei faceva il teschio e l'altre cose' ('not otherwise did Tydeus gnaw Menalippus' / temples in his rage, than this one did the skull and / the other things': *Inferno*, ed. and tr. Robert M. Durling (Oxford: Oxford University Press, 1996), p. 505). In the following canto (XXXIII, l. 150) Dante addresses Alberigo Manfredi with an oxymoron: 'E cortesia fu lui esser villano' ('it was / courtesy to treat him boorishly': *Inferno*, tr. Durling, p. 523).

19   Benvenutus de Imola, *Comentum super Dantis Aldigherij Comoediam*, ed. J. F. Lacaita (Florentiae: typis G. Barbera, 1887), vol. 1, p. 476ff, esp. pp. 479–80 (on *Inferno*, XIV): 'Modo in praesenti capitulo solum in speciali agitur de prima specie in persona Capanaei; unde vide quomodo bene autor scit aliena scripta trahere ad suum propositum.'

20   'Anima fatta la virtute attiva' (*Purgatorio* XXV, l. 52); 'la virtù ch'è dal cor del generante' (59); 'e spira / spirto novo, di vertù repleto'

comment on the *Commedia*, Benvenuto of Imola glossed these words with terms from the scholastic lexicon equivalent to *dynamis*: *potentia*, *potentialiter*. This choice confirms Benvenuto's hermeneutic acumen. Statius's speech in *Purgatory* is a mosaic of quotations from two works by Aristotle: William of Moerbeke's translation of *De generatione animalium* and Albertus Magnus's paraphrase of Aristotle's *De animalibus*.[21] Scholastic teaching had reinforced the ambivalent meaning of *virtus*, emphasizing the disturbing contiguity, and potential tension, between *areté* and *dynamis*, morality and force. Proceeding along this road, Donato Acciaiuoli, in his commentary on Aristotle's *Nicomachean Ethics*, construed the word *virtus* in the sense of *vis* and *potentia*.[22] One of the poles in the contradiction that nourished Machiavelli's use of *virtù* lies here.

5. Language, a distinctive trait of the animal species we belong to, comes to us as a historically stratified legacy. Even a bold and highly imaginative writer like Machiavelli worked within definite constraints, linguistic as well as social and political. But constraints can also be transformed into opportunities.

All this is commonplace, but it needs to be recalled before broaching the famous passage from *The Prince*, chapter 6:

> All armed prophets succeed whereas unarmed ones fail. This happens because, apart from the factors already mentioned, the people are fickle; it is easy to persuade them about something, but difficult to keep them persuaded. Hence, when they no longer believe in you and your schemes, you must be able to force them to believe.

(71–2); 'Quando Lachèsis non ha più del lino, / solvesi dalla carne, ed in virtute / ne porta seco l'umano e 'l divino' (79–81); 'la virtù informativa raggia intorno' (89); 'in quella forma che in lui suggella / virtüalmente l'alma che ristette' (95–6).

21　See Enrico Berti's erudite article 'De generatione animalium' in *Enciclopedia dantesca* (Rome: Istituto della Enciclopedia Iitaliana, 1970), pp. 335–6.

22　See above, chapter 2.

If Moses, Cyrus, Theseus and Romulus had been unarmed, the new order which each of them established would not have been obeyed for very long. This is what happened in our own times to Fra' Girolamo Savonarola, who perished together with his new order as soon as the masses began to lose faith in him; and he lacked the means of keeping the support of those who had believed in him, as well as of making those who had never had any faith in him believe.[23]

And here is Hexter's comment: 'This seems to be about the residue of the *mystique* of *virtù* so dear to the heart of Machiavelli worshipers of a later day.'[24]

Hexter's allusion to the Fascist interpretations of *The Prince* (including a well-known piece by Mussolini himself) does not seem completely out of place. One sentence – 'when they no longer believe in you and your schemes, you must be able to force them to believe' – might put us in mind of the club as a weapon of persuasion, evoked by Giovanni Gentile in a famous speech in 1924. But a contextual, non-anachronistic reading of Machiavelli must, as Hexter himself pointed out, take account of the complexity of the word *virtù*. Not only that, but also the possibility that the contrast between armed and unarmed prophets involves a concealed allusion.

6. In his *Thoughts on Machiavelli*, Leo Strauss wrote, 'Machiavelli is justly notorious or famous for the extraordinary boldness

---

23 Machiavelli, *The Prince*, p. 21. (*Il principe*, pp. 119–20: 'tutti e' profeti armati vinsono e li disarmati ruinorono: perché, oltre alle cose ditte, la natura de' populi è varia, e è facile a persuadere loro una cosa, ma è dificile fermarli in quella persuasione: e però conviene essere ordinato in modo che, quando non credono più, si possa fare credere loro per forza. Moisé, Ciro, Teseo e Romulo non arebbono possuto fare osservare loro lungamente le loro constituzioni, se fussino stati disarmati; come ne' nostri tempi intervenne a fra' Girolamo Savonerola, il quale ruinò ne' sua ordini nuovi, come la moltitudine cominciò a non crederli; e lui non aveva modo a tener fermi quelli che avevano creduto, né a far credere e' discredenti.')

24 Hexter, *The Vision of Politics*, p. 190.

with which he attacked generally accepted opinions. He has received less than justice for the remarkable restraint which he exercised at the same time. This is not to deny that the restraint was, in a way, imposed on him.'[25] An example of such restraint follows:

> Concerning prophets in general, Machiavelli remarks that all armed prophets have conquered and the unarmed prophets have failed. The greatest armed prophet is Moses. The only unarmed prophet mentioned is Savonarola. But as is shown by the expression 'all armed prophets ... and the unarmed ones,' he thinks not only of Savonarola. Just as he, who admired so greatly the contemporary Muslim conquerors, could not help thinking of Muhammad when speaking of armed prophets, so he must have thought of Jesus when speaking of unarmed prophets. This is perhaps the greatest difficulty which we encounter when we try to enter into the thinking of the *Prince*: how can Machiavelli, on the basis of his principles, account for the victory of Christianity?[26]

In this question we can hear the insistent voice of a great scholar. But Strauss was apparently unaware that his interpretation had been anticipated, four hundred years earlier, by a very insightful reader of Machiavelli's writings: Girolamo Cardano.

In *De sapientia libri* (Books on wisdom), published in Nuremberg in 1544, Cardano, astrologer, mathematician and physician, dealt at length with irony as a technique aiming to convey hidden contents in three forms: life, deeds, sayings. Within the third category Cardano analysed 'a way of concealing one's message by means of incomplete communication ... A discourse is obscure when what we wish to convey is stated, but the conclusions are omitted, out of motives of prudence.'[27]

---

25 Strauss, *Thoughts on Machiavelli*, p. 32.

26 Ibid., pp. 83–4.

27 Girolamo Cardano, *De sapientia libri quinque* (Norimbergae: apud Iohan. Petreium, 1544), p. 125ff, esp. 128: 'Est et ratio alia occultandi quae dixeris cum imperfecte dixeris ... Obscura est etiam omnis

This is the case, Cardano continued, with Machiavelli's remark that 'all those who wanted to defend truth unarmed perished. In another passage he says that Christ, being unarmed, was condemned by the Jews who hated him. Who does not see from this that according to him Christ died, not because he wished of his own accord to sacrifice himself, but as a result of a purely human decision – a conclusion the author did not dare to make explicit?'[28]

Cardano's words exemplify the hermeneutic principle formulated by Leo Strauss in his famous essay 'Persecution and the Art of Writing' (1941): 'The influence of persecution on literature is precisely that it compels all writers who hold heterodox views to develop a peculiar technique of writing, the technique which we have in mind when speaking of writing between the lines.'[29]

Research also consists in this: the endeavour to grasp something written between the lines, in invisible ink, on the fragmentary evidence of the past.[30] The hermeneutic strategy suggested by Strauss is obviously risky, but research must take risks; otherwise it is innocuous – that is, irrelevant.

7. The importance of the question raised by Strauss, 'How can Machiavelli, on the basis of his principles, account for the victory of Christianity?', is beyond doubt. But coming up with an answer may be impossible. Machiavelli never commented

---

oratio in qua quod volumus intelligi apertum, silent conclusiones propter honestatem.'

28 Ibid., p. 128: 'Quale illud Machiavelli: omnes qui veritatem tueri sine armis voluerunt male periere. Deinde alibi Christum asserit sine armis quod esset, ob invidiam a Iudaeis condemnatum. Quis non videt ex his Christum humano consilio non quod sponte oblatus sit perijsse illius sententia, quam tamen explicare non ausus est[?]' See Vittorio Frajese, *Profezia e machiavellismo. Il giovane Campanella* (Rome: Carocci, 2002), p. 65; Lorenzo Bianchi, 'Inganno e impostura tra Cardano e Naudé', *I castelli di Yale* I/I (2013), pp. 25–47.

29 Leo Strauss, *Persecution and the Art of Writing* (Chicago: University of Chicago Press, 1980), p. 24.

30 See on this Carlo Ginzburg, *History, Rhetoric, and Proof* (Hanover, NH: University Press of New England, 1999), pp. 22–3.

on the victory of Christianity, but he did dwell on what had made its renewal possible. In book III, chapter 1 of the *Discourses*, entitled 'In Order that a Religious Institution or a Commonwealth Should Long Survive It Is Essential that It Should Frequently Be Restored to Its Start', we read the following:

> As to religious institutions one sees here again how necessary these renovations are from the example of our own religion, which, if it had not been restored to its starting-point by St Francis and St Dominic, would have become quite extinct. For these men by their poverty and by their exemplification of the life of Christ revived religion in the minds of men in whom it was already dead, and so powerful were these new religious orders that they prevented the depravity of prelates and of religious heads from bringing ruin on religion. They also lived so frugally and had such prestige with the populace as confessors and preachers that they convinced them it is an evil thing to talk evilly of evil doing, and a good thing to live under obedience to such prelates, and that, if they did wrong, it must be left to God to chastise them. And, this being so, the latter behave as badly as they can, because they are not afraid of punishments which they do not see and in which they do not believe. It is, then, this revival that has maintained and continues to maintain this religion.[31]

---

31 *Discourses*, vol. I, pp. 462–3. (*Discorsi*, pp. 361–2: 'Ma quanto alle sètte, si vede ancora queste rinnovazioni essere necessarie per lo esempio della nostra religione; la quale se non fossi stata ritirata verso il suo principio da santo Francesco e da santo Domenico sarebbe al tutto spenta: perché questi, con la povertà e con lo esempio della vita di Cristo, la ridussono nella mente degli uomini, che già vi era spenta; e furono sì potenti gli ordini loro nuovi che ei sono cagione che la disonestà de' prelati e de' capi della religione non la rovinino, vivendo ancora poveramente, ed avendo tanto credito nelle confessioni con i popoli e nelle predicazioni, che ei danno loro a intendere come egli è male dir male del male, e che sia bene vivere sotto la obedienza loro, e se fanno errori lasciargli gastigare a Dio: e così quegli fanno il peggio che possono, perché non temono quella punizione che non veggono e non credono. Ha adunque questa rinnovazione mantenuto, e mantiene, questa religione.')

A sarcastic, bitter reflection that associates republics and religious institutions, secular power and religious power (the new religious orders are labelled 'powerful'). The reader of Machiavelli who uttered the sentence – arguably the stupidest of the twentieth century – 'The Pope? How many divisions has he got?' (Stalin), would have done well to remember it. Machiavelli is aware that *virtù* and force can be also immaterial; and that invisible weapons can function as weapons.

8. Machiavelli's reflections on *virtù* have had a profound echo – for example, in Spinoza's use of *virtus* as synonymous with 'power', δύναμις.[32] In other instances Machiavelli is present as an invisible interlocutor – for example, in a famous fragment from Pascal's *Pensées* that has been analysed by Erich Auerbach:[33]

> Right, might.
> It is right that what is just should be obeyed: it is necessary that what is strongest should be obeyed. Justice without might is helpless: might without justice is tyrannical. Justice without might is challenged, because there are always offenders: might without justice is impugned. We must then combine justice and might, and to this end make what is just strong, or what is strong just. Justice is subject to dispute, might is easily recognizable and is not disputed. So we cannot give might to justice, because might has challenged justice and has said, it is I who am just, and thus being unable to make what is just strong, we have made what is strong just.

Auerbach subjects the fragment to an operation that seems inspired by cinematic montage:

---

32   Cf. Emilia Giancotti Boscherini, *Lexicon Spinozanum* (The Hague: Springer Netherlands, 1970), vol. II, pp. 1099–103; Charles Jarrett, "Spinozistic Constructivism," in *Essays in Spinoza's Ethical Theory*, ed. Matthew Kisner and Andrew Youpa (Oxford: Oxford University Press, 2014), p. 57ff., esp. p. 70ff.

33   Erich Auerbach, 'On the Political Theory of Pascal' (1951), in *Scenes from the Drama of European Literature: Six Essays*, tr. Ralph Mannheim (New York: Meridian, 1959), pp. 101–29.

Justice, force.

Il est juste que ce qui est juste soit suivi; il est nécessaire que ce
    qui est le plus fort soit suivi.

La justice sans la force est impuissante;

la force sans la justice est tyrannique.

La justice sans force est contredite, parce qu'il y a toujours des
    méchants.

La force sans la justice est accusée.

Il faut donc mettre ensemble la justice et la force, et pour cela
    faire que ce qui est juste soit fort,

ou que ce qui est fort soit juste.

La justice est sujette à dispute.

La force est très reconnaissable et sans dispute.

Ainsi

on n'a pu donner la force à la justice, parce que la force a
    contredit la justice, et a dit que c'était elle qui était juste.

Et ainsi,

ne pouvant faire que ce qui est juste fût fort,

on a fait que ce qui est fort fût juste.[34]

9. In this way Auerbach highlighted that Pascal's reflection is articulated in symmetrical pairs. In reality, the first pair – *il est juste / il est nécessaire* – immediately introduces an asymmetry, whose implications emerge gradually. Reconciliation of *justice* and *force* is impossible: one of them (the latter) will be bound to prevail. To this asymmetry is added another: *dispute / sans dispute*. *Force* is stronger; and its obviousness is indisputable.

10. Auerbach concluded his analysis by arguing that Pascal was close to the theorists of *raison d'état*, but distant from the initiator of that tradition, Machiavelli. The distance is undeniable, but it was the result of a profound reflection, a genuine grappling

---

34 Blaise Pascal, *Pensées*, ed. Léon Brunschvicg (Paris: Hachette, 1904), vol. II, fr. 298, p. 224 (the edition used by Auerbach). In *Pensées*, ed. Michel Le Guern (Paris: Gallimard, 1977), the text is slightly different: cf. fr. 94, p. 101. See also fragments 76, 78, 79, pp. 94–6.

with the texts. Pascal may have read *The Prince* in Italian, but he will probably also have seen the French translation by Gaspard d'Auvergne, published in 1563 and reprinted many times down to the mid-seventeenth century.[35] (Incidentally, Pascal and the translator of *Il principe* came from the same region – the Auvergne – and belonged to the same social group, the *noblesse de robe*; Gaspard d'Auvergne was *lieutenant au siège royal*.)

In a long dedicatory letter addressed to James Hamilton, Duke of Châtellerault, Gaspard d'Auvergne explained that Machiavelli had not followed the example of his predecessors. They had 'imagined in their writings a perfect Prince, different from any human being'; Machiavelli 'wanted to adapt [*a voulu accommoder*] his precepts' to what is part of our experience (*à ce qui est sujet à l'experience*) and to the most common behaviour.[36] This remark resonates with one of Pascal's fragments, which reads, 'States would perish if their laws were not often stretched to meet necessity, but religion has never tolerated or practised such a thing. So either compromises [*accommodements*] or miracles are needed.'[37] In this instance, Pascal did not

---

35 A (non-exhaustive) list of editions: 1553 (actually 1563); 1571; 1579; 1586; 1597; 1600; 1606; 1613; 1640; 1664. The last edition contains some linguistic revisions.

36 *Le Prince de Nicolas Machiavel, secrétaire et citoyen de Florence, traduit de l'Italien en François* [par Gaspard d'Auvergne] (Rouen: Robert Maillard, 1586), dedicatory letter: 'n'ayant pas voulu suyvre en cela la traditive de ceux, qui ont escrit par devant luy sur semblable argument: lesquels ont figuré en leurs escrits, ie ne sçai quelle perfection de Prince non imitable à tous les humains pour la fragile condition de ceste nature. Ou au contraire cestuy ci a voulu accommoder la forme des ses preceptes seulement à ce qui est sujet à l'experience, et la plus commune mode de faire.'

37 Pascal, *Pensées*, tr. Krailsheimer, fr. 280, p. 118. (*Pensées*, Le Guern edn, fr. 263, p. 196: 'Les États périraient si on ne faisait ployer souvent les lois à la nécessité, mais jamais la Religion n'a souffert cela et n'en a usé. Aussi il faut ces accommodements ou des miracles.') On this passage, see the preface above. Cf. Christian Lazzeri, *Force et justice dans la politique de Pascal* (Paris: Presses Universitaires de France, 1993), p. 246; Hélène Bouchilloux, 'Justice, force: les limites de la raison d'État selon Pascal', in *Raison et déraison d'État. Théoriciens et theories de la raison d'État aux XVII*[e] *et XVIII*[e] *siècle,*

hesitate to use a casuistic argument that had been anticipated by Gaspard d'Auvergne (who called it 'a paradox'). 'Sometimes,' Gaspard d'Auvergne had written, 'depending on the circumstances, our monarchs are allowed to transgress the boundaries of virtue [*extravaguer, selon les affaires, hors les bornes de la vertu*] in order to survive in this evil and rotten world which they rule: and in so doing, their power continues to be approved by God.'[38]

Behind the voice of Machiavelli's translator we hear that of Machiavelli himself. Here is a passage from *The Prince*, chapter 18, first in modern English, then in Gaspard d'Auvergne's French translation, and finally in the original:

> You should know, then, that there are two ways of contending: one by using laws, the other, force. The first is appropriate for men, the second for animals; but because the former is often ineffective, one must have recourse to the latter. Therefore, a ruler must know well how to imitate beasts as well as employing properly human means.[39]

> Et pour bien parler de cecy, il faut entendre que l'on combat en deux manieres. L'une avec les loix, et l'autre par la force. La premiere appartient aux hommes, la seconde aux bestes. Mais parce que le plus souvent la premiere n'est pas suffisante, il faut de nécessité

---

ed. Yves Charles Zarka (Paris: Presses Universitaires de France, 1994), pp. 341–57; Pierre Force, 'Pascal et Machiavel', in *Justice et force. Politiques au temps de Pascal*, ed. Gérard Ferreyrolles, proceedings of the Clermont-Ferrand conference, 20–23 September 1996 (Paris: Klincksieck, 1996), pp. 61–70. Gennaro Maria Barbuto, 'Nel segno di Agostino. Pascal e Machiavelli', in *'Ragionare dello Stato'. Studi su Machiavelli*, ed. Anna Maria Cabrini (Milan: Ledizioni, 2017), pp. 7–19, relies upon the entry 'Agostino, Aurelio' (by G. Lettieri) in *Enciclopedia machiavelliana*, vol. I, pp. 15–26.

38 *Le prince*, 1586 edn, dedicatory letter: 'il est par fois loisible à nos Monarques extravaguer, selon les affaires, hors les bornes de la vertu, pour se faire raison de ce meschant et corrompu monde, qui leur est suiet: et le faisant, leur puissance ne laisse point pourtant d'estre approuvé de Dieu.'

39 Machiavelli, *The Prince*, p. 40.

prendre son recours à l'autre. Parquoy il est de besoin au Prince sçavoir bien jouër le rolle de la beste, et de l'homme ensemble.[40]

Dovete adunque sapere come e' sono dua generazione di combattere, l'uno con le leggi, l'altro, con la forza: quel primo è proprio dello uomo, quel secondo, delle bestie; ma perché el primo molte volte non basta, bisogna ricorrere al secondo: pertanto a uno principe è necessario sapere bene usare la bestia e lo uomo.[41]

11. As has long been recognized, this passage is a translation from Cicero, *De officiis* (I, 34) – except for one detail.[42] Cicero counterposed *disceptatio* (argumentation) and *vis* (force). Machiavelli replaced 'argumentation' with 'laws' (*leggi*).[43] As in the case of *virtù* – a word (as we have seen) also inspired by Cicero – Machiavelli emphasizes that law and force are at once contiguous and heterogeneous, like man and beast in the body of the mythical centaur.[44] Pascal's opposition between *justice* and *force* echoes Machiavelli's but then takes a different route. The prince, says Machiavelli, must turn himself into a centaur, half beast and half man: '*è necessario . . .*' Pascal echoes him: 'It is necessary that what is strongest should be obeyed.' The ensuing sentence – 'Justice without might is helpless / might without justice is tyrannical' – sounds, once again, like a biting comment on Machiavelli: 'All armed prophets succeed whereas unarmed fail (*Tutti e' profeti armati vinsono e li disarmati ruinorono*).'

---

40 *Le prince*, 1586 edn, pp. 57v–58r.

41 *Il principe*, p. 235.

42 'Cum sint duo genera decertandi, unum per disceptationem, alterum per vim; cumque illud proprium sit hominis, hoc beluarum, confugiendum est ad posterius, si uti non licet superiore' (Cicero, *De officiis*, I, 34).

43 Cf. Riccardo Fubini, 'Politica e morale in Machiavelli. Una questione esaurita?', in *Cultura e scrittura di Machiavelli*, pp. 117–43, esp. pp. 123–4, commenting on M. L. Colish, 'Cicero's *De officiis* and Machiavelli's *Prince*', *The Sixteenth Century Journal* 9/4 (1978), pp. 81–93.

44 On the derivation of the reference to the centaur Chiron from Xenophon, see Lucio Biasiori, *Nello scrittorio di Machiavelli. 'Il principe' e la 'Ciropedia' di Senofonte* (Rome: Carocci, 2017), pp. 65–8.

Pascal's conclusion is bitterly ironic: 'And thus being unable to make what is just strong, we have made what is strong just (Et ainsi, ne pouvant faire que ce qui est juste fût fort, on a fait que ce qui est fort fût juste).'[45]

The adjective *fort* echoes the noun, which recurs like a leitmotiv in Pascal's fragment: *force*. A Machiavellian word, taken up and reworked in a different context by a man of science who had also read Galileo's oeuvre and meditated on it. In Pascal's fragment we can read between the lines a passage we have already referred to in the *Lettera a Cristina di Lorena*, first published in Strasbourg in 1636, in Latin translation with the parallel Italian text:

I entreat those wise and prudent Fathers to consider with great care the difference that exists between doctrines subject to opinion and those subject to proof. Considering the force exerted by necessary inferences, they may ascertain that it is not in the power of the professors of demonstrative sciences to change their opinions at will and apply themselves first to one side and then to the other. There is a great difference between commanding a mathematician, or a philosopher, and influencing a lawyer or a merchant, for demonstrated conclusions about things in nature or in the heavens cannot be changed with the same facility as opinions about what is or is not lawful in a contract, bargain, or bill of exchange.[46]

---

45 See the isolated observation by Albert Cherel, *La Pensée de Machiavel en France* (Paris: L'Artisan du livre, 1935), pp. 164–6, esp. p. 166: 'On the impossibility and pointlessness of establishing justice in government; on the people, who must be deceived; on the need to "justify" force and accept absolutism, it is not surprising that Pascal's formulations should sound like *The Prince*'.

46 Galileo Galilei, *Nov-Antiqua Sanctissimorum Patrum, et Probatorum Theologorum Doctrina, De Sacrae Scripturae Testimoniis, in Conclusionibus mere Naturalibus, quae sensata experientia, et necessariis demonstrationibus evinci possunt, temere non usurpandis: in gratiam Serenissimae Christinae Lotharingae, Magnae Ducis Hetruriae* (Augustae Treboc[orum]: impensis Elzeviriorum, typis Davidis Hautti, 1636), p. 27. And see Galileo, *Lettera a Cristina di*

This is the translation provided by *Interdisciplinary Encyclopedia of Religion and Science*, available on the internet. I modified the translation 'logical deductions' into 'necessary inferences', which is closer to Galileo's 'necessarie illazioni'.

'Considering the force exerted by necessary inferences ...' (Con qual forza stringhino le *necessarie* illazioni). If Pascal read Galileo's *Lettera a Cristina di Lorena* (and he must have), he will have been profoundly affected by the distinction between 'doctrines subject to proof' (*dimostrative*) and those 'subject to opinion' (*opinabili*). The root of Pascal's distinction between *esprit de géométrie* and *esprit de finesse* is here. But in the fragment that distinction was profoundly reworked. The force of mathematicians' and natural philosophers' 'demonstrated conclusions' became, literally, force. '*Il est juste que ce qui est juste soit suivi; il est nécessaire que ce qui est le plus fort est suivi* (It is right that what is just should be obeyed; it is necessary that what is strongest should be obeyed).' Justice is debatable; force is not. In the legal and commercial spheres, force, disguised as justice, prevails: 'And thus being unable to make what is just strong, we have made what is strong just.' Distant from Machiavelli and Galileo alike, Pascal was nourished by their thought. Without them, he would not have become wholly himself.

Lorena, Besomi edn, p. 71. ('Io vorrei pregare questi prudentissimi e sapientissimi Padri, che volessero con ogni diligenza considerare la differenza, che è tra le dottrine opinabili e le dimostrative: acciò [rappre] sentandosi bene avanti la mente con qual forza stringhino le necessarie illazioni, accertassero maggiormente come non è in potestà de' professori delle scienze demostrative il mutar l'opinione a voglia loro applicandosi hora a questa, et hora a quella; e che gran differenza è tra il comandare a un matematico, o a un filosofo, e 'l disporre un mercante o un legista; e che non con 'l'istessa facilità si possono mutare le conclusioni dimostrate circa le cose della natura e del cielo, che le opinioni circa quello che è lecito o no in un contratto, in un censo o in un cambio.')

9

Oblique Words: In the Workshop of the Provincial Letters

1. Until a few decades ago casuistry seemed a relic of the past, defeated by the powerful attack that Pascal had launched on it.[1] Its resurrection, primarily bound up with bioethics, makes it possible to read the *Provincial Letters* in a different light: as an intervention in an ongoing battle.[2]

But a conflict of a quite different kind seems to emerge between the *Provincial Letters* and their reception, implicit and explicit, in the era of the Enlightenment. Francesco Orlando has spoken of a 'divergence between the religious ideology that motivated Pascal and the literary code he used, which was destined to become an instrument in the battle against religion. This is a theoretical lesson, as well a historical one, to be pondered deeply'.[3] Here I shall seek to retrace the roots of the

---

1 Different versions of this essay were presented at the Wissenschaftskolleg, Berlin, in a seminar on irony (4 July 2013) and at a conference on casuistry held at UCLA (27 January 2014). I am grateful to Alberto Frigo, Michael Kardamitsis, Martin Rueff and Andrea Di Biase for their bibliographical suggestions and Laura Tita Farinella (Biblioteca dell'Archiginnasio, Bologna) for her valuable help.

2 See Albert R. Jonsen and Stephen Toulmin, *The Abuse of Casuistry: A History of Moral Reasoning* (Berkeley: University of California Press, 1989): a timely, descriptive defence of casuistry, especially in its Jesuit versions (Jonsen was a pupil of the Gonzaga University, Spokane, WA).

3 Francesco Orlando, *Illuminismo e retorica freudiana* (Turin: Einaudi,

divergence in the work itself, in its immediate prehistory, and in the initial responses prompted by it. This is an attempt to continue, in his absence, a dialogue with Francesco Orlando that lasted half a century.[4]

2. The eighteen *Provincial Letters* (in fact, *Letters Addressed to a Provincial*) appeared in quick succession between 1656 and 1657 under a pseudonym: Louis de Montalte. Until Pascal's death, the identity of their author remained unknown to everybody, with the exception of a small group of friends, all connected to the Port-Royal abbey, stronghold of Jansenism. Significantly, the author of the *Provincial Letters* was identified as 'the Secretary of Port-Royal' in an anonymous volume published in 1657 and then, in expanded form, the following year: *Responses aux Lettres provinciales publiées par le sécretaire du Port-Royal, contre les PP. de la Compagnie de Jésus* (Replies to the *Provincial Letters* published by the secretary of Port-Royal, against the Fathers of the Society of Jesus).[5] In this collection, written by Jacques Nouet and other Jesuits, 'Louis de Montalte' was accused of having broached questions of theology, morality and cases of conscience even though he was neither a theologian nor an ecclesiastic. Furthermore, he had shamefully used a sarcastic,

---

1982) (republished as *Illuminismo, barocco, e retorica freudiana* [Turin: Einaudi, 1997]), p. 186 (on Pascal see also pp. 94–6, 186–93). From a not dissimilar standpoint, see Leszek Kolakowski, *God Owes Us Nothing: A Brief Remark on Pascal's Religion and on the Spirit of Jansenism* (Chicago: University of Chicago Press, 1995), pp. 63–4.

4　The last time we met, in 2010, Francesco Orlando (1934–2010) referred to Pascal: see 'Un ricordo', in D. Ragone, ed., *Per Francesco Orlando. Testimonianze e ricordi* (Pisa: Edizioni ETS, 2012), p. 105. On the admiration of Giuseppe Tomasi di Lampedusa (whose pupil Orlando was) for Pascal, see the appendix below.

5　[J. Nouet et al.,] *Responses aux Lettres provinciales publiées par le Secretaire du Port-Royal, contre les PP. de la Compagnie de Jesus* (Liège: Jean Mathias Hovius, 1658). On this collection and its authors, cf. A. de Backer and C. Sommervogel, eds., *Bibliothèque de la Compagnie de Jésus*, new edn (Brussels and Paris: O. Schopens and A. Picard, 1890), vol. I, p. 404 (entry on 'Annat, J.').

comical style, unworthy of a Christian, 'treating holy things like a scoffer or comedian'.[6]

3. The origins of this stylistic option are to be sought in the immediate prehistory of the *Provincial Letters*, starting with an anonymous text entitled *Les enluminures du fameux Almanach des PP. Iesuistes, intitulé la déroute et confusion des Iansenistes, ou Triomphe de Molina Iesuiste sur S. Augustin* (The Miniatures of the Famous Jesuit Almanach, entitled Defeat and Confusion of the Jansenists, or Triumph of the Jesuit Molina over St Augustine).[7] The author, Isaac-Louis Le Maistre de Sacy, a prominent member of the Port-Royal group, appeared as an interlocutor of Pascal in a famous dialogue on Epictetus and Montaigne.[8] In an introductory letter to a friend, dated 18 February 1654, Sacy described the *Enluminures* as a response to the Jesuits' shameful attack on St Augustine and his disciples, using an engraving (mentioned in Pascal's third letter).[9] Sacy's text included the engraving (fig. 4), here and there touched up

---

6 [Nouet et al.,] *Responses aux Lettres provinciales*, p. xvi: 'cet auteur . . . ne se sert que d'un style railleur et bouffon, indigne, je ne dis pas d'un théologien, ou d'un Ecclésiastique, mais même d'un Chrestien, qui ne doit pas traiter en gauffeur et farceur les choses saintes'. See also the English translation *An Answer to the Provinciall Letters published by the Jansenists, under the name of Lewis Montalt, against the Doctrine of the Jesuits and School-Divines, made by some Fathers of the Society in France. There is set before the Answers in this Edition,* The History of Jansenisme, *and at the end,* A Conclusion of the Work, *where the English* Additionalls *are shewed to deserve no Answer: also an* Appendix *shewing the same of the Book called* A further Discovery of Jesuitisme (Paris, 1659), pp. 10–11. The differences between the French original and the translation are listed in the preface, p. a2r. Cf. Louis Cognet's introduction to Blaise Pascal, *Les Provinciales*, ed. Cognet and Gérard Ferreyrolles (Paris: Bordas, 1992), pp. 50–7.

7 The *Almanach* is reproduced in the catalogue of an extraordinary exhibition: see Jean-Marc Chatelain, ed., *Pascal: le coeur et la raison* (Paris: BNF Édition, 2016), pp. 112–15 (ill. p. 114).

8 'Entretien de Pascal avec M. de Sacy sur Épictète et Montaigne', in Blaise Pascal, *Oeuvres complètes*, ed. Michel Le Guern, vol. II (Paris: Gallimard, 2000), pp. 83–98.

9 Pascal, *Les Provinciales*, ed. Cognet and Ferreyrolles, p. 48.

by Abraham Bosse, a prose description of it, and eighteen *Enluminures*, 'miniatures' comprising octosyllabic rhyming couplets. Some allusions were clarified in a series of marginal notes: a scholarly device that contrasted with the deliberately simple metrical form. Sacy's sixth *Enluminure* polemically ascribed the same contrast to the Jesuits, commenting upon a detail of their engraving: in the ranks of the Jansenists driven hither and thither, expelled by the king of France and the pope, we glimpse 'Ignorance', represented 'as an idiot with asinine features', in the act of seizing Jansenius, the author of *Augustinus*, equipped with devil-like wings. How, asked Sacy, could the Jesuits, always quick to seek to 'defeat the learned in front of ladies and the élite', have decided to please a populace of miserable artisans and peasants, presenting the Jansenists as ignorant?[10]

Today, we regard this seeming contradiction as a specific feature of the Jesuit order and its historical novelty. The Jesuits addressed the upper and lower echelons of the social order using carefully differentiated communication strategies, which often included subtle use of images.[11] Sacy decided to challenge the Jesuits on their own ground: the *Enluminures*, commented the Jansenist Pierre Nicole (hiding behind a pseudonym), attracted everybody, from the refined to the vulgar.[12] Over a couple of

---

10   Le Maistre de Sacy, *Les enluminures du fameux Almanach des PP. Iesuistes, intitulé La déroute et confusion des Iansenistes, ou Triomphe de Molina Iesuiste sur S. Augustin* (Paris 1654), p. 26: 'Souffrez-vous, que votre foiblesse / Vous reduise à cette bassesse, / De complaire au petit bourgeois, / Au menu peuple, aux villageois?' See Albert Maire, *Bibliographie générale des oeuvres de Blaise Pascal* (Paris: Giraud-Badin, 1925), vol. II: *Pascal pamphlétaire. Les Lettres provinciales*, part 1: *Les éditions*, p. 19.

11   According to René Rapin, a Jesuit, the image for the *Almanach* was suggested by the Parisian priest Adrien Gambart (*Pascal: le coeur et la raison*, p. 115). But its appropriation by the Jesuits remains crucial.

12   *Ludovici Montaltii litterae provinciales, de morali et politica Jesuitárum disciplina, a Willelmo Wendrockio Salisburgensi* [i.e., Pierre Nicole] *theologo, e Gallica in Latinam linguam translatae; et theologicis notis illustratae*, 6th corrected and expanded edn (Coloniae: apud Nicolaum chouten, 1700) (Staatsbibliothek, Berlin: Ci. 4867 a), vol. I,

Fig. 4 *La déroute et confusion des Iansenistes*, incisione, in Le Maistre de Sacy, *Les enluminures du fameux Almanach des PP. Iesuistes*, [s.e., Paris, 1654], p. non numerata. © Bibliothèque des Arts Décoratifs, Paris, France / Bridgeman Images

months the book was reprinted twice.[13] Then the Jesuit Pierre Le Moyne, criticized in the *Enluminures*, attacked it in an anonymous tract, targeting the foremost representative of the Jansenist movement, Antoine Arnauld, nicknamed 'le Grand Arnauld' (1612–1694).[14] The latter replied with an anonymous work, dated 20 March 1654: *Réponse à la lettre d'une personne*

---

p. 50: 'hunc enim libellum ab infimis ad summos omnes in manibus habebant; erat enim ejusmodi qui vel rudes set imperitos oblectaret, et tamen vel politissimis satisfaceret'. On Nicole's text, see below.

13 The colophon of the edition I have consulted reads as follows: 'Enluminé pour la première fois le 15 Janvier & pour la seconde le 18 février 1654'.

14 [P. Le Moyne,] *L'estrille du Pegase Ianseniste, aux rimailleurs du Port Royal* (Paris, 1654), pp. 8, 10. The allusion to Pegasus, the mythical horse, may have been suggested by a pun (*harnais* [harness]/ Arnauld).

de condition touchant les règles de la conduitte des Saints Pères dans la composition de leurs ouvrages, pour la deffense des veritez combattuës ou de l'ignorance calomniée (Answer to a respectable person concerning the rules followed by Holy Fathers in composing their works, in order to defend either truths that have been attacked or ignorance that has been defamed).[15] With Arnauld's *Réponse* the theme of irony moved centre stage in the debate.

4. In his *Réponse* Antoine Arnauld quoted several passages from a *Lettre d'une personne de condition*: a text, possibly nonexistent, to which he had decided to respond.[16] The anonymous author of the *Lettre* inquired whether 'ancient ecclesiastical authors, in dealing with issues of such importance, like those related to the mysteries of faith, ever employed derision'.[17] Arnauld acknowledged the Church Fathers' 'marvellous gravity' but pointed out that even Jesus 'never condemned spiritual joys and laughter inspired by wisdom and reason',[18] for 'there is

---

15   The quotations from the *Réponse à la lettre d'une personne de condition* ... are taken from the reprint contained in A. Arnauld, *Oeuvres*, vol. XXVII (Paris: Sigismond d'Arnay, 1779), pp. 1–49.

16   Arnauld may have been indirectly inspired by a *Lettre écrite à une personne de condition sur le sujet des secondes enluminures du célèbre et fameux Almanach* (Paris 1654), which is bound with Sacy's *Enluminures* and Arnauld's *Réponse* in a volume preserved in Berlin Staatsbibliothek (shelf-mark: Unter den Linden, Do. 6730). The *Lettre* (which does not contain the passages quoted by Arnauld) was written after 18 February 1654, date of the second edition of *Enluminures*. In a postscript the anonymous author refers 'in astonishment and horror' to the recent publication of Le Moyne's *L'Estrille* (see above). The chronological sequence I am suggesting is very tight – but not incompatible with the rhythm of the debate between Jesuits and Jansenists at the time.

17   Arnauld, *Réponse à la lettre*, p. 5: 'si ces anciens auteurs ecclésiastiques en traitant des matières aussi importantes que sont celles qui régardent les mystères de la foy, ont employé pour sa défense quelques railleries'.

18   Ibid., p. 6: 'une gravité merveilleuse ... il n'a pas condamné les ris des Sages et des vertueux, qui viennent de la lumiere de la prudence, et du discernement de l'esprit'.

a time to weep, and a time to laugh' (Eccl. 3: 4). To substantiate this claim Arnauld selected a series of passages from the Old Testament mentioning laughter or derision.[19] The prophets and saints had a model – God himself, whose first words to Adam after his sin are full of irony: 'Behold, the man is become as one of us' (Gen. 3: 22).[20]

'This is the kind of aggressive irony God uses in the Bible', wrote the Benedictine Rupert of Deutz (eleventh century): a rebuke delivered in ironic, veiled form is much more effective than an open rebuke.[21] Arnauld made these observations his own and added: in the same way, to attack the Jesuits and their false devotions, the *Enluminures* used 'those subtle, elegant ironies that Socrates practised so effectively, and which the Church Fathers deemed necessary in their own polemical writings'.[22] But this was an irony profoundly different from the

---

19 Fortunat Strowski's ironic comment on the 'forme géometrique' of Arnauld's text seems unjustified (*Pascal et son temps* [Paris: Plon-Nourrit, 1908], vol. III, *Les Provinciales et les Pensées*, p. 105).

20 Arnauld, *Réponse à la lettre*, p. 7: 'Voilà l'homme qui est devenu comme l'un de nous' ('Ecce Adam quasi unus ex nobis factus est'). I hope to return to Genesis 3:22 and its reception elsewhere.

21 Ibid., p. 7: 'C'est une ironie sanglante et sensible ... telles que sont celles dont use Dieu dans les Écritures ... Et on le lui fasoit sentir plus vivement par cette expression ironique et affirmative, que l'on n'eut fait par une sérieuse et négative'. Cf. Rupert of Deutz, *De Trinitate et operibus ejus libri XLII. Commentariorum in Genesim liber tertius*, cap. xxviii, PL, 167, 315: 'Gravissima haec more Domini Dei et acerba nimis ironia est ... Ergo non vere sed ironice dictum ... Hoc modo quasi affirmativa enunciatione dictum, gravitate dicentis adjuvante, multo acerbius denegatum est, quam si negativa dictione exclamasset'. On these passages, see Dilwyn Knox, *Ironia: Medieval and Renaissance Ideas on Irony* (New York: Brill, 1989), Name Index, 'Rupert of Deutz'. Cf. also Rupert of Deutz, *Les Oeuvres du Saint-Esprit*, introd. and notes Jean Gribomont, text established and tr. É. de Solms (Paris: Éditions du Cerf, 1967); John H. Van Engen, *Rupert of Deutz* (Berkeley: University of California Press, 1983).

22 Ibid., p. 14: 'ces ironies élégantes et subtiles, que Socrate le premier a si heureusement pratiquées, et que les Peres de l'Eglise ont jugé si nécessaires dans les rencontres'.

'satirical tomfoolery of profane poets', as well as the vulgar sarcasm employed in the Jesuit *Almanach*.[23]

5. Arnauld praised irony, but he did not use it openly. *Théologie morale des jésuites* (Moral theology of the Jesuits), a short tract published in 1643, usually attributed to him, followed an indirect strategy: a series of passages from Jesuit texts, followed by a brief comment.[24] It might be said that the *Provincial Letters* emerged from the interaction of two texts by Arnauld: the attack on casuistry (*Théologie morale des jésuites*) and the defence of irony in writings intended to defend the truth of religion (*Réponse à la lettre d'une personne de condition*). But this provisional conclusion, although not without foundation, immediately proves inadequate when confronted with the richness and complexity of Pascal's text.[25] The technique employed in the *Provincial Letters* is different, and addressed to a different audience: 'To speak publicly of such questions in a familiar language, to make them the subject of mirth, to disseminate them among the people, and expose them even to the eyes of women', we read in the anonymous *Responses aux Lettres provinciales*, 'is an action deserving of punishment ... This is why I am not surprised that the public believes the author of those *Letters* to have spent all his life writing romances. Never would a man of honour have chosen such themes as a target for his mockery.'[26]

---

23   Ibid., p. 18: 'bouffonneries satyriques des poëtes profanes'.

24   [A. Arnauld or F. Hallier?,] *Théologie morale des jésuites, extraite fidellement de leurs livres* (Paris, 1643), reprinted in Arnauld, *Oeuvres*, vol. XXIX, pp. 74–94. See Maire, *Bibliographie générale des oeuvres de Blaise Pascal*, vol. II, part 1, p. 61: 'It is from it [Arnauld's *Théologie morale des Jésuites*] that Pascal borrows the exposition, so blunt and so bold, of the casuistry of the era'.

25   Cf. Gérard Ferreyrolles, 'L'ironie dans les *Provinciales* de Pascal', *Cahiers de l'AIEF* 38 (1986), pp. 39–50; Laurent Thirouin, 'Imprudence et impudence. Le dispositif ironique dans *Les provinciales*', *Courrier du Centre international Blaise Pascal* 18 (1996), pp. 31–42.

26   [Nouet et al.], *Responses aux Lettres provinciales*, p. 125: 'Mais de publier ces questions en termes familiers, mais d'en faire des risées, mais de les semer parmy le peuple, et les exposer mesmes aux

The *Provincial Letters* looked like a transgressive work that defied any classification. But the Jesuits sensed its power of attraction: 'One has to confess that he [Louis de Montalte] knows the art of ridicule better than anybody else, and uses it with the utmost perfection.'[27]

6. Two passages from two letters, the ninth and eighth, will give an idea of this perfection. The ninth letter presents a dialogue between an unnamed Jesuit father and 'I', or Louis de Montalte. The Jesuit asks:

'You see now how important it is to define things properly?'

'Yes, father,' I replied, 'and this brings to my mind your other definitions about assassinations, ambushes, and superfluous goods. But why have you not extended your method to all cases, and given definitions of all vices in your way, so that people may no longer sin in gratifying themselves?'

'It is not always essential', he replied, 'to change the definitions of things in that way. I may illustrate this by referring to the subject of eating well, which is accounted one of the greatest pleasures of life, and which *Escobar* thus sanctions in his *Practice* n. 102, according to our Society: "Is it sinful for a person to eat and drink their fill, unnecessarily, and solely for pleasure? Certainly he may, according to Sanchez, provided he does not thereby injure his health; because the natural appetite may be permitted to enjoy its proper functions: *An comedere et bibere usque ad satietatem absque necessitate, ob solam voluptatem, sit peccatum? Cum Sanctio negative respondeo, modo non obsit*

---

yeux des femmes; je dis que c'est une action digne de chastiment ... C'est pourquoy je ne m'étonne pas si l'on croit dans le monde que l'autheur de ces *Lettres* a passé toute sa vie à faire des romans. Car jamais homme d'honneur n'eust voulu prendre cette matière pour sujet de ses railleries.'

27   Ibid., p. 62: 'Car il faut avouër qu'il sçait mieux qu'homme du monde l'art du ridicule, et qu'il s'en sert avec toute la perfection qu'on peut souhaiter.' See Maire, *Bibliographie générale des oeuvres de Blaise Pascal*, vol. II, part 2: *Les documents*, 1926, pp. 350, 351-3.

valetudini, quia licite potest appetitus naturalis suis actibus frui."'

'Well, Father, that is certainly the most complete passage, and the most finished maxim in the whole of your moral system! What comfortable inferences may be drawn from it! Why, is gluttony not even a venial sin?'

'Not in the shape I have just referred to', he replied, 'but, according to Escobar, n. 56, it would be a venial sin *"if a man without any necessity should so overload himself with eating and drinking as to vomit: si quis se usque ad vomitum ingurgitet."*'[28]

7. The ironic effect derives, above all, from the absence of comments. In the eleventh *Provincial Letter*, largely based on

---

28 *The Provincial Letters of Blaise Pascal*, tr. Thomas M'Crie (Edinburgh and London: John Johnstone 1847), pp. 138–9; trans. modified. Blaise Pascal, *Les Provinciales*, ed. Michel Le Guern (Paris: Gallimard, 1987), p. 149: 'Comprenez-vous bien par là combien il importe de bien définir les choses? Oui, mon Père, lui dis-je; et je me souviens sur cela de vos autres définitions de l'assassinat, du guet-apens et des biens superflus. Et d'où vient, mon Père, que vous n'étendez pas cette méthode à toutes sortes de cas, et pour donner à tous les péchés des définitions de votre façon, afin qu'on ne péchât plus en satisfaisant ses plaisirs? Il n'est pas toujours nécessaire, me dit-il, de changer pour cela les définitions des choses. Vous l'allez voir sur le sujet de la bonne chère, qui est sans doute un des plus grands plaisirs de la vie, et qu'Escobar permet en cette sorte, n. 102, dans la pratique selon notre Société: *Est-il permis de boire et manger tout son saoul sans nécessité, et pour la seule volupté ? Oui, certainement, selon notre Père Sanchez, pourvu que cela ne nuise point à la santé, parce qu'il est permis à l'appétit naturel de jouir des actions qui lui sont propres. An comedere, et bibere usque ad satietatem absque necessitate ob solam voluptatem, sit peccatum? Cum Sanctio negative respondeo, modo non obsit valetudini, quia licite potest appetitus naturalis suis actibus frui.* O mon Père! lui dis-je, voilà le passage le plus complet, et le principe le plus achevé de toute votre morale, et dont on peut tirer d'aussi commodes conclusions. Et quoi! la gourmandise n'est donc pas même un péché véniel? Non pas, dit-il, en la manière que je viens de dire. Mais elle serait péché véniel selon Escobar, n. 56, *si, sans aucune nécessité, on se gorgeait de boire et de manger jusqu'à vomir: si quis se usque ad vomitum ingurgitet.*'

Arnauld's aforementioned *Réponse à la lettre d'une personne de condition*, Pascal quoted Rupert of Deutz's comment on Genesis 3:22 as an example of irony but tacitly excised the remark on the greater effectiveness of veiled irony as regards reproof.[29] Pascal may have thought it made his own rhetorical strategy in the *Provincial Letters* too explicit. But in the imperturbable tone in which Louis de Montalte listens, without reacting (except, as we shall see, in one passage), to the absurdities of the Jesuit father, we hear a silent echo of Pascal's interminable inner conversation with Montaigne.[30] At the very end of his essay 'On Cannibals', Montaigne described the (probably fictitious) comments made by a group of Brazilian natives who had been brought to France. They were savages, commented Montaigne, hence close to nature, their minds unclouded by presuppositions or prejudices. Confronted with an unfamiliar reality, they were able to see French society in its naked truth: 'And they thought it strange that these needy halves [poor folk] . . . did not take the others by the throat, or set fire to their houses.'[31]

The apparent naivete of the character in the *Provincial Letters* who says 'I' prompts the Jesuit father to reveal ('even to the eyes of women', as Jacques Nouet wrote in horror) a truth known only to those who belonged to the circle of theologians – namely, the arguments that justified Jesuit casuistry as regards morality. Hence, in the replies of the Jesuit father, the brusque alternation between Latin and French, with irresistibly comic effects. But the clash between everyday language and the theologians' jargon had a political implication. When St Thomas and St Anthonin

---

29 Fortunat Strowski, *Pascal et son temps*, vol. III, p. 105 (and see above, p. 186 n. 24).

30 Pascal, *Entretien de M. Pascal avec M. de Sacy*.

31 See Carlo Ginzburg, 'Montaigne, Cannibals, and Grottoes', in *Threads and Traces: True False Fictive*, tr. Anne C. Tedeschi and John Tedeschi (Berkeley: University of California Press, 2011), pp. 34–53. Michel de Montaigne, 'On Cannibals', in *The Complete Works*, tr. Donald M. Frame (London: Everyman, 2003), p. 193. Cf. Orlando, *Illuminismo e retorica freudiana*, p. 189.

faced special cases (noted Jacques Nouet), they used a language unknown to common people; making those cases accessible to everybody in the vernacular, as the Jansenists did, was 'horribly malicious'.[32]

8. Yet Pascal's decision to deal with sensitive theological issues in French would have been much less effective if some of the *Provinciales* had not been constructed in the form of dialogues. Pascal had written the eighteen letters at a frantic pace, as a theological *feuilleton*: the first letter was dated 23 January 1656; the last, 24 March 1657. Soon afterwards they were assembled and published as a volume. In his anonymous 'Avertissement' the editor, the Jansenist Pierre Nicole (who subsequently translated them into Latin), remarked that in the central section 'verisimilitude (*vraysemblance*), which must be always preserved in dialogues, is scrupulously observed'. The Jesuit father is a good man, who 'ingenuously (*naïvement*)' discloses the principles of his order. The person who listens to him receives his teaching on casuistry with 'ambiguous mockery' (*une raillerie ambiguë*). 'All this shows the advantage of dealing with this topic through a series of dialogues', Nicole commented.[33]

A passage from the eighth *Provincial Letter* illustrates the possibilities afforded by the dialogical form. The roles have been reversed; now the Jesuit father is asking questions:

> 'Answer this time', said he, 'with a little more circumspection. Tell me now, "is a man who deals in divination obliged to make restitution of the money he has acquired in the exercise of his art?"'

32　[Nouet et al.,] *Responses aux Lettres provinciales*, pp. 116–17: 'C'estoit une action de sagesse à saint Thomas et saint Antonin, d'écrire en une langue qui n'est pas connuë au peuple, ces decisions que vous appellez extravagantes; mais c'est une horrible malice à vous [Jansenists] dc les avoir publiées en des termes vulgaires'.

33　Pierre Nicole, 'Avertissement' (1657), in Maire, *Bibliographie générale des oeuvres de Blaise Pascal*, vol. II, part 1, pp. 149–64, esp. p. 153.

'Just as you please, Father', said I.

'What! – just as I please! You really are extraordinary! It would seem, according to your way of talking, that the truth depends on our will and pleasure. I see that you would never find it out yourself. So see how *Sanchez* resolves this problem – no less a man than *Sanchez*. In the first place he distinguishes, in his *Summary*, l. 2, c. 38, n. 91, 95 and 96. "*Either this Fortune teller makes use of astrology and other natural means, or he does his work by the black arts. For he says, he is obliged to make restitution in one case, and not in the other.*" Now, will you tell which of them it is?'

'It is not difficult', said I.

'I see what you mean to say', he replied. 'You think that he ought to make restitution in the case of his having employed the agency of demons. But you know nothing about it; it is just the reverse. See *Sanchez*'s resolution in the same place: "If", says Sanchez, "the sorcerer has not taken care and pains to discover, by means of the devil, what he could not have known otherwise, he must make restitution – *si nullam operam apposuit ut arte diaboli id sciret*, but if he has been at that trouble, he is not obliged."'

'Why so, Father?'

'Don't you see?' he answered. 'It is because men may truly divine by the aid of the devil, whereas astrology is a mere sham.'

'But, Father, should the devil not tell the truth (and he is no more to be trusted than astrology), the magician must, I should think, for the same reason, make restitution?'

'Not always', he replied: '*Distinguo*, as Sanchez says, here. If the magician is ignorant of the diabolic art – *si sit artis diabolicae ignarus* – he is bound to restore: but if he is an expert sorcerer, and has done all in his power to arrive at the truth, the obligation ceases; for the industry of such a magician may be valued in monetary terms, *diligentia a mago apposita est pretio aestimabilis.*'

'This is good sense, Father', said I, 'for this is a way of inducing sorcerers to aim at proficiency in their art, in the hope of making an honest livelihood, as you would say, by faithfully serving the public.'

'You are making a jest of it, I suspect', said the Father: 'that is very wrong. If you were to talk in that way in places where you were not known, some people might take it amiss and charge you with ridiculing sacred subjects.'

'That, Father, is a charge against which I can very easily defend myself; for I believe that whoever takes the trouble to examine the true meaning of my words will find my object to be precisely the reverse; and perhaps, before our conversations are ended, I may find an opportunity to make this fully apparent.'[34]

---

34 *The Provincial Letters of Blaise Pascal*, pp. 124–5; trans. modified. (Pascal, *Les Provinciales*, pp. 148–9: "Je vous demande maintenant: *Un homme qui se mêle de deviner, est-il obligé de rendre l'argent qu'il a gagné par cet exercice?* Ce qu'il vous plaira, mon Révérend Père, lui dis-je. Comment, ce qu'il me plaira? Vraiment vous êtes admirable! Il semble, de la façon que vous parlez, que la vérité dépende de notre volonté. Je vois bien que vous ne trouveriez jamais celle-ci de vous-même. Voyez donc résoudre cette difficulté-là à Sanchez; mais aussi c'est Sanchez. Premièrement il distingue en sa Som., l. 2, c. 38, n. 94, 95 et 96: *Si ce devin ne s'est servi que de l'astrologie et des autres moyens naturels, ou s'il a employé l'art diabolique.* Car il dit qu'il est obligé de restituer en un cas, et non pas en l'autre. Diriez-vous bien maintenant auquel? Il n'y a pas là de difficulté, lui dis-je. Je vois bien, répliqua-t-il, ce que vous voulez dire. Vous croyez qu'il doit restituer au cas qu'il se soit servi de l'entremise des démons? Mais vous n'y entendez rien. C'est tout au contraire. Voici la résolution de Sanchez au même lieu: *Si ce devin n'a pas pris la peine et le soin de savoir par le moyen du diable ce qui ne se pouvait savoir autrement, si nullam operam apposuit ut arte diaboli id sciret, il faut qu'il restitue; mais s'il en a pris la peine, il n'y est point obligé.* Et d'où vient cela, mon Père? Ne l'entendez-vous pas? me dit-il. C'est parce qu'on peut bien deviner par l'art du diable, au lieu que l'astrologie est un moyen faux. Mais, mon Père, si le diable ne répond pas à la vérité, car il n'est guère plus véritable que l'astrologie, il faudra donc que le devin restitue par la même raison? Non pas toujours, me dit-il. *Distinguo*, dit Sanchez sur cela. *Car si le devin est ignorant en l'art diabolique, si sit artis diabolicae ignarus, il est obligé à restituer; mais s'il est habile sorcier, et qu'il ait fait ce qui est en lui pour savoir la vérité, il n'y est point obligé. Car alors la diligence d'un tel sorcier peut être estimée pour de l'argent: diligentia a mago apposita est pretio aestimabilis.* Cela est de bon sens, mon Père, lui dis-je: car voilà le moyen d'engager les sorciers à se rendre savants et experts en leur art, par l'espérance de gagner du bien légitimement selon vos maximes, en servant fidèlement le public. Je

9. In an earlier passage (third letter) the Jesuit father 'answered laughing, as if he had been amused by my naiveté'.[35] This is a game of Chinese boxes: the person reading is amused at the naive amusement of the Jesuit who does not realize he is being fooled by the person who says 'I'. The former is monstrously innocent; the latter is full of ill-repressed indignation, which suddenly bursts out when he is accused of making fun not only of Jesuit casuistry but also of sacred things in general. It is possible that this accusation stirred among the readers of the *Provincial Letters*. But how far was Pascal aware that irony about casuistry and its implications could be turned into an attack on religion? To what extent can we identify the character who says 'I' with the author of *Provincial Letters*?[36] Pascal's dialogues, as Pierre Nicole noted, are full of subtle ambiguities.

10. To insist on Pascal's greatness as a writer would be superfluous. But his role in the composition of the *Provincial Letters* should not be taken for granted. Let me quote a passage from a recent book: *Saint Cicero and the Jesuits: The Influence of the Liberal Arts on the Adoption of Moral Probabilism* (2008). In a paragraph devoted to *Provincial Letters* as political invective, the author, Robert A. Maryks, editor-in-chief of the *Journal of Jesuit Studies*, writes, 'The theological and political

---

crois que vous raillez, dit le Père; cela n'est pas bien. Car si vous parliez ainsi en des lieux où vous ne fussiez pas connu, il pourrait se trouver des gens qui prendraient mal vos discours, et qui vous reprocheraient de tourner les choses de la religion en raillerie. Je me défendrais facilement de ce reproche, mon Père. Car je crois que, si on prend la peine d'examiner le véritable sens de mes paroles, on n'en trouvera aucune qui ne marque parfaitement le contraire, et peut-être s'offrira-t-il un jour dans nos entretiens l'occasion de le faire amplement paraître.')

35 *The Provincial Letters of Blaise Pascal*, p. 35; trans. modified. (Pascal, *Les provinciales*, p. 45: 'A quoi il me répondit en riant, comme si il eût pris plaisir à ma naïveté'.)

36 See Alain Cantillon, 'Énonciation individuelle et énonciation collective 1: La position auctoriale dans *Les Provinciales*' (an essay combined with that of Dinah Ribard), *La Campagne des Provinciales 1656–1658* (Paris: Bibliothèque Mazarine, 2008), pp. 165–76 (many thanks to Martin Rueff for having drawn my attention to this essay).

controversies over Jansenism that we have just pictured are all mirrored in a series of letters that Arnauld and his friend Pierre Nicole (1625–1695) produced secretly with the assistance of Pascal.'[37]

'With the assistance of Pascal': deliberately provocative and paradoxical words. When I read them, I thought: the *Provincial Letters* are still an open wound. But even those incapable of regarding Pascal as a mere 'assistant' must take the provocation seriously. The *Provincial Letters* were undoubtedly the fruit of a collective enterprise, which involved other members of the Port-Royal group. Many scholars (including Robert Maryks) mention Arnauld and Nicole in this context: a reasonable conjecture, even if it is not supported by precise evidence. But there is something more to be said on this subject. We need to enter the workshop of the *Provincial Letters* in order to understand how they took shape.

11. Charles Perrault, author of the most famous collection of fairy tales in the Western tradition (*Tales of Mother Goose*), as well as of the *Parallelle des anciens et des modernes*, had one sister and five brothers. One of them, Nicolas, was a theologian, who openly sided with the Jansenists. In 1656 he defended Arnauld and, as a result, was expelled from the Sorbonne.[38] In his autobiography Charles Perrault recalled Nicolas's intervention in the debate on grace and predestination, sparked by the accusation of heresy against Arnauld. Speaking with Pierre, another brother, Nicolas clarified the distinction between *pouvoir prochain* (proximate power) and *pouvoir éloigné* (distant power). Subsequently, Pierre had a conversation on the same subject with various people, some of them close to Port-Royal. Eight days later, one of them brought him the first

---

37 Robert A. Maryks, *Saint Cicero and the Jesuits: The Influence of the Liberal Arts on the Adoption of Moral Probabilism*: (Burlington VT: Ashgate, 2008), p. 131.

38 On Nicolas Perrault see Gérard Namer, *L'abbé Le Roy et ses amis. Essai sur le jansénisme extrémiste intramondain*, preface by Lucien Goldmann (Paris: S.E.V.P.E.N., 1964).

Provincial Letter, saying 'this is the result of what you told me last week'. The first letter, which deals with *pouvoir prochain*, was followed by seventeen more: 'And this', commented Charles Perrault, 'was the subject and origin of the *Provincial Letters*.'[39]

The anecdote might be of little relevance were it not reinforced by additional evidence. First of all, a passage from the life of Pascal that Charles Perrault included in his imposing collection of biographies of famous men in seventeenth-century France, published in 1696: *Les hommes illustres qui ont paru en France pendant ce siècle*.[40] (Both the life of Pascal and that of Arnauld were censored, then published independently, and ultimately reintegrated into later editions; in some of these the passage I am going to quote is missing.)[41] Charles Perrault warmly praised the *Provincial Letters*, without naming them, but entered a reservation concerning their 'accuracy' (*exactitude*), not their doctrinal content: 'Someone has argued that those who provided him [Pascal] with materials [*mémoires*] for his work, were not always very accurate.'[42]

---

39 Charles Perrault, *Mémoires de ma vie*, preceded by an essay by Antoine Picon, 'Un moderne paradoxal' (Paris: Macula, 1993), pp. 119–20.

40 Charles Perrault, *Les hommes illustres qui ont paru en France pendant ce siècle, avec leurs portraits au naturel*, 2 vols (Paris: Antoine Dezallier, 1696–1700) (Biblioteca dell'Archiginnasio, Bologna: 10.u.III.2–3)

41 See Charles Perrault, *Les Eloges de MM Arnauld et Pascal, composés par M. Perrault, de l'Académie française, imprimés d'abord et supprimés ensuite par la cabale de quelques envieux de la gloire de ces deux grands hommes* (Cologne: Marteau, 1697).

42 Perrault, *Les hommes illustres*, vol. I, p. 66: 'Quelques-uns ont prétendu que ceux qui luy fournissoient des mémoires pour cet ouvrage, ne l'ont pas toujours servi avec la dernière exactitude.' In some editions the passage is omitted: see Charles Perrault, *Les hommes illustres qui ont paru en France*, 3rd edn, revised and corrected, 2 vols (The Hague: Matthieu Roguet, 1707) (Biblioteca dell'Archiginnasio, Bologna: 5. gg. III. 22): the life of Pascal appears at the end of vol. II, pp. 194–6; Charles Perrault, *Les hommes illustres qui ont paru en France pendant ce siècle, augmenté des éloges de Messieurs Arnauld et Pascal* (Paris: Antoine Dezaillier, 1698), in 12°, without illustrations (Biblioteca dell'Archiginnasio, Bologna: 5. gg. IV.13): the missing passage should have been on p. 239. Yvonne

In his posthumously published *Mémoires*, the Jesuit René Rapin wrote that the Marquise de Sablé, a writer favourable to Port-Royal, had raised doubts with Pascal about the accuracy of the quotations in the *Provincial Letters*. Pascal had answered 'that this business did not concern him, but those who had provided him with the materials [*mémoires*] he used in his work'.

The coincidence is worth noting, because the two texts are completely independent. René Rapin died in 1687, nine years before the publication of Charles Perrault's *Hommes illustres* (which, as has been said, included a life of Pascal); Rapin's *Mémoires* (which featured the dialogue between the Marquise de Sablé and Pascal) were published only posthumously, in 1865.[43] But to whom did Charles Perrault's critical remark refer? In all probability to his brother, Nicolas. More precisely, Nicolas's posthumous work, *La morale des jésuites, extraite*

Bézard, 'Autour d'un éloge de Pascal. Une affaire de censure tranchée par Louis XIV en 1696', *Revue d'histoire littéraire de la France* 33 (1926), pp. 215–24, quotes the passage (p. 217) as 'restriction sur la doctrine'. (I am grateful to Laura Tita Farinella who pointed out this essay to me.)

43 René Rapin, *Mémoires sur l'église et la société, la Cour, la Ville et le Jansénisme*, published for the first time from the original manuscript, ed. L. Aubineau, 3 vols (Paris: Gaume frères and J. Duprey, 1865) (facsimile reprint, Gregg, Farnborough 1972), vol. II, p. 395: 'la marquise de Sablé qui, se trouvant dans les intérêts de Port-Royal plutôt par l'estime qu'elle avoit pour les personnes qui en étoient que pour la doctrine, qu'elle n'entendoit pas comme les autres femmes du party, ne put toutefois s'empêcher de reprocher à Pascal, qui l'étoit allé voir, la liberté qu'il prenoit de décrier une compagnie célèbre, qui servoit bien l'Eglise. "Car que seroit-ce, luy dit-elle, si ce que vous leur reprochez étoit faux, comme on le dit depuis que les *Impostures* que le P. Nouet, jésuite, a commencé a donner au public ont detrompé le monde?" Pascal luy répondit que c'étoit à ceux qui luy fournissoient les mémoires sur quoy lesquelles il travailloit à y prendre garde et non pas à luy, qui ne faisoit que les arranger. C'est une particularité que j'ay apprise de cette marquise, dans les derniéres années de sa vie, la voyant assez souvent'. Rapin's passage is mentioned by Maire, *Bibliographie générale des oeuvres de Blaise Pascal*, vol. II, part 1, p. 68.

fidelement de leurs livres, published as the work of 'a doctor of the Sorbonne' in 1667 and then repeatedly reprinted.[44]

The title echoed Arnauld's *Théologie morale des jésuites*, published in 1643, but the content was 'prodigiously enlarged', as the eighteenth-century editors of Arnauld's works put it.[45] The first edition – a quarto – contains two anonymous introductions: one by the editor (probably Alexandre Varet) the other by the author, Nicolas Perrault. They both mention the publication of the *Provincial Letters*.[46] So Nicolas Perrault was working on *La morale des jésuites* between 1656 or 1657 and 1661 – the year of his death. But so vast a project must have commenced much earlier. Is it possible that Pascal, in the frantic months spent writing the *Provincial Letters*, had access to the still-unpublished material – the *mémoires* – on Jesuit casuistry that

---

44 [N. Perrault,] *La morale des jésuites, extraite fidelement de leurs livres* (Mons: chez la Veuve Waudret, à la Bible d'Or, 1667) (BNF: Rés. D. 4041). The importance of the material collected by Nicolas Perrault in the composition of the *Provincial Letters* has been highlighted by Michel Le Guern, 'Pascal, Arnauld et les casuistes', in *La casuistique classique*, ed. S. Boarini (Saint-Étienne: Publications de l'Université de Saint-Étienne, 2009), pp. 115–22, esp. pp. 119–21. The documentation presented here provides further evidence in support of Le Guern's argument.

45 Cf. Arnauld, *Oeuvres*, vol. XXXII, 1780, p. 11 note b: 'M. Perrault, docteur de Sorbonne, avoit depuis prodigieusement augmenté le project de M. Arnauld. Son ouvrage fut publié en 1667, dix ans [actually six] après sa mort, in 4°, sous ce même titre: *La Théologie morale des Jésuites* [actually *La morale des jésuites*].'

46 [N. Perrault,] *La morale des jésuites*, 'Avertissement sur la publication de cet ouvrage' (by Alexandre Varet?), p. 2r: 'L'Auteur l'avoit entrepris [ce livre] dans le temps du monde qui paroissait le plus favorable. La morale des jesuites estoit devenüe l'objet de l'aversion et de l'horreur de tous ceux qui avoient quelque lumiere, ou quelque pieté. Les *Lettres ingenieuses de Montalte à un Provincial*, et les sçavants écrits des Curez de Paris avoient découvert la corrruption de la pluspart de leurs maximes'; preface by the author, p. 2r: 'Mais il est arrivé par un ordre particulier de la providence divine que celuy qui depuis quelques années a entrepris de les découvrir, les a exprimées d'une maniere si agreable, qu'il a attiré tout le monde à les lire par la grace de son stile, et les a en suite aisément fait paroistre odieuses et insupportables par leur propre excés et leur propres extravagances'.

Nicolas Perrault must have been amassing over the years? This is a plausible hypothesis: as Jacques Nouet stressed in the *Responses aux Lettres provinciales*, 'Louis de Montalte' knew very little about casuistry besides Arnauld's *Théologie morale des jésuites* and the *Summula* written by the Jesuit Antonio Escobar y Mendoza.[47] But the range of texts quoted in the *Provincial Letters* is much wider. Pascal may have used the material collected by Nicolas Perrault to find his bearings in the labyrinth of casuistical literature.

This hypothesis is confirmed when we discover that the most unexpected passages in the *Provincial Letters* are based on quotations which feature, under relevant headings, in the materials assembled by Nicolas Perrault. For example, the texts by Escobar excusing the sin of gluttony, unless 'eating and drinking [so much] as to vomit', and the text by Sanchez arguing for the magicians' right to demand a fee for their work, appear in *La morale des jésuites*, in the chapters entitled, respectively, 'De la gourmandise' and 'De la magie'.[48] Taken out of context, these quotations have an aggressive tone; in Pascal's hands they became very powerful weapons. It will be remembered that in the *Responses aux Lettres provinciales* Jacques Nouet had observed, 'One has to confess that he [Louis de Montalte] knows the art of ridicule better than anybody else, and he uses it with the utmost perfection. Can one imagine anything subtler than the *pouvoir prochain* of his first letter or more surprising than the *Mohatra* in the eighth?'[49] Now, the comments on *pouvoir prochain* were (according to Charles Perrault) suggested by his brother, Nicolas; and as to *Mohatra* – a kind of usurious contract very

---

47   [Nouet et al.,] *Responses aux Lettres Provinciales*, p. 118.

48   [N. Perrault,] *La morale des jésuites*, 'De la gourmandise' pp. 35–6 and 'De la magie', pp. 387–8.

49   [Nouet et al.,] *Responses aux Lettres provinciales*, p. 62: 'Car il faut avouër qu'il sçait mieux qu'homme du monde l'art du ridicule, et qu'il s'en sert avec toute la perfection qu'on peut souhaiter. Se peut-il rien dire de plus délicat que *le pouvoir prochain* de sa première lettre, de plus surprenant que le Mohatra de la huitième ...?'

few people had ever heard of – we find it commented on in Nicolas Perrault's *La morale des jésuites*, in the chapter 'De l'usure'.[50] But there is one more piece of evidence, which is decisive: in his seventh letter Pascal attributed to the Jesuit Lessius a passage in which he argued that it was lawful to kill to defend one's honour.[51] The same passage is cited in Perrault's *La morale des jésuites*, in a chapter entitled 'Que selon Lessius il est permis de tuer pour defendre son honneur'.[52] Perrault did not realize that Lessius had quoted Francisco de Vitoria in order to refute him. Vitoria's point of view (Lessius concluded) was admissible in theory, but scarcely acceptable in practice. In his thirteenth letter Pascal, who had taken up Perrault's incomplete (and hence distorted) reference, was obliged to defend himself against the charge, levelled by Jacques Nouet in the *Responses aux Lettres provinciales*, that he had falsified the texts.[53] In the 1659 edition of the *Provincial Letters*, the passage on Lessius was reshaped.[54]

To suppose that Nicolas Perrault, theologian, *docteur de Sorbonne*, was following in the footsteps of Louis de Montalte, who by his own admission was ignorant of theology, is theoretically possible – but extremely unlikely. The reverse hypothesis seems unavoidable.

---

50 [N. Perrault,] *La morale des jésuites*, p. 695ff. Cf. Emilio Bussi, 'Contractus Mohatrae', *Rivista di storia del diritto italiano* 5 (1932), pp. 492–519.

51 Pascal, *Les Provinciales*, p. 115: 'Voyez Lessius, *De Just.* Lib. II, C. IX, d. 12, n. 79: 'Celui qui a reçu un soufflet ne peut pas avoir l'intention de s'en venger; mais il peut bien avoir celle d'éviter l'infamie, et pour cela de repousser à l'instant cette injure, et même à coups d'épée: etiam cum gladio.' And see the embarrassed correction in the thirteenth letter, ibid., pp. 203–7.

52 [N. Perrault,] *La morale des jésuites*, p. 407ff.

53 See [Nouet et al.,] *Responses aux Lettres Provinciales*, pp. 284–5, with a reference to Lessius, *De justitia*, book II, chapter 9, par. 80: 'Ob has rationes haec sententia est speculative probabilis, tamen in praxi non videtur facile permittenda'.

54 Pascal, *Les provinciales*, pp. 120, 349 n. 13.

12. Casuistry was not the only point of contact between Nicolas Perrault and Pascal. The editor of *La morale des jésuites* informs us that Nicolas was passionately keen on mathematics – the only passion which, at least for a while, distracted him from his devotion to the truth of religion.[55] To explore the relationship between Nicolas Perrault and Pascal would help us to understand more about the composition of the *Provincial Letters*. In any event, the reliance on Perrault's *La morale des jésuites* sheds light on the way that Pascal worked, transforming the material submitted to him. In a sense, the *Provincial Letters* were a collective work. But without Pascal, their short- and long-term effects would have been inconceivable.

Pascal's imagination reaches its peak in the sudden dialogic turn whose ironic implications are unfolded from the fourth to the tenth letters.[56] Its source has never been identified. The text I am going to refer to is far from unknown, although apparently nobody has spotted its connection with the *Provincial Letters*. It appeared, anonymously, with a false place of publication (Villefranche) in 1622. Its title reads as follows: *Les*

---

55 [N. Perrault,] *La morale des jésuites*, p. 3r: 'La seule chose qu'il eut à combattre dans cette loüable entreprise, fut la passion qu'il avoit pour les mathematiques. Car comme cette science est la plus assurée des sciences humaines, et presque l'unique où l'on trouve quelque chose de certain et capable de satisfaire un esprit qui aime la verité, l'amour qu'il avoit pour cette mesme verité formoit en luy une pente si violente vers cette science, qu'il ne pouvoit s'empescher de s'y appliquer et de s'occuper à inventer quelque nouvelle machine. Mais enfin l'esprit saint qui le conduisoit dans ces études luy fit surmonter en peu de temps l'inclination qu'il avoit pour ces curiositez et ces recherches innocentes, et il crut que ce n'estoit pas assez à un théologien de mépriser les divertissemens du monde, mais qu'il falloit encore qu'il se privast de ceux de l'esprit, et qu'il cherchast uniquement la verité où elle se pouvoit trouver, c'est à dire dans les Écritures Saintes et les livres de Saints Peres.' See also BNF, mss. fr., 23467, p. 109 (an arithmetical triangle comparable to Pascal's: see Namer, *L'abbé Le Roy et ses amis*, p. 44). The same manuscript contains Nicolas Perrault's *Raisons moralles et Chrestiennes contre la Banque ou lotteries*.

56 Cf. Strauss, 'Persecution and the Art of Writing', esp. p. 35 n. 19.

mystères des Pères Jésuites, par interrogations et responses, extraictes fidèlement des éscrits par eux publiés. Pour précaution en ce temps, au public et au particulier (The mysteries of the Jesuit fathers, by way of questions and answers, faithfully extracted from writings published by them).[57]

The book, republished in 1624 with the same false place of publication, had been translated into English the year before; a Latin translation, with some additions, was reprinted multiple times (1631, 1633 and 1637).[58] In the catalogue of the Bibliothèque Nationale de France, both the Latin translation, *Mysteria patrum Iesuitarum*, and a Latin response to a Jesuit who had attacked it, are recorded under the name of Kaspar Schoppe, along with an alternative attribution to André Rivet.[59] I shall return to this double attribution later.

The book consists of a series of questions and answers, which make us think of a catechism. But an inverted catechism: the novice, who would like to enter the order, asks the questions; the Jesuit father answers them. A previous attempt in this direction – Étienne Pasquier's *Catéchisme des Jésuistes, ou examen de leur doctrine* (Catechism of the Jesuits, or examination of their doctrine), published in 1602 – ultimately turned into a prolix, erudite treatise.[60] *Les mystères des Pères Jésuites* is quite different. Readers are confronted with a concise self-presentation of what the Jesuit order really is. 'I am not going to conceal

---

57 BNF: 8-LD39-106. In this copy the pagination has been altered.

58 *The State-Mysteries of the Iesuites, by way of Questions and Answers, Faithfully extracted out of their owne Writings by themselves published* (London: G. E. for Nicholas Bourne, 1623) (Cambridge University Library); *Mysteria patrum Jesuitarum, ex ipsorum scriptis* (Lampropoli: apud Robertum Liberum, 1631) (Berlin, Staatsbibliothek); 1633 (UCLA, Special Collections); (Lugduni: apud Gelasium Nomimelcum, 1637) (BNF).

59 In the UCLA catalogue the *State-Mysteries* (1623) are attributed to André Rivet.

60 [É. Pasquier,] *Le catechisme des Jesuites, ou Examen de leur doctrine* (Ville-franche: Guillaume Grenier, 1602). See the critical edition by Claude Sutto (Quebec: University of Sherbrooke, 1982).

anything of our mysteries', says the Jesuit father, 'on one condition: you must receive my answers under the seal of confession . . . We want the theory, related to many things whose practice cannot be concealed, to remain secret.' The novice swears to remain silent.

In the virtually contemporaneous English translation, the mysteries unveiled by the Jesuit father became 'State-Mysteries' – an allusion to the *arcana imperii*. Indeed, politics plays a prominent role in *Les mystères des Pères Jésuites*. The father reveals, for instance, that the Jesuit order aims to establish a universal monarchy under the king of Spain: 'A mystery that should not be revealed until the plan has become a reality.'[61] But *Les mystères* also deals with issues relating to the present and everyday life. 'Since I see your good will', the Jesuit father says, 'I shall give you twenty-five aphorisms selected from among many others.'[62] What follows is a list of short casuistical maxims, touching on all kinds of topics, from confession to vengeance, from food to sex. This list may have elicited Pascal's curiosity. But the unusual structures of *Les mystères des Pères Jésuites* was even more important for the composition of the *Provincial Letters*. Its inversion of the catechistic form recalls the asymmetry between the questions asked by Louis de Montalte and the long answers given by the Jesuit father. However, despite this morphological resemblance, there is a striking difference. In *Les mystères des Pères Jésuites* there is no trace of irony. Why?

13. This question demands a twofold answer, historical and morphological. First of all, who wrote *Les mystères des Pères Jésuites*? The names of two very different possible authors have been suggested: Kaspar Schoppe and André Rivet. Schoppe, born into a Lutheran family in Bavaria, went to Rome, where he converted to Catholicism. In his tempestuous literary career, he attacked Protestant men of learning and Jesuit scholars on

---

61 *Les mysteres des Peres Jesuites* (Ville Franche: Eleuthère Philalèthe, 1622), pp. 90–1.
62 Ibid., p. 96ff.

theological and philological subjects. Rivet, a rigid Calvinist born in France, near Poitiers, spent more than thirty years at the University of Leiden teaching theology and biblical exegesis.

The case for attributing *Les mystères des Pères Jésuites* to Rivet rests on strong, if not definitive, evidence. In 1635 the Swiss Jesuit Laurenz Forer published a book attacking a group of anti-Jesuitical works, including *Mysteria patrum Societatis Jesu* – more precisely, *Mysteria patrum Iesuitarum*, the Latin translation of *Les mystères des Pères Jésuites*. Forer argued (a) that *Mysteria patrum Iesuitarum* had originally been written in German and (b) that its author was Anatomicus Melander, one of the alleged pseudonyms of Kaspar Schoppe.[63] Both arguments were refuted in a book, likewise published under a pseudonym (Renatus Verdaeus: an anagram), and later included in André Rivet's complete works. Verdaeus/Rivet emphatically pointed out that (a) *Mysteria patrum Iesuitarum* had originally been written in French, not German, and subsequently translated into Latin and (b) the author of the book was not Kaspar Schoppe.[64]

---

63 Laurenz Forer, *Mantissa anti-anatomiae jesuiticae, opposita famosis contra Societatem Jesu sparsis libellis, quorum tituli sunt: I. Mysteria Patrum Societatis Jesu; II. Consultatio Fr. Juniperi de Ancona Minoritae; III. Fr. Lud. Soteli Relatio, de Ecclesiae Iaponicae statu* (apud Joannem Gächium Oeniponte, 1635). This was a sequel to a book by the same author against Kaspar Schoppe: *Anatomia anatomiae Societatis Jesu* (apud Joannem Gächium, 1634). A handwritten note on the frontispiece of the copy of *Mysteria patrum Iesuitarum* held by the Bayerischen Staatsbibliothek, Munich, reads: 'a Casp. Scioppio'.

64 *Renati Verdaei Statera qua ponderatur Mantissae Laurentii Foreri Jesuitae* (Lugduni: apud Gelasium Nomimelcum, 1637) (Biblioteca Angelica, Rome: +.3.38. On the frontispiece we read: 'sub hoc nomine latet Andreas Rivetus'); at p. 10: 'Libellus ille [*Mysteria Patrum Jesuitarum*] Gallice primum conscriptus est, et postea Latine'. The BNF online catalogue comments on the 1644 reprint of this work: 'Cet ouvrage, réimprimé au T. III des *Opera* d'André Rivet, éd. de Rotterdam, 1560, et attribué communément, entre autres par Barbier, les bibliographies hollandaises, le Catalogue du British Museum, à cet auteur, dont Renatus Verdaeus est l'anagramme, est cependant attribué nommément à Scioppius par Niceron, qui s'appuie sur les *Generales vindiciae adversus famosos Gasparis Scioppii libellos*, du P. Alberti, et par Jöcher'.

We are probably dealing with a masked claim to authorship. The Frenchman André Rivet is certainly a more likely author of *Les mystères des Pères Jésuites* than the Bavarian Kaspar Schoppe, who may have translated the book into Latin. In his lectures on the *Decalogue* Rivet attacked the Jesuits and their casuistry, venturing his own interpretation of 'so-called *casus conscientiae*'.[65] On the subjects of grace and predestination, as has been remarked, Rivet felt close to the Jansenists.[66] In 1644 he planned to publish in Amsterdam a volume collecting some texts against the Jesuits, including Antoine Arnauld's *Théologie morale des Jésuites, extraict fidèlement de leurs livres* (The moral theology of the Jesuits, faithfully extracted from their books) – a work from 1643 I have already mentioned among the precedents of *Les Provinciales*.[67] Arnauld, who certainly knew Rivet's writings, may have pointed out *Les mystères des Pères Jésuites* to Pascal. As we can see, the connection between Jansenism and Calvinism, polemically suggested in the pro-Jesuit print entitled 'The Defeat and Confusion of the Jansenists' (fig. 4), was not wholly unfounded.

Pascal's debt to *Les mystères des Pères Jésuites* did not escape some of his contemporaries. The frontispiece of the first English translation of the *Provincial Letters*, published in London in 1657, reads as follows: *Les Provinciales, or, The Mysterie of*

---

65 André Rivet, *Praelectiones in cap. XX Exodi in quibus ita explicatur Decalogus, ut casus conscientiae, quos vocant, ex eo suborientes, ac pleraeque controversiae magni momenti, quae circa legem moralem solent agitari, fuse et accurate discutiantur, opus, ut varietate jucundum, sic, non solum sacra, sed etiam politica tractantibus, profuturum* (Lugduni Batavorum: apud Franciscum Hegerum, 1632). A second, enlarged edition, including a commentary on the whole book of Exodus, appeared in 1637.

66 See Gustave Cohen, *Écrivains français en Hollande dans la première moitié du XVIIe siècle* (Paris: Champion, 1920), pp. 293–310; Paul Dibon, *Inventaire de la correspondance d'André Rivet (1595–1650)* (The Hague: Nijhoff, 1971).

67 *Correspondance intégrale d'André Rivet et de Claude Sarrau*, ed. Hans Bots and Pierre Leroy, vol. II (Amsterdam: APA-Holland University Press, 1980), pp. 223–4 (letter from Rivet to Sarrau). See also pp. 184–5 (letter from Sarrau to Rivet).

Jesuitisme, discover'd in certain Letters ... Displaying the corrupt Maximes and Politicks of that Society.[68]

14. Morphologically, Pascal's probable reworking of *Les mystères des Pères Jésuites* suggests that the ironic effect of the *Provincial Letters* is the result of two different, but related, stylistic moves: the absence of comments and the contiguity between the narrator and the main character, the person who says 'I'.[69] In *Les mystères des Pères Jésuites* there is no 'I': the dialogue between the novice and the Jesuit father is staged by the narrator, but the narrator himself is offstage. Literally, *Les mystères des Pères Jésuites* reminds us of a theatrical play more than the *Provincial Letters* do – notwithstanding the recurrent comparison between the dialogic section of the *Provincial Letters* (letters 4–10) and Molière's plays.[70]

In the *Provincial Letters*, the narrator asks the reader to guess the reactions of the character who says 'I' and the Jesuit father, reading their dialogue as if it were a musical score. Let me quote a tiny fragment of the *Provincial Letters* once again:

'Well, Father, that is certainly the most complete passage, and the most finished maxim in the whole of your moral system! What comfortable inferences may be drawn from it! Why, is gluttony not even a venial sin?'

'Not in the shape I have just referred to,' he replied, 'but, according to Escobar, n. 56, it would be a venial sin *"if a man without any necessity should so overload himself with eating and drinking as to vomit: si quis se usque ad vomitum ingurgitet."* '

---

68 Cf. P. Jansen, *De Blaise Pascal à Henry Hammond. 'Les Provinciales' en Angleterre*, preface by G. Le Bras (Paris: Vrin, 1954), who attributes the English translation, with convincing arguments, to the Anglican theologian Henry Hammond.

69 See Pierre Kuentz, 'Un discours nommé Montalte', *Revue d'histoire littéraire de la France* 71/2 (1971), pp. 195–206, esp. p. 202.

70 Ibid., p. 197.

The *Provincial Letters* are a supreme example of the art of the unsaid.

15. But also a case of unintended consequences. The point is worth repeating: an attack on casuistry, written by a profoundly religious individual, helped in the long run to discredit not only casuistry but also religion, paving the way for the Enlightenment and its contentious legacy. Today, in a largely secular world, marked by the clash between (and with) religious fundamentalisms, casuistry has re-emerged in a different, secularized version. A text decisive for the history of irony invites us to reflect on the irony of history.

10

Ironic and Ambiguous Euclid: Two Notes in Connection with Bayle

I

1. Indirect, unexpected light on the initial reception of the *Provincial Letters* comes from a tract published in Paris in 1658: *De ludicra dictione* (On the jocular style).[1] The author, the Jesuit François Vavasseur, professor of theology at Clermont College in Paris, had written, nearly always in Latin, on theology, philology and poetry (in addition to being a poet himself).[2] The tract opens with a dedicatory letter dated 'Paris, 5 January 1655', in which Vavasseur addresses Guez de Balzac, a celebrated man of letters, who had asked him what he thought 'of the jocular and ridiculous style that our contemporaries call *burlesque*'.[3] Balzac

---

1 I am very grateful to Perry Anderson and Sanjay Subrahmanyam for their comments.

2 François Vavasseur, *De ludicra dictione liber in quo tota iocandi ratio ex veterum scriptis aestimatur* (Lutetiae Parisiorum: apud Sebastianum Cramosium, Architypographum Regium, 1658). I have also consulted the volume *Francisci Vavassoris e Societate Jesu Opera omnia antehac edita, theologica et philologica. Nunc primum in unum volumen collecta, ad quae accesserunt inedita et sub ficto nomine emissa, cum Latina, tum Gallica* (Amstelodami: apud Petrum Humbertum, 1709) (*De ludicra dictione* takes up pp. 1–84, plus two unnumbered sheets, given over to the dedicatory letter and the index). I have not seen another edition of Vavasseur's works published in 1722.

3 Vavasseur, *De ludicra dictione*, p. 1 (subsequently in *Opera*

had been dead for a year.[4] His *Entretiens*, published posthumously in 1657, included some pages '*Du stile burlesque*', followed by a comment in Latin by the editor announcing the imminent publication of a text by Vavasseur on the subject.[5]

The word '*burlesque*', from the Italian '*burlesco*', had been common in France for fifteen years.[6] Its presence on the streets, in theatres and in markets is indirectly documented by polemical writings for immediate consumption, addressed to a large audience, like those ridiculing Cardinal Mazarin (the *Mazarinades*).[7] Addressed to a smaller audience were epic-burlesque poems, which often rewrote ancient epic poems in a mocking key: a genre that referred to Italian models like Alessandro Tassoni's *La secchia rapita* (The abducted bucket – 1622, but circulating for some years in manuscript form); Francesco Bracciolini's *Dello scherno degli dei* (On mockery of the gods – 1618); and Giovanni Battista Lalli's *L'Eneide travestita* (The disguised Aeneid – 1632). In the case of Tassoni,

---

omnia, p. 1): 'De ioculari et ridicula dictione, quam homines nostri, *burlesque*, appellant, petis a me, praestantissime Balzaci, ut perscribam tibi iudicium meum.'

4 See F. E. Sutcliffe, *Guez de Balzac et son temps: littérature et politique* (Paris: Nizet, 1959); and the rich bibliography in Bernard Beugnot, *Guez de Balzac* (Paris: Memini, 2001).

5 *Les Entretiens de feu Monsieur Balzac* (Paris: Augustin Courbé, 1657), p. 421ff. (Entretien 38, 'Du stile burlesque'). Cf. ibid., p. 430: 'Quid de ludicro hoc, ut vocant, scribendi genere, et, ut ego interpretor, de hoc nugarum ludo, sentiat Vavassor, interrogatus a Balzacio, scire interest Reipublicae litterariae'. Vavasseur was identified as the literary heir of the Jesuit scholar Jacques Sirmond, of whom he had written an obituary (*Jacobi Sirmondi Societatis Jesu longaevitas* [Parisiis: apud S. and G. Cramoisy, 1652]).

6 See Francis Bar, *Le Genre burlesque en France au XVIIe siècle. Étude de style* (Paris: D'Artrey, 1960).

7 *Dialogue burlesque de Gilles de Niais et du Capitan Spacamon* (Paris: Theodore Pepingué, 1649); *Le Festin burlesque du fourbe ou la Micaresme des Partisans, traittez à la Cour par leur chef et protecteur le C[ardinal] M[azarin]* (Paris: chez la veuve André Musnier, 1649) (Biblioteca di Discipline Umanistiche, Bologna: Antico, AA.380, opp. 83 and 87). On the genre and its context, cf. Christian Jouhaud, *Mazarinades: la Fronde des mots* (Paris: Aubier, 1985).

derision of ancient models intertwined with a reflection on the relationship between the ancients and the moderns (*Paragone degli ingegni antichi e moderni*, 1620).[8]

Some decades later, this nexus was reprised in France. Charles Perrault, future author of the *Parallele des anciens et des modernes* (1688), wrote, along with his brothers Claude, Nicolas and Pierre, a parody of the *Aeneid* entitled *Les murs de Troye, ou l'origine du burlesque*, which was presented in the preface as a detached, deliberate 'satire directed against the poetry of the ancients, or rather against the poetry of the moderns who have sought to imitate the ancients'.[9] An ambiguous formula, which emphasized the originality, if not the superiority even, of the moderns. In *De ludicra dictione*, Vavasseur too disdainfully rejected the scurrilous reprise of the gravity of ancient poems, or the *burlesque* of his contemporaries.[10] But the objective of his text was broader: to

---

8 Alessandro Tassoni, *La secchia rapita*, critical edn ed. Ottavio Besomi, 2 vols (Padua: Antenore, 1987–90); Francesco Bracciolini, *Dello scherno degli dei. Poema piacevole* (Florence: Giunti, 1618); Giovanni Battista Lalli, *L'Eneide travestita* (Venice: Stefano Curti, 1675).

9 Cf. Charles Perrault, *Les murs de Troye, ou l'origine du burlesque* (Paris: Louis Chamhourdry, 1653); Charles, Claude, Nicolas and Pierre Perrault, *Le Burlesque selon les Perrault. Oeuvres et critiques*, ed. Claudine Nédelec and Jean Leclerc (Paris: Champion, 2013), p. 186: 'ce poeme est une satyre contre la poësie des Anciens, ou plutost contre celle des Modernes qui ont affecté d'imiter les Anciens'. The cultural superiority of the Italian precursors of the *Querelle* is insisted upon by Marc Fumaroli, 'Les abeilles et les araignées', introduction to *La Querelle des Anciens et des Modernes*, ed. Anne-Marie Lecoq (Paris: Gallimard, 2001), p. 57 and passim. Cf. Bar, *Le Genre burlesque*; Paul Scarron, *Le Virgile travesti*, ed. Jean Serroy (Paris: Bordas, 1988); Paul Scarron, *Le Roman comique*, ed. Claudine Nédelec (Paris: Classiques Garnier, 2010); Antoine Picon, 'Un moderne paradoxal', introduction to Charles Perrault, *Mémoires de ma vie* (Paris: Macula, 1994).

10 Vavasseur, *De ludicra dictione*, unnumbered and pp. 3–4 (subsequently in *Opera omnia*, unnumbered and p. 1): 'de ioculatoria et futili dictione, quae per hosce annos increbuisset ... Nec vero satis habent, inepte cogitata sua ineptis efferre verbis, inepta dictione: nisi scripta etiam summorum poetarum, plena prudentiae, plena gravitatis, mimice et scurriliter tractent, detorquendis aliorsum carminis sententiis.'

demonstrate that in Greek and Roman antiquity the jocular style had never existed. Those who had utilized it, like Aristophanes and Plautus, had never lapsed into the vulgarity displayed by unnamed contemporary French authors. An outright condemnation, reiterated by the titles of the five parts of the tract: 'Greek writers never used the jocular style' (*Ludicra dictione non usi Graeci scriptores*); 'Roman writers never used the jocular style' (*Ludicra dictione non usi scriptores Latini*); 'Antique writers never taught how to use the jocular style' (*De ludicra dictione nihil praeceperunt scriptores antiqui*); 'There is no reason to use the jocular style' (*Ludicra dictione utendi nulla causa est*); 'There are many reasons not to use the jocular style' (*Ludicra dictione non utendi causae multae sunt*).

In this insistent, paradoxical sequence, one chapter focuses on Socrates: an obvious choice in a volume dedicated to Guez de Balzac, author of the celebrated *Socrate chrestien* (1652) – a work that Pascal had read and a passage of which he implicitly criticized at the end of the sixteenth *Provincial Letter*.[11] But here a question inevitably arises.

2. At the end of *De ludicra dictione* Vavasseur contrasts good authors, prone to employ antiquated words, with those, inspired by Rabelais or Marot or fashionable romances like *Amadis de Gaule*, that use words taken from the streets, taverns and fish and fruit markets.[12] The allusion to a Calvinist poet like Marot,

---

11 *Socrate chrestien par le Sr de Balzac, et autres oeuvres du mesme Autheur – Dissertation ou diverses remarques sur divers escrits. À Monsieur Conrart, conseiller et secretaire du Roy* (Paris: Augustin Courbé, 1652); critical edn ed. Jean Jehasse (Paris: Champion, 2008). Cf. Blaise Pascal, *Oeuvres*, ed. Léon Brunschvicg, Pierre Boutroux and Félix Gazier, vol. VI (Paris: Hachette, 1914), p. 292 n. 3. See also the conjecture ventured by Brunschvicg in Pascal, *Oeuvres*, vol. XIV, *Pensées III* (Paris: Hachette, 1921), p. 226 n. 1.

12 Vavasseur, *De ludicra dictione*, p. 459 (subsequently in *Opera omnia*, p. 84): 'Vos certo iudicio verba vetusta, et ab usu quotidiani sermonis iamdiu intermissa, crebro usurpari, aut continenter in oratione poni vetatis. Illi a Rabelasio, a Maroto, ab Amadisiis nescio quibus revocant, atque operibus immiscent suis, aut ex iis etiam solis opera omnino

and to an author with a reputation for atheism like Rabelais, makes it clear that Vavasseur's polemic against the jocular style also had religious implications. And yet, from a Jesuit who had written a polemical treatise against Jansenism (*Cornelius Iansenius iprensis, suspectus*), we would expect, in a text on the jocular style published in 1658, mention of Arnauld's *Réponse* (1654) and, above all, the *Provincial Letters* (1656–1657).[13] Yet Vavasseur is silent on both. A contemporary reader might have detected in the very brief section dedicated to scripture and the Church Fathers (26 pages out of 462) an implicit refutation of the thesis advanced by Arnauld in his *Réponse*: namely, that the Bible and the Fathers, in confronting religious subjects, had sometimes employed an aggressive irony similar to that first practised by Socrates.[14] The same reader might have spotted an allusion to the *Provincial Letters* in Vavasseur's reference to contemporary *Gelasimi*, or writers who use the jocular style vainly searching, 'in poetry, long letters [*longis epistolis*], and books of every sort', to transform an ephemeral experience like laughter into something stable and permanent.[15] Why, in 1658, did the Jesuit Vavasseur avoid openly referring to the *Provincial Letters*, the book everyone was talking about, which openly derided the Jesuits? And what was the eighteenth-century editor of Vavasseur's works referring to when he compared *De ludicra dictione* to Erasmus's *Alcibiades's Silenus*, or Socrates, 'who conceals many things that do not appear on the surface'?[16]

---

sua construunt. Vos plebeiis et abiectis sententiis locum esse nullum vultis, nullum pretium. Illi ex tabernis, ex triviis, ex olitorio aut piscatorio foro accersunt, et in honorem, si superis placet, adducere conantur.'

13 François Vavasseur, *Cornelius Iansenius iprensis, suspectus* (Parisiis: apud Sebastianum et Gabrielem Cramoisy fratres, 1650) (subsequently in *Opera omnia*, pp. 343–74).

14 See above, p. 183 and n. 22.

15 Vavasseur, *De ludicra dictione*, p. 431 (subsequently in *Opera omnia*, p. 78).

16 Preface to Vavasseur, *Opera omnia*, p.*2r: 'hujus libri eadem est ratio ac Silenorum Alcibiadis; multo plus in recessu occultat, quam in fronte pollicetur'.

3. We shall attempt to answer these questions later. But first it must be remembered that the quality of Vavasseur's writings did not escape the eye and ear of Sainte-Beuve. In the dense pages of his *Port-Royal*, Sainte-Beuve frequently returned to the Jesuit's works (though not to *De ludicra dictione*), signalling his erudition, incisive elegance and stylistic awareness.[17] In particular, Sainte-Beuve dwelled on the attack that Vavasseur, in a polemical text directed at Arnauld, had launched against the style of *Port-Royal*, deploring 'the length of the interminable sentences', the repetitions, the inability to use brief and concise sentences (*quid caesim sit, quid membratim dicere*).[18] Some years later, observed Sainte-Beuve, the *Provincial Letters* refuted the accusations formulated by Vavasseur. (We are immediately put in mind of the unforgettable incipit to the first letter: 'Nous étions bien abusés. Je ne suis détrompé que d'hier' [We were completely mistaken. I was only disabused yesterday]).[19]

It has recently been assumed that Pascal had read Vavasseur and absorbed his arguments, as well as (we might add) his style.[20] A few lines will suffice to convey the rhythm of Vavasseur's prose. Arnauld had attributed to him an anonymous text written in Latin directed against Jean Callaghan, a Jansenist prior. Vavasseur responded contemptuously: 'What is my defence? Easy and rapid, it can be summed up in two words: read, compare.'[21] Albeit reluctantly, Arnauld and Pascal will have

---

17 Charles Augustin Sainte-Beuve, *Port-Royal*, ed. Maxime Leroy (Paris: Gallimard, 1954), vol. II, pp. 74–6, 468–70, 861–2, 979–84. Sainte-Beuve constantly used the Latin spelling 'Vavassor' (see p. 981).

18 Ibid., pp. 74–6 on François Vavasseur, *Dissertatio de libello supposititio. Ad Antonium Arnaldum doctorem et socium Sorbonicum* (Paris: apud Sebastianum and Gabrielem Cramoisy fratres, 1653), pp. 70–1 (subsequently in *Opera omnia*, pp. 403–12, esp. p. 410).

19 Pascal, *Les Provinciales*, ed. Michel Le Guern (Paris: Gallimard, 1987), p. 41.

20 Cf. Yuka Mochizuki, 'Les *Provinciales* et le style janséniste', *Chroniques de Port-Royal* 58 (2008) (issue entitled *La Campagne des 'Provinciales'*), pp. 137–51.

21 Vavasseur, *Dissertatio de libello supposititio*, p. 11

admired this ironic variation on the famous passage in the *Confessions* where St Augustine recalled the words, similar to a children's lullaby, which had propelled him from the abyss of dejection to the letters of St Paul: 'Tolle lege, tolle lege' (Pick it up and read it, pick it up and read it).[22] And Pascal will have been able to learn from Vavasseur's incisive style. But all this renders the silence of the treatise *De ludicra dictione* on the *Provinciales* even stranger.

4. A winding track begins here, which will lead us to reject a hypothesis advanced by Pierre Bayle. In the entry 'Nicolle, Pierre' in his *Dictionnaire historique et critique*, Bayle referred to a refutation of the Latin translation of the *Provincial Letters*, which had appeared under a pseudonym: *Notae in notas Willelmi Wendrockii ad Ludovici Montaltii Litteras, et in disquisitiones Pauli Irenaei, inustae a Bernardo Stubrockio Viennensi theologo* (Cologne: Joannem Busaeum Bibliopolam, 1659).[23] Some of these pseudonyms are familiar: Wilhelm Wendrock is Pierre Nicole; Ludovicus Montaltius is Pascal; Paulus Irenaeus is, once again, Pierre Nicole. But who is Bernardus Stubrockius? Bayle, followed by many scholars, has identified him with Honoré Fabri, a Jesuit known for his theological writings, and for a many-sided erudition put to good use in various fields:

(subsequently in *Opera omnia*, p. 404): 'Quae est igitur mea defensio? Facilis et expedita, quam verbis duobus complecti licet: Lege, confer.' Antoine Arnauld, *L'innocence et la verité defendues, contre les calomnies et les faussetez que les jesuites ont employées en divers libelles, pour déchirer les vivans et les morts*, [no publisher, no place] 1652 (subsequently in *Oeuvres*, vol. XXX, 1779, pp. 13–378), had attributed to Vavasseur the anonymous opuscule *Calaghanus natione Hybernicus, Chiverniensis Curio, an Satyrus ille qui nuper in lucem prodiit*. Cf. Jules Gallerand, 'Le jansénisme en Blésois. Le conflit entre le P. de Brisacier et Jean Callaghan (1651–1653)', *Revue d'Histoire de l'Église de France* 55/154 (1969), pp. 29–47.

22 Augustine of Hippo, *Confessiones*, book VIII, 12, 29: 'et ecce audio vocem de vicina domo cum cantu dicentis et crebro repetentis, quasi pueri an puellae, nescio: "tolle lege, tolle lege".'

23 I have consulted the copy preserved in the Berlin Staatsbibliothek: Da 8188 (2) (rightly 3).

astronomy, botany, anatomy.[24] As was customary, Bayle mentioned his sources in the notes: three statements by Arnauld, confirmed by the fact that Fabri had reprinted Stubrock's *Notae* in the second edition of a volume edited by him, *Apologeticus* (1672). In fact, this inclusion proves that Stubrock and Fabri were not the same person. Let us see why.

In the first edition of *Apologeticus* (1670), Stubrock's *Notae* do not feature, even though Fabri mentioned their author several times – in particular, in a passage from the dialogue *De opinione probabili* in which Pithanophilus (a pseudonym of Fabri himself) addresses Antimus (pseudonym of Anthyme-Denis Cohon, Bishop of Nîmes), alluding to Stubrock as 'one of your friends'.[25] Here, as in another passage where Fabri says that he sails 'in the same boat' as Stubrock (*in eadem navi navigamus*), we are manifestly dealing with two different people.[26] Both the first edition of the *Apologeticus* and the second (much larger) one contain writings by Fabri and other authors, duly listed in the table of contents. The 1672 edition includes a reprint of Stubrock's *Notae*, followed by an appendix and Stubrock's comment 'on the new index by Wendrock [i.e., Nicole]' (*de novo indice Wendrockiano*).[27] Once again,

---

24 Fabri played an important part in the *Provinciales* being placed on the Index. This is demonstrated, on the basis of new documents, by Jean-Louis Quantin, '"Si mes *Lettres* sont condamnées à Rome . . ." Les *Provinciales* devant le Saint-Office', *XVIIe siècle* 265 (2014), pp. 587–617 (at pp. 597–8 and passim is repeated the erroneous attribution of Stubrock's *Notae* to Fabri). In an introduction to the *Provinciales*, Louis Cognet writes that in 1666 Fabri (identified as the author of Stubrock's *Notae*) 'also published a refutation of the *Provinciales*' (Paris: Garnier, 1965, p. 77, n. 3). I have not managed to verify this claim.

25 Honoré Fabri, *Apologeticus Doctrinae Moralis eiusdem Societatis* (Lugduni: sumptibus Laurentii Anisson, 1670), p. 92.

26 Ibid., p. 109.

27 Honoré Fabri, *Apologeticus doctrinae moralis ejusdem Societatis. In quo variis tractatibus, diversorum auctorum opuscula confutantur ... in duas partes commode sectus ... editio altera* (Coloniae Agrippinae: sumptibus viduae Joannis Busaei, 1672), pp. 673–9 ('Appendix ad praemissas confutationes'), pp. 680–2 ('Bernardus Stubrockius lectori de novo indice Wendrockiano').

we can clearly see that Fabri and Stubrock were two different people. In 1698 this was underlined by the anonymous author of the *Apologie des Lettres provinciales* (a work by the Benedictine Mathieu Petitdidier).[28]

A letter by Hermann Conring (1601–1681), a highly learned jurist and doctor, refers to Stubrock as a Jesuit. Stubrock himself, as we shall see, forcefully invoked his adherence to the Society of Jesus. Stubrock was a Jesuit, but he was not Honoré Fabri. Who was he?

On the flyleaf of the copy of Stubrock's *Notae* published in 1659 and held by Bibliothèque Nationale de France, we read a note in Latin written by a seventeenth-century hand: 'The true author of these *Notes*, published under the pseudonym Stubrock, was a Jesuit, Father Vavasseur.' The author of the treatise *De ludicra dictione* is said to have written the *Notae* in 1659 in Clermont College, Paris.[29] This attribution is confirmed by an internal factor, which is much more persuasive, based on a comparison between two texts written by Stubrock and Vavasseur, respectively.

Here is Stubrock's reaction to the insinuation by Hermann Conring, who had identified him as a Jesuit: 'I am Stubrock as he is Wendrock; I am Bernardus as he is Willelmus; I am a

---

28 [Mathieu Petitdidier,] *Apologie des Lettres provinciales de Louis de Montalte contre la dernière réponse des PP. Jésuites, intitulée Entretiens de Cléandre et d'Eudoxe* (Rouen: Henri van Rhin, 1698), vol. I, pp. 211–12. In this work the true identities of Louis de Montalte (Pascal) and Wilhelm Wendrock (Nicole) are taken for granted.

29 BNF: D.34676: *Notae in notas Willelmi Wendrockii ad Ludovici Montaltii Litteras, et in Disquisitiones Pauli Irenaei, inustae a Bernardo Stubrockio Viennensi theologo* (Coloniae: apud Joannem Busaeum Bibliopolam, 1659), verso of the flyleaf: 'Harum notarum sub nomine Bernard Stubrockii Vienn. Theologi scriptarum verus author est R.P. Vavassor Societ. Jesu theol. qui has in collegio Claromontano scripsit anno 1659 ut a multis et omni exceptione [*struck through*: dignis] maioribus viris accepi.' In the record for this volume in the BNF's electronic catalogue, we read: 'A hand-written note on the flyleaf attributes to P. Vavasseur the pseudonym of Stubrockius, generally recognized as being that of P.H. Fabri, S.J.'

theologian from Vienna just as he is from Salzburg; I am German as is he; I am a Jesuit as he is a Jansenist [*tam ego Jesuita, quam ille Jansenista*].'[30]

These analogies, which follow hard upon one another, are all fallacious except for the last. Stubrock and Wendrock are both pseudonyms; their first names are not Bernardus or Willelmus; Stubrock is not a theologian from Vienna, just as Wendrock is not a theologian from Salzburg; neither of them is German. But Stubrock is indeed a Jesuit, just as Wendrock is a Jansenist. The truth of the last statement is submerged in the falsity of the preceding ones. A similar hodgepodge of the true and the false, here concentrated in three sentences, reappears in Vavasseur's reaction to Antoine Arnauld's insinuation, which had identified him as the author of an anti-Jansenist text: 'A book has been published, entitled *Iansenius suspectus*, attributed to Denis Petau. Another book has been published, entitled *Iansenius damnatus*, written, it is said, by François Vavasseur. Both claims are false.'[31]

In reality, the author of *Iansenius suspectus* was precisely Vavasseur, who immediately afterwards vigorously, if indirectly, reiterated his identity: 'The editor knows it; the style speaks for itself; the learned, intelligent reader recognizes [the author's identity].'[32]

---

30 Fabri, *Apologeticus*, 1672 edition, p. 677: 'tam sum ego Stubrockius, quam ille Wendrockius; tam Bernandus [!], quam ille Willelmus; tam Viennensis Theologus, quam ille Salisburgensis; tam ego Germanus, quam ille; tam ego Jesuita, quam ille Jansenista.'

31 Vavasseur, *Dissertatio de libello supposititio*, pp. 54–85 (subsequently in *Opera omnia*, p. 411): 'Prodit liber, qui *Iansenius suspectus* inscribitur: Dionysij Petavij est, inquiunt. Alter prodit, qui inscribitur *Iansenius damnatus*: Francisci Vavassoris est. Utrumque falsum.' Cf. *Triumphus catholicae veritatis adversus novatores, sive Jansenius damnatus a conciliis, pontificibus, episcopis . . . opera et studio S.E.R.T* [Sanctae Ecclesiae Romanae Theologi] (Parisiis: apud S. and G. Cramoisy, 1651). The anonymous author of this work is generally identified as the Jesuit Philippe Labbé.

32 Vavasseur, *Dissertatio de libello supposititio*, p. 85 (subsequently in *Opera omnia*, p. 411): 'Scit librarius: stilus loquitur: doctus, et intelligens lector agnoscit.'

The same reader would have understood, from the playful juxtaposition of true and false statements, the ironic use of mental reservation, the unmistakable staccato, that Vavasseur and Stubrock were the same person: *stilus loquitur,* 'the style speaks for itself'. At this point the absence of any references to Jansenism in the *De ludicra dictione* is explicable: behind the mask of a pseudonym (Bernardus Stubrockius), Vavasseur was preparing a frontal attack on two targets that were likewise concealed by a pseudonym: Ludovicus Montaltius and his translator, Willelmus Wendrockius, that is, Pierre Nicole. Some years later (1669), without the veil of a pseudonym, Vavasseur once again attacked Nicole in his *De epigrammate liber.*[33]

5. As Bayle noted, the reception of the *Provinciales* was curious. The French original was placed on the Index; its Latin translation, annotated and glossed by Wendrock-Nicole, was never proscribed.[34] Instead, what would be placed on the Index, on 30 July 1678, was the refutation, written by Stubrock alias Vavasseur, of the Latin translation of the *Provinciales.*[35]

---

33 François Vavasseur, *De epigrammate liber et Epigrammatum libri tres* (Parisiis: e typographia Edmundi Martini, 1669). See also Sainte-Beuve, *Port-Royal,* Vol. II, pp. 468–70.

34 Bayle, *Dictionnaire historique et critique,* vol. III, pp. 501–2 (the entry 'Nicolle, Pierre').

35 It should be noted that a subsequent Italian translation of the *Provinciales* with Nicole's notes, preceded by a violently anti-Jesuit preface, was placed on the Index: *Le Provinciali o lettere scritte da Luigi di Montalto ad un provinciale de'suoi amici colle annotazioni di Guglielmo Wendrok, tradotte nell'italiana favella con delle nuove annotazioni,* 6 vols (Venice: stamperia de' PP. Gesuiti nel foro deretano [printing house of the Jesuit fathers in the back hole] [sic!], 1761). This new translation ('Or io mi sono indotto a intraprenderne una nuova traduzione': ibid., vol. I, p. 9) is not – as stated by Giovanni Melzi, *Dizionario di opera anonime e pseudonime di scrittori italiani* (Milan: Luigi di Giacomo Pirola, 1852, vol. II, p. 384) – the one by Cosimo Brunetti subsequently included in the polyglot edition of the *Provinciales* published in Cologne in 1684, but the work of Ludovico Maria Carrara. The 1761 preface does not feature in subsequent editions of the *Provinciales* (Venice: Giuseppe Bettinelli, 1766, 1st edn in Italy; Domenico Fracasso, Venice 1789, 2nd edn in Italy).

We glimpse a profound ambivalence about Pascal's work at the top of the Catholic hierarchy. But the condemnation of the French original and the non-condemnation of the Latin translation are easily explained. As was immediately noted by the Jesuit Jacques Nouet, it was permissible to discuss the most delicate theological issues in Latin, but not in an everyday language accessible to everyone, including women.[36] But, observed Nouet, there was another danger: atheists and freethinkers might convert the mockery of casuistry into mockery of the Bible. They might mock Moses, who prohibited usury to his people except when it involved foreigners, regarding this as an example of casuistry. Similarly, they might regard David's command to put Joab and Shimei to death (I Kings 2: 1–9), 'for good reasons that the Bible does not specify', an example of 'an excellent politician capable of adapting his conscience to the dictates of the state, directing his intention'.[37]

---

36 See above, pp. 187–8.

37 [Jacques Nouet et al.,] *Responses aux Lettres provinciales publiées par le secretaire du Port-Royal, contre les PP. de la Compagnie de Jésus* (Liège: Jean Mathias Hovius, 1658), pp. 213–14: 'Or qui ne void que s'il est permis de faire le plaisant en des questions de cette sorte, de traitter en comedien les matieres de theologie, et de faire passer des railleries indignes d'un bon esprit, pour des solides raisons: non seulement la morale des casuistes, mais encore celle de l'Ecriture est exposée à l'impudence des libertins, et que le Janseniste n'a rien dit en ce poinct contre le Iesuites, qu'un athée ne puisse reprocher aux prophetes et aux Apostres?

'Moyse defend l'usure aux Israëlites avec ceux de leur nation, et la tolere avec les idolatres, *Non foenerabis fratri tuo ad usuram, sed alieno*. Deut. 23. Le Janseniste aprend au libertin à rire de cette tolerance, disant que ce sage legislateur avoit des methodes à choisir pour enrichir son peuple, et justifier l'usure en dirigeant l'intention.

'Judith se pare avec soin pour surprendre son ennemy: quelque innocente que soit cette action, le libertin instruit dans l'Echole des Jansenistes dira que Judith estoit habile femme, et qu'elle a apris à son sexe à sanctifier le luxe et la volupté en purifiant son intention.

'David estant proche de sa fin commande à son fils de se défaire de Joab, et de Semeï pour des justes raisons que l'Ecriture ne nous a pas si clairement expliquées: le libertin s'en mocque, disant que David estoit un excellent politique qui sçavoit bien accorder les maximes de la conscience avec celles de l'Etat, en dirigeant son intention.

'Samuel par un merveilleux jugement de Dieu parut à Saul apres sa

A similar reaction had emerged some years earlier, after the publication of *Théologie morale des jésuites,* an anonymous text commonly attributed to Arnauld. A Jesuit, Nicolas Caussin, had objected that 'some irreverent individuals could pick out a series of passages in the Bible, taking them out of context, distorting and travestying them just as our opponents do with our writings, in order to induce the people to believe that the Bible is a blasphemous, reprobate book'.[38] The Jesuits themselves were aware that casuistry was an ambiguous tool. Cases based on a contextual perspective could be taken out of their context and turned against those who had constructed and disseminated them: a hypothesis that is quite the reverse of far-fetched, as had been demonstrated by the ferocious irony of the *Provinciales.*

II

1. Johann Ludwig Fabricius, born in Schaffhausen, Switzerland, in 1632, studied in Utrecht and Paris (1652–1656). He revisited France in 1658, became professor of theology at the University of Heidelberg in 1661, and died in 1696.[39] His name is

---

mort selon l'opinion des plusieurs Peres: le libertin suivant la morale des Jansenistes, dira que ce prophete estoit fort charitable, puis qu'il aidoit méme les sorciers à gagner legitimement le prix de leurs detestables crimes.'

38 Nicolas Caussin, *Apologie pour les religieux de la Compagnie de Iesus,* 2nd rev. and expanded edn (Lyon: [no publisher] 1644), p. 93: 'J'asseure, mon Lecteur, avec toute verité, que si quelque impudent vouloit compiler divers passages de la Bible, en les arrachant de leur sens, et de leur suite, en les estropiant, en les déguisant comme font nos adversaires sur nos ouvrages, il la feroit passer dans la creance du peuple comme un livre impie et damnable.'

39 Cf. Albert de Lange, 'Die *Dissertatio de Amicitia* (1656) von Johann Ludwig Fabricius (1632–1696)', in *Mentis amore ligati. Lateinische Freundschaftsdichtung und Dichterfreundschaft in Mittelalter und Neuzeit. Festgabe für Reinhard Düchting zum 65. Geburtstag,* ed. Boris Körkel, Tino Licht and Jolanta Wiendlocha (Heidelberg: Mattes, 2001), pp. 191–215. (I am grateful to Sanjay Subrahmanyam for having pointed out this essay to me.)

remembered for an exchange of letters in 1673 with Spinoza, known at the time as the presumed author of a scandalous book, the *Tractatus theologico-politicus*, published anonymously in 1670. On behalf of the elector of the Palatinate, Fabricius invited Spinoza to take up a professorship at Heidelberg University, where he would enjoy 'the most ample freedom to philosophize [*philosophandi libertatem*]' – an allusion to the subtitle of the *Tractatus* – on condition that he did not abuse it. Spinoza declined the invitation, declaring that he did not know what limits could be imposed on the freedom to philosophize.[40]

Often characterized as 'an orthodox theologian', Fabricius knew Spinoza's writings well.[41] In summer 1670 he had sent a letter to Leibniz's patron, Baron Johann Christian von Boyneburg, informing him that during a journey in the Netherlands he had seen an anonymous *Tractatus theologico-politicus* at a book shop. From a friend he learned it had been written by Spinoza, the author of *Renati Des Cartes Principiorum Philosophiae pars I et II, more geometrico demonstratae* (1663).[42] Reference to this work – the only one published by Spinoza under his own name – was significant. Fabricius, hiding behind a pseudonym (Janus Alexander Ferrarius coenobite augustinianus), had echoed its title in a book published in 1667:

40 Benedict de Spinoza, *Opera*, ed. Carl Gebhardt (Heidelberg: Carl Winters Universitätsbuchhandlung, 1924), vol. IV, *Epistolae*, pp. 234–6 (letters 47–8).

41 W. N. A. Klever, 'Spinoza's Life and Works', in Don Garrett, ed., *The Cambridge Companion to Spinoza* (Cambridge: Cambridge University Press, 1995), pp. 42–3.

42 See Otto Rüdiger, *Studien zur Spinozarezeption in Deutschland im 18. Jahrhundert* (Frankfurt am Main: Lang, 1994), p. 19 n. 22. (Fabricius cited the title incorrectly: 'Ibidem primum incidi in tractatum philosophico-politicum'); Steven Nadler, *A Book Forged in Hell: Spinoza's Scandalous Treatise and the Birth of the Secular Age* (Princeton: Princeton University Press, 2011), p. 221. Cf. *Commercii epistolici Leibnitiani, ad omne genus eruditionis comparati, per partes publicandi, tomi prodromi pars altera, quae itidem Boineburgica est, accedit appendix Conringiana ... recensuit Io. Daniel Gruber* (Hanoverae-Gottingae: apud Jo. Wilhelmum Schmidium, 1745), pp. 1314–20, esp. 1315–16.

Euclides Catholicus, sive demonstratio Romanae Fidei ex primis, certis et evidentibus principiis, Mathematicâ methodo et connexis continua serie propositionibus deducta.[43]

Everything, or virtually everything, on the frontispiece is misleading: the author's name (Ferrarius, Latinate-Italian version of Fabricius); the self-description (Augustinian brother); the subtitle ('Demonstration of the Roman Faith'); the place of publication (Paris, as opposed, probably, to Heidelberg).[44] Few contemporaries took the demonstration in Euclidean style literally: the majority of them, it seems, read the book as a satire. A Latin annotation, probably written by an eighteenth-century hand, on the ante-frontispiece of the copy preserved in the Berlin Staatsbibliothek runs as follows: 'A satire that reveals the uncertainty of papal dogmas.' There follows the author's real name.[45] But even this description was, as we shall see, inadequate and, in the final analysis, misleading.

---

43   The frontispiece of the copy consulted by me (Staatsbibliothek, Berlin: Dh. 6720, 'ex Bibl. Frid. Jac. Roloff'), bears the indication in print 'juxta exemplar impressum Parisiis', followed by a handwritten date '1667'. From p. 37 (repeated twice) the pagination is partially altered. For passages cited from these pages, the correct numbering is indicated in brackets.

44   In the important entry on 'Janus Alexander Ferrarius', David Clément, *Bibliothèque curieuse historique et critique, ou catalogue raisonné des livres dificiles à trouver,* vol. VIII (Leipzig: Jean Fred. Gleditsch, 1759), pp. 281–2 and 282–5 n. 26, suggested Heidelberg as place of printing. Cf. also *La Biblioteca di Samuel Pufendorf. Catalogo dell'asta di Berlin del settembre 1697,* ed. Fiammetta Palladini (Wiesbaden: Harrassowitz, 1999), p. 136 n. 570. The catalogue of the library of Wolfenbüttel conjectures that this edition was printed in the Low Countries. Cf. also the copy held by the library of the University of Erfurt (location: 03 – Hn. 8° 00811 [03]), ex Bibliotheca Boineburgica, with handwritten annotations on the frontispiece and final page.

45   J. A. Ferrarius, *Euclides Catholicus* (Parisiis: [no publisher], 1667): 'Satira incertitudinum dogmatum Pontificiorum exponens. Auctoris verum nomen Jo. Lud. Fabricius Professor Theol. Heidelb.' The edition published in London in 1676 displayed on its frontispiece an epigraph inspired by a verse of Horace (*Sermones,* I, 1, 24): 'Ridenti dicere Verum/ Quis vetat?' (What stops one telling the truth while smiling?).

2. *Euclides Catholicus* takes the form of a series of letters followed by definitions, axioms, postulates, proofs and corollaries. They are addressed to Adrian and Peter von Wallenburg: two brothers, both Catholic bishops *in partibus infidelium* (Adrianople and Mainz, respectively). Peter von Wallenburg and Johann Ludwig Fabricius (the real author of *Euclides Catholicus*) are mentioned in the introduction to Leibniz's *Theodicy* (1710). In a passage, Leibniz discreetly alluded to his own attempts to reconcile the various Christian creeds: 'I had opportunity on my journeys to confer with some excellent men of different parties, for instance with Bishop Peter von Wallenburg, Suffragan of Mainz, with Herr Johann Ludwig Fabricius, premier theologian of Heidelberg, and finally with the celebrated M. Arnauld' – a Catholic bishop, a Calvinist theologian, and a foremost figure in Jansenist circles.[46] Even if Fabricius met Leibniz many years after the publication of *Euclides Catholicus*, the reference to Arnauld and his circle is eloquent. In the structure of *Euclides Catholicus* we sense an echo of Pascal's *Provinciales* (which Fabricius will have read in 1658 during his trip to France): seven letters, one of which (the fifth) includes a section of dialogue, which are supposed to have been sent from Paris in close succession, between the beginning of August 1666 and the beginning

---

46   G. W. Leibniz, *Theodicy: Essays on the Goodness of God, the Freedom of Man, and the Origin of Evil* (New York: Cosimo, 2009), p. 67; *Essais de Théodicée sur la bonté de Dieu, la liberté de l'homme, et l'origine du mal* (Amsterdam: François Changuion, 1734), vol. I, pp. 35–6: 'Je ne négligeois point les enseignemens de nos théologiens; et la lecture de leurs adversaires bien loin de me troubler, servoit à me confirmer dans les sentimens moderés des Eglises de la Confession d'Ausbourg. J'eus occasion dans mes voyages de conferer avec quelques excellens hommes de differens partis; comme avec M. Pierre de *Wallenbourg* Suffragant de Mayence, M. *Jean-Louïs Fabrice* premier théologien de Heidelberg, et enfin avec le célèbre M. *Arnauld*, à qui je communiquai même un Dialogue Latin de ma façon sur cette matiere, environ l'an 1673, où je mettois déjà en fait que Dieu ayant choisi le plus parfait de tous les Mondes possibles, avoit été porté par sa sagesse à permettre le mal qui y étoit annexé, mais qui n'empêchoit pas que tout compté et rabbatu ce Monde ne fût le meilleur qui pût être choisi.'

of December 1667. Even Ferrarius's ironic tone presupposes Pascal.

3. A reprint of *Euclides Catholicus* in Latin, published in London in 1673, contains a preface informing readers that the letters addressed to the two bishops were not 'proofs but mockeries of the *Roman* Catholic faith, presented under a cloak of *politeness* and an ostentatious reverence'.[47] The passage was taken from an English translation of *Euclides Catholicus* published in London in the same year – 1673 – at the end of whose title the ambiguity of the 'demonstration of the Roman faith' displayed in the Latin title is dissolved, stressing as it does instead the anti-Catholic element: *His Epistle to the Two Brethren of Wallenburgh, Concerning the Usefulness and Necessity of the Roman Catholick Faith, wherein the Ambition and Avarice of the Church of Rome Are Lively Demonstrated in a Mathematical Method, by a Continued Series of Connected Propositions, from the Original Latine.*[48]

The abrupt transition from 'usefulness and necessity' to 'ambition and avarice' alerts readers straight away. The same desire for clarity emerged in the dedicatory letter (only included

---

47 J. A. Ferrarius, *Euclides Catholicus* (Londini: Guil. Gilbert, 1673), pages unnumbered.

48 J. A. Ferrarius, *His Epistles to the Two Brethren of Wallenburgh* (London: Thomas Ratcliffe and Nathaniel Thompson, 1673). A reprint of *Euclides Catholicus* exists, followed (with different pagination) by a new edition of Erasmus's *Julius Exclusus: Julius Secundus. Dialogus anonymi cujusdam Authoris festivus sane ac elegans* ... Lector, risum cohibe. *Dialogo praefixum est ab Editore* Colloquium, *Dialogistae, qua fieri potuit,* Exquirendo *destinatum:* Quem magnum *illum fuisse* ERASMUM, *tam Rationibus, quam Testimoniis efficitur. Julio secondo accessit EUCLIDES CATHOLICUS, Rom. Ecclesiae Fidem non minus lepide Demonstrans, quam Mores Artesque Rom. Pontificum graphice depinxit Erasmus* (Oxonii, 1680). This edition of *Euclides Catholicus* was preceded by four Latin poems (addressed to the Pope, the Jesuits, etc.), and by the preface that had already appeared in various reprints: 1673 edn (London: [no publisher], 1676). Clément, *Bibliothèque curieuse*, p. 284 n. 26, mentions two copies of this last edition, only one of which includes the preface to the reader.

in the translation) signed 'J.D.' – in all likelihood, the translator's initials. The letter, addressed to Anthony Cooper, Earl of Shaftesbury, the Lord Chancellor (a post he was removed from shortly afterwards, at the start of November), extolled his 'zeal in *protecting* and *defending* the Protestant religion, *firmly established* in the Realm'.[49] Established but, or so it seemed to many, threatened. Both the English reprint of the Latin original and the English translation of the Latin original were published in the course of the strident anti-Catholic campaign provoked by the announcement of the imminent marriage of the Duke of York (later James II) to a Catholic princess, Maria of Modena: a campaign rendered even more strident by the Test Act, which imposed an anti-Catholic oath on all public servants.[50] Both editions warned that the author of the book was 'English by birth … and of not ignoble family'. To this observation, whether truthful or not we do not know, there followed a passage in the Latin edition where the editor made it clear that the author's true name was known to him, but could not be revealed, so as not to expose him to Catholic retribution.[51]

In the English reception of *Euclides Catholicus*, which pivoted around the book's anti-Catholic content, we hear a discordant element. In a passage of the preface (a passage present in the reprint of the Latin edition but absent from the translation), the

---

49 K. H. D. Haley, *The First Earl of Shaftesbury* (Oxford: Clarendon Press, 1968), esp. p. 326ff; John Spurr, 'Shaftesbury and the Politics of Religion', in *Anthony Ashley Cooper, First Earl of Shaftesbury 1621–1683*, ed. Spurr (Farnham: Ashgate, 2011), pp. 127–51.

50 See John Spurr, *England in the 1670s: 'This Masquerading Age'* (Oxford: Blackwell, 2000), p. 35ff.

51 Ferrarius, *Euclides Catholics*, 1673 edn, preface: 'natione sc. *Anglus* … Nex ex *ignobili* oriundus *familia* … De *authore* nihil est quod amplius praefari ausim: cum ipsi etenim sub *ementito* nomine visum est delitescere nollem ego committere, ut nomen *verum* in publicum proferendo exacerbatis *papicolarum* odiis ultricibusque (*sacrificulorum* praesertim) iris, aut *ferro* aut *veneno* petendum exponerem.' Clément, *Bibliothèque curieuse*, p. 284 n., attributes this passage to the translator, who would have suggested the 1673 reprint.

caustic style of *Euclides Catholicus* was compared to that of Hobbes's *Leviathan*.[52] The recipient of the dedicatory letter inserted in the English translation, Lord Shaftesbury, will have regarded this reference to Hobbes, which echoed the text of Ferrarius, favourably.[53] But the reference to Hobbes makes it plain that *Euclides Catholicus* is something very different from a pure and simple anti-Catholic satire.[54]

4. In the first letter Janus Alexander Ferrarius, the Augustinian pseudo-brother, addresses his interlocutors, the two Wallenburg bishops, recalling that 'controversies between Catholics and heretics pertain to a sphere that is not sacred and religious, but juridical and political'. The power of the Roman pontiff, observes Ferrarius, clearly demonstrates all this: 'For who can doubt that, in order to establish so extensive an empire, such as to cover the earth and impose itself on the most powerful emperors, kings and princes,

---

52 Ferrarius, *Euclides Catholicus*, 1673 edn, preface: 'Perpetua nempe per omnes epistolas *ironia* lepidissime luditur; *jocis* adeo facetis, dentatis *salibus*, mordacibusque dicteriis, [ut magnus ille in isthoc scribendi genere *Ichardus* noster, *Anglicano* usus idiomate nihilo felicius cum *Hobbio* (majori ipsomet, quam scripserat, *Leviathane*)] egisse videatur, quam lingua romana (rebus Romanae Ecclesiae transigendis aptiori) *Walenburghicos* (novos istos coeli papalis Atlantes) tractasse noster hic consendus est *Author*.' In the English translation the passage in square brackets is missing. '*Ichardus* noster' probably refers to Richard Flecknoe: see his *Aenigmatical Characters: Being Rather a New Work, than New Impression of the Old* (London: Wood, 1665).

53 Paul Seaward, 'Shaftesbury and the Royal Supremacy', in *Anthony Ashley Cooper*, p. 76, cites a letter from John Aubrey to John Locke, dated 11 February 1673: 'I have a conceit that if your Lord sawe it [Hobbes's *Behemoth*] he would like it.' Cf. also Spurr, 'Shaftesbury and the Politics of Religion', p. 134.

54 What follows presupposes Leo Strauss, *Persecution and the Art of Writing* (Chicago: Chicago University Press, 1988), pp. 22–37. Cf. now Leo Strauss, 'Lecture Notes for "Persecution and the Art of Writing"' (1939), critical edn, ed. Hannes Kerber, in *Reorientation: Leo Strauss in the 1930s*, ed. Martin D. Yaffe and Richard S. Ruderman (New York: Palgrave Macmillan, 2014), pp. 293–304.

vanquishing their resistance, a more than human power was required?'[55]

The discerning reader will have immediately identified the source of Ferrarius's rhetorical (and ironic) question: chapter 11 of Machiavelli's *The Prince*, devoted to ecclesiastics and their principalities. Here is the incipit:

> Only they have states and do not defend them, and subjects whom they do not trouble to govern; and although their states are undefended, they are not deprived of them. And their subjects, although not properly governed, do not worry about it; they cannot get rid of these rulers, nor even think about doing so. Only these principalities, then, are secure and successful.
>
> However, since they are controlled by a higher power, which the human mind cannot comprehend, I shall refrain from discussing them; since they are raised up and maintained by God, only a presumptuous and rash man would examine them. Nevertheless . . .[56]

---

55 Ferrarius, *Euclides Catholicus*, 1667 edn, p. 4: 'Controversias, quae catholicos inter et haereticos agitantur, non in sacro et religioso, sed forensi atque politico causarum genere versari ... Quis enim postea dubitaverit, ad stabiliendum tantum tamque late per omnes terrarum regiones diffusum, et in ipsos potentissimos imperatores, reges ac principes quantumvis invitos atque reluctantes extensum imperium, cujus nec par, nec simile unquam extitit, prudentiâ opus fuisse, plus quam humanâ?'

56 Niccolò Machiavelli, *The Prince*, ed. Quentin Skinner and Russell Price, tr. Russell Price (Cambridge: Cambridge University Press, 2016), p. 40. ('Costoro soli hanno stati, e non li defendano, sudditi, e non li governano, e li stati per essere indifesi non sono loro tolti, e' sudditi per non essere governati non se ne curano né pensano né possano alienarsi da loro. Solo adunque questi principati sono sicuri e felici; ma sendo quelli retti da cagione superiori, alle quali mente umana non aggiugne, lascerò el parlarne, perché, sendo essaltati e mantenuti da Dio, sarebbe offizio di uomo prosuntuoso e temerario discorrerne. Nondimanco . . .': *Il principe*, ed. Mario Martelli, Edizioni nazionale delle Opere, section 1, vol. I (Rome: Salerno, 2006), pp. 175–6.)

Here Machiavelli inverts the casuistic sequence of which he was fond, transforming the alleged exception (the state of the Church) into the rule.[57] One hundred and fifty years later, Fabricius, under the mask of an Augustinian brother, inspects a papacy that had extended its power over the oceans to new worlds. Machiavelli was read through a satirical grid inspired by Spinoza, using the language of Euclid.[58] 'Three basic elements' were identified. A definition: 'The Church is a spiritual, but visible, power, through which men profess the prescribed faith under a spiritual but visible head, or the Roman Pope, and render him the obedience that is due to him.' An axiom or proposition: 'That, and only that, which contributes to the defence and growth of this Church is to be considered true, pious and holy.' A postulate: 'That this Church can expand to the ends of the earth.'[59]

5. If you are disposed to accept all this, wrote Fabricius/Ferrarius addressing the von Wallenburg brothers, I shall set about 'explaining in the most straightforward and simplest fashion, in so far as I can, all the arts of the Catholic religion'.[60] The ingenuousness displayed by Louis de Montalte in Pascal's *Provincial Letters* comes to mind. Here an Augustinian brother (Ferrarius), behind whom is concealed a Calvinist theologian (Fabricius), proposes an ambiguous definition – 'To obtain salvation, some religion is absolutely necessary' (*Ad obtinendam salutem religio aliqua est absolute necessaria*) – followed by a provocative gloss: 'For us salvation signifies simply this: the grandeur and perpetuity of the visible dominion that in Christ's name his Vicar exercises on this earth.'[61] There follows a warning: the papacy

---

57 See chapter 1 above.

58 *Euclides Catholicus* is not mentioned in Enrico De Angelis, *Il metodo geometrico nella filosofia del Seicento* (Florence: Le Monnier, 1964).

59 Ferrarius, *Euclides Catholicus*, 1667 edn, pp. 6–7.

60 Ibid., p. 7: 'Omnesque catholicae religionis artes, quâ potero simplicitate atque ingenuitate explicabo.'

61 Ibid., p. 14: 'Propositio I. Ad obtinendam salutem religio aliqua est absolute necessaria ... voce SALUTIS nihil aliud nobis significari, quam *aspectabilis illius, quod sub Christi nomine*

exemplifies universal rule. Political power is always based upon religion: a thesis that Ferrarius proposes through a series of citations, ranging from Montaigne to Campanella, from Polybius to the 'most wise' Machiavelli.[62]

The impression of finding ourselves face to face with a freethinker, or deist, might seem to be contradicted by the conclusion: 'But natural religion is not sufficient for salvation.' Ferrarius offers a succinct definition of natural religion according to the deists, citing Father Garasse (who had attacked them) and Herbert of Cherbury (who had defended them). But given that, as we recall, Ferrarius had identified salvation with the universal power of the pope, the thesis that 'natural religion is not sufficient for salvation' obviously sounds ironic, as can be inferred from its corollary: 'Hence from natural light it does not follow that the Roman Pope is the lord of the universe, or that this mystery has been revealed to the gentiles.' The thesis is repeated in the subsequent proposition: 'To obtain salvation, or to establish and preserve the regal Roman pontificate, alongside natural religion another is necessary, which is called super-natural.'[63]

6. A series of tautologies, or semi-tautologies, ironically presented as proofs, introduces a thesis whose implications emerge gradually. It begins with a terminological clarification, which once again refers to Machiavelli:

And yet, this religion which we call *super-natural*, might also be called *civil*, for it has been contrived solely in order to build and

---

Vicarius Ejus in terris exercet, Doninij magnitudinem atque perpetuitatem.'

62 Ibid., p. 16.

63 Ibid., p. 17: 'Propositio II. Religio autem naturalis ad salutem non sufficit'; p. 18: 'Corollarium. Ergo, ex solo lumine naturae non constat Pontificem Romanum esse dominum universi, nec mysterium hoc omnibus Gentibus est revelatum'; p. 22: 'Propositio III. Ad obtinendam salutem, sive ad regalem Pontificatum Romae stabiliendum atque conservandum opus est praeter religionem naturalem aliâ aliquâ, quae supernaturalis dicitur.'

preserve the city: and if God is its true author, and it is destined to fulfil a more sublime, eternal goal, its goal is the same. We might add that observance of this religion is commanded by the civil laws, and hence also in this sense we can define it as *civil*. But we have preferred to abstain from this word, given that it does not elicit religious veneration in those who hear it. Similarly, we have abstained from the word *preternatural*, which has a connotation that is in some way strange and unpleasant. Hence we have used the term *super-natural*, because it is composed of a nobler particle, which impresses a more solemn idea on our minds.[64]

Ferrarius's argument is clear: what matters is the civil religion, conveniently characterized as 'super-natural'. Revelation is simply a possibility ('if God is its true author'): the power of the Roman pope is not based on it. Are we dealing with a deist modelled on Machiavelli, who disguises himself as an Augustinian brother in order to conceal his own identity as a Calvinist theologian? In truth, this conclusion likewise proves too simple.

In a world dominated by relentless religious conflicts, the Roman pope (suggests Ferrarius) finds himself faced with two alternatives, which are presented in these terms:

Consequently, super-natural religion that does not conduce to salvation must be destroyed immediately, at a stroke, violently, so that this can happen without risks and difficulties. But if this is not possible, it must be changed one piece at a time, step by

---

64   Ibid., p. 23: 'Enimvero et hanc, quam *supernaturalem* dicimus, *civilem* quoque nominare possemus: vel enim ad civitatem solum constituendam atque conservandam est excogitata, vel, si ipsum Deum revera autorem habeat et ad sublimiorem aeternumque finem destinetur, non minus tamen huc conducit. Ne dicam quod legibus civilibus observantia ejus ut plurimum imperetur, adeoque et illo sensu *civilis* dici possit. Istâ tamen appellatione, quoniam nullam audientibus ingerit religionis venerationem, abstinere maluimus, quemadmodum et voce *praeternaturalis*, utpote quae nescio quid alienum et odiosum sonat. *Supernaturalem* igitur diximus, vocabulo ex nobiliori particula composito, quodque menti nostrae augustiorem quandam ideam imprimit.'

step, gradually, always preserving the external aspect, as long as it is not perfectly *qualified* to obtain salvation.[65]

But what is the 'super-natural religion that does not lead to salvation'? According to Ferrarius, it is the Christian religion:

> Because the apostles did not aspire to anything exalted or sublime, but in their mediocrity praised plebeian virtues such as modesty, patience and humility, which endanger not only the condition of the Church, but its whole structure ... it follows that the religion transmitted by them is in and of itself supremely ill-suited to salvation.[66]

Once again we hear an echo of Machiavelli's voice: Christianity, condemned as a meek, weak, pusillanimous religion, is contrasted with the heroic, bellicose religion of the Romans.[67] Fabricius/Ferrarius reworks Machiavelli's *Discourses*, but to what end? What exactly does he mean when he speaks of 'Christian religion'? A thesis (number IX) proposed in the seventh and last letter of *Euclides Catholicus* counterposes the 'Christian religion' to the Catholic Church:

> Although the Christian religion is as far as ever from the goal of our Roman Church, where it is approved by reason, become

---

65   Ibid., p. 25: 'Propositio VI. Illa igitur religio supernaturalis, quae ad salutem non conducit, quam ocyssime uno impetu et aperta vi destruatur, modo id tuto et commode fieri possit: [si non] sit, carptim ac sensim lentisque artibus immutetur, servatâ semper eâdem externa specie, donec ad salutem comparandam sit perfecte *qualificata*.'

66   Ibid., p. 43: 'Demonstratio. Cum Apostoli nihil altum spiraverint, nihil sublime, sed fractis dejectisque animis nonnisi plebejas virtutes patientiam scilicet, modestiam, humilitatem commendaverint, quibus Ecclesiae non salus solum impeditur, sed universa structura funditus labefactatur ... adeoque religionem quam tradiderunt ex se et principiorum suorum natura ad salutem comparandam esse ineptissimam.'

67   See Niccolò Machiavelli, *Discourses on Livy*, tr. Julia Conaway Bondanella and Peter Bondanella (Oxford: Oxford University Press, 2008), bk. I, 11–15, pp. 50–61.

customary, and established by the authority of princes, it does not seem opportune to seek to destroy it suddenly, violently.[68]

Are we to suppose that the Calvinist theologian Johann Ludwig Fabricius, via his alter ego Janus Alexander Ferrarius, was attacking any attempt to alter the religious map of Europe by force? Was Fabricius/Ferrarius perhaps arguing that the status quo, based on confessional divisions, must be protected on the grounds of the principle *cuius regio eius religio*? An interpretation of the sort immediately sounds absurd. Why hide behind the mask of an Augustinian brother, why write a bizarre satire of the Church of Rome in Euclidean form, to propose, in contorted fashion, an utterly respectable thesis – one that was in fact commonly accepted in Protestant countries?

7. Ferrarius's thesis was less respectable. We see it emerge through a series of examples, intended to prove that the Christian religion should be changed slowly from within rather than violently suppressed. This strategy had been employed by Mohammed, 'a most clever man, as is shown by the facts'. He 'judged that the Christian religion, although contrary to his plan and profoundly harmful, should not be destroyed in one blow, in a frontal attack'.[69] For that reason he required his followers to acknowledge the truth of the prophets and apostles.

The heretics (that is, in the fiction of *Euclides Catholicus*, Protestants) regard Mohammed and the pope as two faces (or horns) of the Antichrist. In reality, comments Ferrarius, the pontiff should take Mohammed as a model and follow his example. Mohammed's empire was 'material and physical'. The pope's will

---

68 Ferrarius, *Euclides Catholicus*, 1667 edn, p. 44: 'Quamvis religio Christiana a scopo Romanae nostrae Ecclesiae immane quantum abhorreat minime tamen consultum videtur, ut ubi rationibus approbata, consuetudine introducta et principum auctoritate stabilita est, aperta ejus ruina violento molimine et uno impetu tentetur.'

69 Ibid., p. 45: 'Homo, ut eventus docuit, perspicacissimus ... eam sibi noxiam et perniciosam omnino credidit, neque tamen uno ictu et vi aperta judicavit demoliendam.'

have to be very different, because it will have to fuse together 'divine and human things in order to be *spiritually physical and invisibly visible*'. In this way, 'profane and sacred, heaven and earth, truth and falsehood' will blend. The person who will employ these arts 'to give life to the sacred empire will form a veritable Leviathan, more robust and more fearsome than that of Hobbes'.[70]

Mohammed is offered as a model because he had adapted himself to the pre-existing context. Equally exemplary, concludes *Euclides Catholicus*, is the strategy adopted by the Jesuit missionaries in Asia:

When they realised that what remained of the teaching of the apostles in Europe, although very little, contained something noxious and repugnant which, as in the past, seemed mad to the Gentiles and scandalous to the Jews, they did not preach Christ crucified, the only Christ Paul professed to know, but a different Christ: beautiful, magnificent, dressed in a Chinese costume, who long ago descended from heaven to Europe in great pomp and announced the reign of our Pontiff.[71]

---

70 Ibid., p. 46: 'Nam si ille [Mohammed] non nisi crassum quoddam et corporeum imperium erat exstructurus, et tamen adeo exquisitas artes sibi adhibendas credidit, quando subtiliori industriâ nobis opus erit in condendo mystico nostro et spiritali regno . . . Tale imperium cum ex divinarum et humanarum rerum mixtura ita contemperari debeat, ut *spiritaliter-corporeum et invisibiliter visibili* existat, necesse est utique ut artes, quibus exstruitur, utrique isti rerum generi conveniant. Ita demum profana sacris, coelum terris, vera falsis feliciter immiscebuntur . . . qui his omnibus ad sacri imperii stabilimentum utetur, ex utroque existet verus Leviathan, ipso *Hobbiano Leviathane* longe robustior et formidabilior.'

71 Ibid., p. 43 [rightly 51]: 'Hi enim, cum animadverterent ipsas illas licet exiguas, quae in Europa permanserunt, apostolicae doctrinae reliquias etiamnum nescio quid continere horridum et durum, et quod, ut olim, stultitia Gentibus videatur, Judaeisque sit scandalo, non Christum docuere crucifixum, quem unicum tamen Paulus se scire professus est, sed alium formosum, magnificum, Chinensi habitu indutum, qui mira cum magnificentia aliquando de coelo in Europam descenderit, et Pontificis nostri praedicaverit regnum.'

8. Ferrarius illustrated this 'method of Christian catechism', disseminated by the Jesuits 'in the provinces of East Asia',[72] with citations from three authors hostile to the Jesuits: the Jansenist Louis de Saint-Amour, the Bishop of Puebla Juan de Palafox y Mendoza, and the theologian Tomás Hurtado.[73] Along with other authors, the last-named had been mentioned by Pascal in the fifth *Provincial Letter* in a passage dedicated to the Jesuits, who in India and China 'suppriment la scandale de la Croix, et ne prêchent que Jésus-Christ glorieux, et non pas Jésus-Christ souffrant' (abolish the scandal of the Cross, and preach only the glorious Jesus Christ, not the suffering Jesus Christ).[74] Ferrarius avoided mentioning Pascal and converted the charges levelled against the Jesuits into eulogies. The Jesuit exception had proved capable of transforming itself into the norm; shame over a suffering Jesus could have been the starting point of a trajectory that would have ended with the disappearance of the Christian religion:

This being the case, I believe that the safest route is the one followed by the emperors, when they were on the point of transforming the Roman republic into an empire. They left a simulacrum of the

---

72   Ibid., p. 43 [rightly 51]: 'Talem Christianae catecheseos methodum jam nostris temporibus in extimis Asiae provinciis observarunt Ignatianae fidei propagatores solertissimi.'

73   Cf. *Journal de Mr de Saint Amour, docteur de Sorbonne, de ce qui s'est fait à Rome dans l'affaire des cinq propositions* (Paris: [no publisher], 1662), followed, with different pagination, by *Recoeuil de diverses pieces dont il est parlé dans ce Iournal ou qui en regardent la matiere* (at pp. 11–26 we find the original Latin version of Palafox's letter to Innocent X, which mentions Christ 'pulchrum, gloriosum, formosum (sicut ipsum Iesuitae Chinico habitu depingunt)', p. 26; see also *Journal*, p. 163). Cf. Tomás Hurtado, *Resolutiones orthodoxomorales, scholasticae, historicae, de vero, unico, proprio et catholico martyrio fidei* (Coloniae Agrippinae: apud Cornelium ab Egmond, 1655), pp. 426–30: 'Resolutio LXIX. Utrum in catechesi Indorum et Chinensium Crucis mysterium ante baptismum debeat edoceri, et Christi crucifixi imago in publico monstrari?'; Theophilus Raynaud, *Hoplotheca contra ictum calumniate robur,* in *Miscella sacra* (Lugduni: sumpt. Horatii Boissat, et Georgii Remeus, 1665), vol. XII, pp. 554–5.

74   Pascal, *Les provinciales,* p. 87.

previous liberty, even though liberty had been completely abolished. Thus it will be opportune to display some images of Christ, even if Christ will have been abolished bit by bit.[75]

Thus warns, in fact, the 'most religious' (*religiosissimus*) Machiavelli:

Anyone who desires or tries to reform the government of a city in a way that is acceptable and capable of maintaining it to everyone's satisfaction will find it necessary to retain at least the semblance of its ancient customs, so that it will not seem to the people that its institutions have changed, though in fact the new institutions may be completely dissimilar from those of the past, because men in general live as much by appearances as by realities: indeed, they are often moved more by things as they appear than by things as they really are.[76]

Comparing Machiavelli with the Jesuits was part of a widespread stereotype. But here the perspective was different and

---

75 Ferrarius, *Euclides Catholicus*, 1667 edn, p. 44 [rightly 52]: 'Quae cum ita sint, tutissimum credo eandem viam inire, quam olim tenuerunt imperatores, cum Remp. Romanam in Dominium essent conversuri. Ut enim illi simulacra quaedam libertatis pristinae reliquerunt, ipsâ libertate funditus sublatâ, ita etiam juvabit imaginem quandam Christi ostendere, Christo ipso sensim abolito.'

76 Ibid., p. 44 [rightly 52]: 'Qui Reip. formam vult innovare, in id incumbat necesse est, ut rerum, quae antea fuerunt, umbram aliquam retineat. Sic enim efficietur, ut plebs non putet quicquam esse mutatum, quamvis omnia re ipsa sint innovata. Nam populus non solet res profundius intueri, sed quae videntur et foris ita apparent, eas perinde ac si ita sint accipit. Quamvis Magistratus plane novi creentur, planeque nova munera hominibus imponantur, sunt tamen eadem retinenda nomina, ut putentur esse eadem.' The quotation merges, with minimal changes, two passages from the Latin translation of the *Discorsi*, I, 25: Niccolò Machiavelli, *Disputationum de republica, quas Discursus nuncupavit, libri III, quomodo in rebuspub. ad Antiquorum Romanorum imitationem actiones omnes bene maleve instituantur, ex Italico Latine facti*, [tr. T. T.] (Mompelgarti: per Iacobum Folietum, 1588), pp. 122–4.

more complex. *Euclides Catholicus* is a text made up of super-imposed strata, at least in the version given to the press. (According to Gerhard von Mastricht, professor at Duisburg, only the 'general part' of *Euclides Catholicus* was published; the 'special part' was suppressed on the orders of the elector of the Palatinate, who seemingly had no objections to the rest.[77]) As we have seen, Ferrarius, the Augustinian brother, had begun by saying that he sought to explain 'all the arts of the Catholic religion'. A different (albeit connected) theme emerged subsequently: how to free oneself of Christianity. Three models, aimed at ensuring its gradual disappearance, had been proposed: (1) Mohammed's abstention from polemic over Moses and Jesus; (2) the Jesuit missionaries' strategy in Asia, based on adaptation to local context; and (3) the gradual transition from the Roman republic to the empire. The three models converge in the model of political transition outlined by the 'most religious' Machiavelli. In this context, 'religion' signifies 'civil religion': a concept derived, once again, from Machiavelli. But who is speaking here? Ferrarius, the Augustinian brother, or Fabricius, the Calvinist theologian at Heidelberg University? Are we dealing with a joke – or are the two voices, the satirical one of Ferrarius and the serious one of Fabricius, in reality only one?

9. For nearly three decades *Euclides Catholicus* was reprinted and translated under the name of Ferrarius. In 1693 Fabricius republished it in a volume collecting some of his writings, thus revealing the identity of Ferrarius.[78] Someone had already sniffed

---

77 See Clément, *Bibliothèque curieuse*, p. 283 n., which cites Gerhard von Mastricht from Vicentius Placcius, *Theatrum anonymorum et pseudonymorum* (Hamburgi: tipis Spieringianis, 1708), p. 281 n. 1040: 'hanc partem generalem tantum quae edita est . . . Pars specialis est jussu sereniss. Electoris Palatini suppressa'. On Placcius, see Martin Muslow, 'Practices of Unmasking: Polyhistors, Correspondence, and the Birth of Dictionaries of Pseudonymity in Seventeenth-Century Germany', *Journal of the History of Ideas* 67/2 (2006), pp. 219–50.

78 J. L. Fabricius, *Opuscula varia* (Heidelberg, 1693), pp. 279–346; subsequently in *Opera omnia, quibus praemittitur historia*

out the truth: Johannes Gezelius the Younger, Lutheran Bishop of Turku, in lauding the book for its anti-Catholic polemic, made a play on words on the Latin word *fabricare*.[79] Other readers, in some cases ignorant of the true identity of Ferrarius, reacted less favourably. 'I wish this book [*Euclides Catholicus*] had never seen the light of day ... because it undoubtedly smacks of atheism', commented the scholar Dorotheus Ascianus, alias Matthias Zimmermann.[80] The Dutchman Adrian Beverland, author of a scandalous dissertation that identified the first parents' sin with sexual intercourse, included Ferrarius in a list of blasphemous writers such as Spinoza, Hobbes and Machiavelli.[81] Another scholar, Johannes Diecmann, expressed his disagreement: *Euclides Catholicus* 'is not a serious book, but a playful satire ... a work by a famous Calvinist theologian, who holds a chair in a celebrated German university'.[82] But the most significant comment was that of Pierre Bayle. In July 1684, Jacques Lenfant wrote to him that he knew the name of the author of *Euclides Catholicus*, which he characterized as 'the most ingenious and

---

vitae et obitus ejusdem, authore Joh. Henrico Heideggero (Tiguri: typis Davidis Gessneri, 1698), pp. 301–49.

79 Johannes Gezelius the Younger, *Jubilaeus Antichristi Romani ipsius exitium* (Aboae: Johannes Winter, 1675), p. 75: 'recens scriptor, qui in *Catholico Euclide* methodo mathematica, *Fabricatus* est Romanae fidei hodiernae demonstrationem'.

80 Dorotheus Ascianus [Matthias Zimmermann], *Montes Pietatis Romanenses ... detecti* (Leipzig: Johannis Bauerianis, 1670), pp. 551–2, 555: 'Qui libellus [*Euclides*] utinam nunquam solem vidisset! ... Verba ejus, merum atheismum sapientia, integre adscribemus' (a long quotation from Ferrarius follows).

81 H. Beverland, *Peccatum originale κάτ' ἐξοχήν sic nuncupatum* (Eleutheropoli [Lugduni Batavorum], 1678), p. 86. Cf. Antonello Gerbi, *Il peccato di Adamo ed Eva. Storia della ipotesi di Beverland* (Milan: La Cultura, 1933) (new edn, ed. Sandro Gerbi [Milan: Adelphi, 2011]).

82 Johannes Diecmann, *De naturalismo, cum aliorum, tum maxime Jo. Bodini, ex opere ejus manuscripto et usque adhuc ανεκδότω, de abditis rerum sublimium arcanis, Schediasma inaugurale* (Kiel: Joachim Reumann, 1693) (reprinted Jena 1700), pp. 11–12: *Euclides Catholicus* 'scriptum non serium, sed jocosum et satyricum ... a celebri quodam Calvinianae cathedrae in Illustr. Germ. Acad. Professore theologo'.

vigorous satire [*la plus ingenieuse et la plus nerveuse satyre*] of the Roman Church that I have ever read'.[83] A few weeks later, Bayle replied to Lenfant, informing him that he had published a long review of Fabricius's works in *Nouvelles de la République des Lettres*, 'doing him the justice he deserves'. 'I knew', continued Bayle, 'who the author of *Euclides Catholicus*, which I recently read with great pleasure, is. But I have not revealed his name to the public, thinking that the author wished to remain unknown [*craignant que l'auteur ne souhaite d'etre caché*].'[84]

But why should a Calvinist theologian have to fear being identified as the author of an anti-Catholic satire? Bayle, who held Fabricius in high esteem – 'Everything this scholar publishes pleases me immensely', he wrote to Lenfant a year later – had doubtless registered a message in *Euclides Catholicus* addressed to a select audience.[85]

10. But what message? Deism? Atheism? It is not easy to say. In a dialogue published under his own name, Fabricius asked whether populations without religion ever existed and concluded

---

83   Pierre Bayle, *Correspondance*, ed. Elisabeth Labrousse et al. (Oxford: Voltaire Foundation, 2005), vol. IV, *Janvier 1684–juillet 1684, lettres 242–308*, p. 225 (letter of 12 July 1684, Heidelberg): 'Monsieur Spener . . . m'a montré un autre ouvrage qu'il m'assure être de M. Fabrice. En voicy le titre . . . C'est la plus ingenieuse et la plus nerveuse satyre que j'aye jamais veuë contre l'Eglise Romaine.'

84   Ibid., vol. V, *Août 1684–fin juillet 1685, lettres 309–450*, 2007, pp. 18–22 (Bayle's letter of 8 August, from Rotterdam): 'Vous y trouveres mes *Nouvelles*, and dans celles de juillet un extrait assez long des 3 dissertations de Mr Fabrice, à qui j'ai taché de rend[re] la justice qui luy est deue. Je savois qu'il est l'auteur de l'*Euclides Catholicus* que j'ay leu depuis peu avec beaucoup de plaisir, mais je n'ay pas voulu l'apprendre au public, craignant que l'auteur ne souhaite d'etre caché' (p. 20). On Fabricius, cf. ibid., vol. IV, p. 70, letter 259 n. 3 (and see also pp. 58, 114, 219); Pierre Bayle, *Oeuvres diverses* (The Hague: P. Husson, T. Johnson et al., 1727), vol. I, pp. 86–9; ibid., vol. III, from *Continuation des pensées diverses*, p. 196 n. f; p. 207 n. h; pp. 219–20. Cf. also Sergio Landucci, *I filosofi e i selvaggi* (Turin: Einaudi, 2014), p. 181ff.

85   Bayle, *Correspondance*, vol. V, p. 323: 'Tout ce que cet habile homme met au jour plait infiniment.'

that the human kind could not be accused of atheism, because some form of natural religion was to be found in every part of the world.[86] But Fabricius made a sceptical observation that cast a shadow over his conclusion: travellers in far-off lands often misconstrued the attitudes of the natives, because they did not know their language.[87]

In the case of *Euclides Catholicus*, the possibility of a misunderstanding had a different root. 'There is irony here, but it is not straightforward', wrote his long-standing friend and colleague Johann Heinrich Heidegger, in a posthumous biography of Fabricius.[88] Often irony generates irony. Jacques Bernard, who edited the *Nouvelles de la République des Lettres*, praised *Euclides Catholicus*, characterizing it as 'a work full of intelligence and imagination', and observed, 'The reader can see the beautiful conclusions [*les belles consequences*] that can be drawn from robust and fertile principles such as its.'[89] The target of this ironic (and possibly ambiguous) eulogy was the Roman Church. But Ferrarius had not confined himself to describing the consequences of a religion in which the teaching of Christ had become 'a mere pretext': he had wished that these consequences would take place.

11. Machiavelli, Hobbes, the Jesuit missionaries in China and, before them, Mohammed, were regarded as a precursor of a

---

86   J. L. Fabricius, *Apologia generis humani, contra calumniam atheismi*, in *Opera omnia*, pp. 119–42.

87   See ibid., pp. 139–40, where a passage from Garcilaso de la Vega is cited, which is commented on by the present writer in *Ethnophilologie. Deux études de cas, Socio-anthropologie* 36, 'Manières de croire' (2017), pp. 157–77.

88   Johann Heinrich Heidegger, *Historia vitae et obitus Johannis Ludovici Fabricii, sanctae memoriae theologi, et consultoris ecclesiastici Archipalatini celeberrimi* (Tiguri: typis Davidis Gessneri, 1697), p. 58: 'Ironia equidem est, sed non simplex'.

89   *Nouvelles de la République des Lettres*, April 1701, pp. 401–25, esp. p. 411: 'Le lecteur voit assez les belles consequences qu'on peut tirer de principes si fécondes et si solides. Il y a beaucoup d'esprit et d'imagination dans toute cette pièce.'

strategy based upon adaptation (*accommodatio*) and the corrosion of Christianity from within. Fabricius/Ferrarius looked to the past to decipher a world in which the secular power struggled to appropriate the venerable instruments of religion.[90] A new world, on which the author of the *Euclides Catholicus* cast a derisive, ferocious, far-sighted eye.

90   On *accommodatio*, see Amos Funkenstein, *Theology and the Scientific Imagination: From the Middle Ages to the Seventeenth Century* (Princeton: Princeton University Press, 2018). On secularization as an unfinished trajectory, readers are referred to my *Fear, Reverence, Terror: Five Essays in Political Iconography* (New York: Seagull, 2017).

Appendix

Reading between the Lines: A Short Note on The Leopard

1. Terms like *gattopardesco* and *gattopardismo* have been part of the Italian language for some time.[1] As is well known, they refer to the passage in *Il Gattopardo* (*The Leopard*) in which the young Tancredi Falconeri addresses his uncle Don Fabrizio, Prince of Salina, commenting on Garibaldi's advance in Sicily: 'Unless we ourselves take a hand now, they'll foist a republic on us. If we want everything to stay as it is, everything will have to change. D'you understand?'[2] According to current opinion, the sentence 'If we want everything to stay as it is, everything will have to change', which became famous immediately, encapsulates the meaning of Giuseppe Tomasi di Lampedusa's novel. In the heated discussion that followed the posthumous publication of *The Leopard*, someone on the left referred to 'anti-historicism'; and many criticized the author, attributing a static view of history to him. In a talk given in 1959, and posthumously published under the title 'Contro *Il Gattopardo*', Franco Fortini did not mince his words: 'The rejection of history in this book is not the rejection of some particular history, but a

---

1 The following text is based on a lecture given at the Université Sorbonne Nouvelle – Paris 3, 19 February 2015.

2 Giuseppe Tomasi di Lampedusa, *The Leopard* (1958), tr. Archibald Colquhoun (London: Everyman, 1998), p. 22; trans. modified. ('Se non ci siamo anche noi, quelli ti combinano la repubblica. Se vogliamo che tutto rimanga come è, bisogna che tutto cambi. Mi sono spiegato?': *Il Gattopardo*, new edn revised by Gioacchino Lanza Tomasi [Milan: Feltrinelli, 2013], p. 50.)

rejection of change in itself.'[3] Often, as Nunzio La Fauci has noted, such judgements presuppose 'the hasty identification between the protagonist of the novel and its author ... that ... is a characteristic feature of the critical literature on *The Leopard*'. Not only that, but the current interpretation of the sentence – the vulgate of *gattopardismo* – is based (as La Fauci has highlighted) on a misunderstanding: 'The extremely famous "If we want everything to stay as it is, everything will have to change" cannot but represent a way of thinking that assigns times and spaces to the human capacity for projection, which situates action in the universe of possibilities rather than that of limits. The thought of someone who feels part, and an active part, of history.'[4]

2. These are pertinent observations. But for a clearer understanding of the famous passage, it is useful to identify its 'source', or the text which, inverted, forms its starting point. This is a passage in Machiavelli's *Discourses* from the chapter 'Whoever Wishes to Reform a Long-Established State in a Free City Should Retain at Least the Appearance of Its Ancient Ways' (book I, chapter 25):

> Any who desires or tries to reform the government of a city in a way that is acceptable and capable of maintaining it to everyone's satisfaction will find it necessary to retain at least the semblance of its ancient customs, so that it will not seem to the people that its institutions have changed, though in fact the new institutions may be completely dissimilar from those of the past, because men in general live as much by appearances as by

---

3 Franco Fortini, 'Contro *Il Gattopardo*', in *Saggi ed epigrammi*, ed. and introd. Luca Lenzini with a text by Rossana Rossanda (Milan: Mondadori, 2003), pp. 720–30, esp. p. 730. See the remarks by Francesco Orlando, *L'intimità e la storia. Lettura del 'Gattopardo'* (Turin: Einaudi, 1998), pp. 156–7 n. 54.

4 Nunzio La Fauci, 'Analisi e interpretazioni linguistiche del *Gattopardo*', *Annali della Scuola Normale Superiore di Pisa. Classe di Lettere e Filosofia*, 3rd ser., 23/3–4 (1993), pp. 1145–85, esp. pp. 1163–4.

realities: indeed, they are often moved more by things as they appear than by things as they really are.[5]

As far as I know, this (inverted) derivation from Machiavelli has not been signalled. Francesco Orlando nearly hit the target. Rejecting the standard use of the terms *gattopardesco* and *gattopardismo*, derived from Tancredi's 'regrettably famous' sentence, he asked, 'A prejudice that has become part of the language is definitively incorrigible – for how many centuries has it been futile to seek to purge *Machiavellianism* and *Machiavellian* of their pejorative sense?'[6] A near miss.

3. In the course of the novel, Don Fabrizio, thinking to himself, frequently returns to his nephew's words, whose profound significance he gradually comes to understand: 'Tancredi, he considered, had a great future; he could be the standard-bearer of a counter-attack which the nobility, under changed trappings, could launch against the new political order.'[7] Here, for an instant, Machiavelli's lexicon surfaces: 'Though in fact the new orders may be completely dissimilar from those of the past.' But over and above the formal echo, the inverted relationship between Tancredi's words and Machiavelli's passage is manifest. If we want everything to change,

---

5 Niccolò Machiavelli, *Discourses on Livy*, tr. and introd. Julia Conaway Bondanella and Peter Bondanella (Oxford: Oxford University Press, 2008), p. 79. (Ch. I, 25: 'Chi vuole riformare uno stato anticato in una città libera, ritenga almeno l'ombra de' modi antichi': 'Colui che desidera o che vuole riformare uno stato d'una città, a volere che sia accetto e poterlo con satisfazione di ciascuno mantenere, è necessitato a ritenere l'ombra almanco de' modi antichi, acciò che a' popoli non paia avere mutato ordine, ancorché in fatto gli ordini nuovi fussero al tutto alieni dai passati; perché lo universale degli uomini si pascono così di quel che pare che di quello che è; anzi molte volte si muovono più per le cose che paiono che per quelle che sono': *Discorsi sopra la prima deca di Tito Livio*, ed. Corrado Vivanti [Turin: Einaudi, 1983], p. 108.)

6 Orlando, *L'intimità e la storia*, pp. 142, 14.

7 *The Leopard*, p. 52; tr. modified. ('Tancredi, secondo lui, aveva dinanzi a sé un grande avvenire; egli avrebbe potuto essere l'alfiere di un contrattacco che la nobiltà, sotto mutate uniformi, poteva portare contro il nuovo ordine politico': *Il Gattopardo*, pp. 85–6.)

some things must remain as they are (*Discourses*); 'if we want everything to stay as it is, everything will have to change' (*The Leopard*). The ends are opposite: revolution in the first case, conservation in the second. The means are the same: change (partial in the first case, total in the second). The one who pushes the paradox to extremes ('everything ... everything') is the conservative, not the revolutionary. But can we define someone who regards the transformation of 'everything' as the only solution as a 'conservative'? Would it not be better to define him as a reactionary?, asked Fortini. And which of them is it: the characters or the author? Tancredi, followed by Don Fabrizio, or Lampedusa? In the allusion to 'the uneducated Machiavellianism of Sicilians', which we read in a passage of *The Leopard*, there resonates the contemptuous voice of the most cultured and Sicilian of authors.[8] Other passages are less transparent. In a letter to his friend Guido Lajolo of 31 March 1956, Lampedusa wrote of his novel, 'It must be read with great attention because every word is weighed and every episode has a hidden meaning.'[9] In his beautiful *Ricordo di Lampedusa*, Orlando recalls Lampedusa's preference for the implicit, in which the taste of the man of letters (the choice of 'lean' writers) converged with aristocratic ostentation.[10] And dealing with Machiavelli, the implicit was de rigueur, as Lampedusa observed in his lectures on English literature: 'Machiavelli is an author whom one can, and perhaps must, follow in politics, provided one repudiates him publicly. If not, one is no longer Machiavellian.'[11] Thus, when

---

8   Ibid., p. 77; tr. modified ('machiavellismo incolto dei Siciliani': *Il Gattopardo*, p. 117). See also Orlando, *L'intimità e la storia*, p. 107.

9   Andrea Vitello, *Giuseppe Tomasi di Lampedusa. Il Gattopardo segreto*, rev. and updated edn (Palermo: Sellerio, 2008), pp. 335–6. The limitations of this flat, reticent biography emerge, for example, from an essay by Fabien Kunz-Vitali, '"Un po' di convenzionale ruggine antisemita ..." Giuseppe Tomasi di Lampedusa e la questione ebraica', *Italienisch* 67 (2012), pp. 47–70.

10   Francesco Orlando, *Ricordo di Lampedusa* (1963) (Milan: All'Insegna del Pesce d'Oro, 1985), p. 50ff.

11   Giuseppe Tomasi di Lampedusa, *Letteratura inglese*, ed. Nicoletta Polo, in *Opere*, introd. Gioacchino Lanza Tomasi, 5th expanded and rev. edn (Milan: Mondadori, 2004), p. 818.

Tancredi adopts, in inverted form, a maxim of Machiavelli's that inspired his matrimonial strategy, he could not have declared his debt. Reading *The Leopard* (and any other book) between the lines is not only possible, it is compulsory: if only to catch undeclared allusions, addressed to the 'happy few' to whom Stendhal, beloved of Lampedusa, had dedicated *The Charterhouse of Parma*.[12] Decipherment of these allusions, literary or otherwise, formed part of the critic's craft even in the distant past, when the term 'intertextuality' had yet to appear. For this reason I cannot accept the page in which Orlando, in his book on *The Leopard*, rejects intertextuality (a term that is certainly superfluous), emphasizing, in a tone which is seemingly jocular but in truth serious, that reading cannot do without focusing on a single text: '*One at a time, for heaven's sake!*' Elsewhere Orlando himself has demonstrated the wealth of what he here curtly dismisses as a 'reflexive procedure imitating the laboratory'.[13] It is enough to think of a book like *Illuminismo e retorica freudiana*, which reads implicit echoes of Pascal behind the anti-religious polemic of the *philosophes*.[14] But what does identification of the (inverted) debt to the passage from the *Discourses* add to a reading of *The Leopard*?

4. According to Francesco Orlando, 'The vulgate has transformed into the moral of the story a proposition that is triply unreliable: not invented by the free will of the author, not confirmed by ultimate developments of the narrative, echoing the historical material predominantly as an illusion.'[15] I shall try to examine these objections starting with the last. In a context that is not Sicilian but European, the strategy delineated and then implemented by Tancredi (come to terms with the bourgeoisie to ensure the survival of the aristocracy) was far from illusory, as Arno Mayer demonstrated in an original book that analyses the

---

12 See Orlando, *Ricordo di Lampedusa*, p. 50.
13 Orlando, *L'intimità e la storia*, p. 8.
14 Francesco Orlando, *Illuminismo e retorica freudiana* (Turin: Einaudi, 1982), p. 186ff.
15 Orlando, *L'intimità e la storia*, p. 15.

persistence of elements of the ancien régime until the First World War.[16] The second objection seems more to the point: at the end of *The Leopard*, the embalmed corpse of the dog Bendicò, thrown out of the window, is momentarily transfigured into the heraldic animal of the Salinas and symbolizes their end. But the title chosen by Lampedusa for this final paragraph, 'Fine di tutto' (end of everything), is (as we shall see) ironic.

There remains the first objection entered by Orlando: 'not invented [Tancredi's sentence] by the free will of the author.' I imagine that Orlando wished to underscore that the person who utters the sentence is not the narrator but a character, who, once created, represents a constraint for the author himself. But Tancredi's words resurface insistently in the monologues of the protagonist Don Fabrizio, who makes them his own: '"Just negotiations punctuated by a little harmless shooting, then all will be the same though all will be changed." Into his mind had come Tancredi's ambiguous words, which he now found himself really understanding . . . "For everything to remain same", just as it is now: except for a gradual substitution of classes.'[17] In the last line the voice of the protagonist and that of the narrator merge. Lampedusa may have sensed the proximity between the two voices as a danger. In some instances he sought to distinguish them, as in Don Fabrizio's reflections on the manipulation of the referendum results approving Sicily's annexation to the Kingdom of Italy:

> At this point calm descended on Don Fabrizio, who had finally solved the enigma; *now he knew* who had been killed at Donnafugata, at a hundred other places, in the course of that night of dirty wind: a new-born babe: good faith . . . Don Fabrizio

---

16   Arno J. Mayer, *The Persistence of the Old Regime: Europe to the Great War* (1981) (London: Verso, 2010).

17   Ibid., pp. 26, 28; trans. modified. ('"Trattative punteggiate da schioppettate quasi innocue e, dopo, tutto sarà lo stesso mentre tutto sarà cambiato." Gli erano tornate in mente le parole ambigue di Tancredi che adesso però comprendeva a fondo . . . "'Perchè tutto resti com'è.' Come è, nel fondo: soltanto una lenta sostituzione di ceti"': *Il Gattopardo*, pp. 54, 56.)

could not know it then, but a great deal of the slackness and acquiescence for which the people of the South were to be criticised during the next decades, was due to the stupid annulment of the first expression of liberty ever offered them.[18]

But the impulse that prompts the author to speak through one of his characters suggests to him, in the case of Colonel Pallavicino (the sole character in the novel who actually existed), an expedient not without awkwardness:

'For the moment, due partly to your humble servant, no one mentions red shirts any more; but they'll be back again. When they've vanished, others of different colours will come; and then red ones once again. And how will it end? There's Italy's Lucky Star they say. But you know better than me, Prince, that even fixed stars are so only in appearance.' Perhaps he was a little tipsy, making such prophecies. But at such disquieting prospects Don Fabrizio felt his heart contract.[19]

5. The autobiographical implications of this passage are obvious. The 1948 elections, when the symbol of the Popular Democratic Front displayed Garibaldi's image (the return of the red shirts),

---

18 Ibid., pp. 82–3, 84; my emphasis. ('A questo punto la calma discese su Don Fabrizio che finalmente aveva sciolto l'enigma; *adesso sapeva* chi era stato strangolato a Donnafugata, in cento altri luoghi, nel corso di quella nottata di vento lercio: una neonata, la buonafede ... Don Fabrizio *non poteva saperlo allora*, ma una parte della neghittosità, dell'acquiescenza per la quale durante i decenni seguenti si doveva vituperare la gente del Mezzogiorno, ebbe la propria origine nello stupido annullamento della prima espressione di libertà che a questo popolo si era mai presentata': *Il Gattopardo*, pp. 123–5.)

19 Ibid., pp. 172–3. (' "Per il momento, per merito anche del vostro umile servo, delle camicie rosse non si parla più, ma se ne riparlerà. Quando saranno scomparse queste ne verranno altre di diverso colore; e poi di nuovo rosse. E come andrà a finire? C'è lo Stellone, si dice. Sarà. Ma Lei sa meglio di me, principe, che anche le stelle fisse veramente fisse non sono." Forse un po' brillo, profetava. Don Fabrizio dinanzi alle prospettive inquietanti sentiva stringersi il cuore': *Il Gattopardo*, p. 231.)

were followed by the agrarian reform of 1950 which irreversibly sanctioned the decline of the Sicilian aristocracy. The novel's most impressive pages (the ball, the protagonist's death) feed off awareness of this decline, which is very different from the 'rejection of change in itself' erroneously pointed out by Fortini. In *The Leopard*, political change exists, as does, at a more profound level, the 'gradual substitution of classes' evoked by the author through Don Fabrizio's reflections on Tancredi's words. But there is something more profound still – the Sicilian landscape stamped by immutable backwardness: 'He ... looked up at the scorched slopes of Monte Pellegrino, scarred like the face of misery by eternal ravines.'[20] The person looking is Don Fabrizio: 'The view of the mountain near Palermo crystallizes a desperation that is conceived as meta-historical' – that is, eternal – 'because no human lifetime would be sufficient to prove it illusory', comments Orlando.[21] But another scholar, Edward Reichel, has argued that a perspective emerges here shared by Lampedusa himself. The image of history presented in *The Leopard* is structured according to three rhythms: quasi-immobile, conditioned by geography and climate; slow, based on social history; rapid and ephemeral, depicted in the goings-on of the characters. Reichel has highlighted the analogy between this image of history and that proposed by Fernand Braudel in his book on the Mediterranean.[22] This would be a mere coincidence, even if (Fabien Kunz-Vitali reports) a copy of Braudel's work was found in what survives of Lampedusa's library.[23]

---

20   Ibid., p. 26 ('Guardava i fianchi di Monte Pellegrino arsicci, scavati ed eterni come la miseria': *Il Gattopardo*, p. 54).

21   Orlando, *L'intimità e la storia*, p. 116.

22   Edward Reichel, 'Geschichtsdenken und Gegenwartsdeutung in *Il Gattopardo*. Tomasi di Lampedusa, die "*nouvelle histoire*" und das Ende der Nachkriegsepoche in Italien', *Italienische Studien* 4 (1981), pp. 31–54, on which see also Orlando, *L'intimità e la storia*, p. 159 n. 61.

23   F. Braudel, *La Méditerranée et le monde méditerranéen à l'époque de Phillip II* (Paris: Colin: 1949). (Personal communication from Fabien Kunz-Vitali, to whom I am grateful.)

6. Less hypothetical, and closer to Lampedusa, seems to me to be a reading based on words that recur several times in the novel: 'eternal', 'eternity'. Here is Don Fabrizio speaking to the Jesuit Father Pirrone: 'We live in a changing reality to which we try to adapt ourselves like seaweed bending under the pressure of water. Holy Church has been granted an explicit promise of immortality; we, as a social class, have not. *Any palliative which may give us another hundred years of life is like eternity to us.*'[24] And here is Don Fabrizio once again after his conversation with the Piedmontese noble Chevalley di Monterzuolo:

> The Prince was depressed. 'All this shouldn't last; *but it will, always; the human "always" of course, a century, two centuries . . .* and after that it will be different, but worse. We were the Leopards and Lions; those who'll take our place will be little jackals, hyenas; and the whole lot of us, Leopards, jackals and sheep, we'll all go on thinking ourselves the salt of the earth.'[25]

In this passage, the character steps back from himself ('we were') and the author steps back from the character ('we'll all go on thinking ourselves'). We are in the slow time of social history, where one hundred or two hundred years are equivalent to eternity. The history conditioned by climate is even slower: 'He . . . looked up at the scorched slopes of Monte Pellegrino, scarred like the face of misery by eternal ravines.' But from a

---

24 *The Leopard*, p. 31; my emphasis. ('Viviamo in una realtà mobile alla quale cerchiamo di adattarci come le alghe si piegano sotto la spinta del mare. Alla Santa Chiesa è stata esplicitamente promessa l'immortalità; a noi, in quanto classe sociale, no. *Per noi un palliativo che promette di durare cento anni equivale all'eternità*': Il Gattopardo, p. 59.)

25 Ibid., p. 137; my emphasis. ('Il Principe era depresso: "Tutto questo" pensava "non dovrebbe poter durare; *però durerà, sempre; il sempre umano, beninteso, un secolo, due secoli . . .*; e dopo sarà diverso, ma peggiore. Noi fummo i Gattopardi, i Leoni; quelli che ci sostituiranno saranno gli sciacalletti, le iene; e tutti quanti Gattopardi, sciacalli e pecore, continueremo a crederci il sale della terra"': Il Gattopardo, p. 185.)

non-human perspective eternity is something else entirely: it is the eternity of the stars, which the astronomer prince contemplates with his telescope. When it comes, death seems to him like a woman, like a star, 'lovelier than she ever had when glimpsed in stellar space'.[26]

7. 'Le silence éternel de ces espace infinis m'effraie' (the eternal silence of these infinite spaces scares me).[27] 'Anyone wishing to call himself a man, not a two-legged animal', said Lampedusa, 'must have read Pascal's *Pensées*.'[28] *The Leopard*, a novel about history and the attempts to alter it made by some of the characters, in a determinate time and place, is framed by Pascal read in a sceptical key. History has a meaning for those who make it, or believe they make it, motivated by more or less Machiavellian strategies; it has no sense from the viewpoint of the stars. The 'end of everything', with which the analytical index composed by Lampedusa concludes, refers to the end of the Salinas and the end of the novel. But it is a patently ironic phrase. Human history is not the entire reality: on this, beyond any possible divergence, we cannot but agree with Lampedusa.

---

26 Ibid., p. 185 ('Più bella di come mai l'avesse intravista negli spazi stellari': Il Gattopardo, p. 246).

27 Blaise Pascal, *Pensées*, ed. Michel Le Guern (Paris: Gallimard, 1977), fr. 187 (Brunschvicg fr. 206), p. 161 (tr. A. J. Krailsheimer [Harmondsworth: Penguin, 1983], fr. 201, p. 95; tr. modified). And see above the postscript to chapter 7.

28 Quoted in Orlando, *Ricordo di Lampedusa*, p. 70.

Name Index